The Science Fiction
Dimensions of
Salman Rushdie

The Science Fiction Dimensions of Salman Rushdie

YAEL MAURER

McFarland & Company, Inc., Publishers
Jefferson, North Carolina

A shorter version of the chapter "Rage Against the Machine: Cyberspace Narratives in Rushdie's *Fury*" was published in *The Journal of Commonwealth Literature* (47:1). March, 2012.

LIBRARY OF CONGRESS CATALOGUING-IN-PUBLICATION DATA

Maurer, Yael, 1966–
　　The Science Fiction Dimensions of Salman Rushdie / Yael Maurer.
　　　p.　　cm.
　　Includes bibliographical references and index.

　　ISBN 978-0-7864-7496-7 (softcover : acid free paper) ∞
　　ISBN 978-1-4766-1402-1 (ebook)

　　1. Rushdie, Salman—Criticism and interpretation.
I. Title.
PR6068.U757Z7656 2014
823'.914—dc23　　　　　　　　　　　　　2013044230

BRITISH LIBRARY CATALOGUING DATA ARE AVAILABLE

© 2014 Yael Maurer. All rights reserved

No part of this book may be reproduced or transmitted in any form or by any means, electronic or mechanical, including photocopying or recording, or by any information storage and retrieval system, without permission in writing from the publisher.

On the cover: Paolo Galetto, *Salman Rushdie "Everywhere Is Love,"* watercolor on paper, 11¾" × 11¾", 2012

Manufactured in the United States of America

McFarland & Company, Inc., Publishers
　Box 611, Jefferson, North Carolina 28640
　www.mcfarlandpub.com

In memory of Miriam Baruch,
my beloved mother.

And to my father, Joseph Baruch,
my inspiration and ongoing
tower of strength.

Acknowledgments

I thank Professor Hana Wirth-Nesher for her unwavering support and for being a true inspiration.

My deepest thanks go to Professor Elana Gomel for her much needed advice and encouragement.

My heartfelt thanks goes to Professor Graham Huggan and Professor John McLeod for their kind and generous support of this project.

I thank my colleague and friend Dr. Amy Garnai for being my inspiration and for her invaluable support. This book wouldn't be the same without her.

My love and thanks go to my friends and colleagues at the Department of English and American Studies at Tel Aviv University. And last, but not least, I thank my students for their wonderful insights on Rushdie.

Table of Contents

Acknowledgments vi

Preface: Rereading Rushdie 1

1. Rushdie's Peripheries: Imagined Histories of Nation 3
2. Rage Against the Machine: Cyberspace Narratives in Rushdie's *Fury* 30
3. "The World Is (Not) What It Is": *The Ground Beneath Her Feet* 50
4. The Year of the Reverse: *The Antagonist* and *Midnight's Children* 75
5. *Haroun* and *Shalimar*: Kashmir and Koshmar 121
6. Immortality Now: *Luka and the Fire of Life* 149

Conclusion: The Genre That Isn't: Rereading Rushdie 178

Chapter Notes 187

Works Cited 195

Index 201

Preface: Rereading Rushdie

The one duty we owe to history is to rewrite it.
— Oscar Wilde, *The Artist as Critic*

When I first began work on this book, I found myself having to defend my view of Rushdie as a writer of science fiction. Rushdie's well known persona, more so than his writing, has come to define him in many ways: a postmodernist writer who delights in puns; a "Third World Cosmopolitan" writer of "magical realist" fiction; a writer who addresses postcolonial concerns. But the science fictional mode that, as I show in this book, is at the heart of his oeuvre has not been extensively commented on. This book aims to put this aspect of Rushdie's work at the center.

Salman Rushdie had become, at least since the infamous *fatwa* in 1989, a celebrity figure.[1] He was seen as a representative of the just fight against censorship by his supporters, or as an arrogant blasphemer by his detractors, either in the Muslim world or by the Western Left. His controversial stance regarding the book that sparked the "Rushdie Affair" is still a matter of public debate. With the recent publication of his memoir *Joseph Anton*, the debate was rekindled.[2]

This view of Rushdie as a public figure seems to have taken over our perception of the author. "Rushdie" had become a code name, a symbol for a political stance and a worldview. Rushdie's many fictional alter egos best demonstrate the controversy that surrounds him. Is he the "Shah of Blah" or Rashid, the teller of tales and the maker of worlds with the power to change reality?[3] Conflicting views of the man and the author abound.

In my attempt to locate a different trajectory for Rushdie, I will therefore not relate to *The Satanic Verses* explicitly. I choose to focus on Rushdie's rewriting of Indian and Western histories as science fictional. This aspect of his work, though widely discussed in its postmodern and postcolonial aspects, has yet to be treated employing the distancing lens of speculative fiction. This is what this book sets out to do.

In my rereading of Rushdie's work, I trace the science fictional imaginary of the author, going back to the first novel he wrote, *The Antagonist* (never published). This novel imagines a post–Imperial England in the "year of the Reverse," 1974, the mirror image of the year of India's independence from British rule. Although Rushdie chose not to publish this early work, his most successful novel, *Midnight's Children*, reinvents the main character and some of the themes of the earlier piece.

Rushdie's first published novel *Grimus* (1975) is a science fictional meditation on the migrant condition. It was not well received and Rushdie seemed to abandon the science fictional mode. However, as I show in this book, the science fictional elements that were so prominent in his early work continue to influence his later writing in varying degrees.

My aim is therefore to relocate the author, and his work, within what I see as a postcolonial science fictional imaginary: I show how Rushdie represents the migrant condition by employing science fictional tropes like the alien, the stranger in a strange land and the shape-shifter for the creation of what I termed "imaginary cosmopolitan" sites. These sites of alterity create an alternative to the conflicted history of self and nation.

I use the term *science fiction* in the broadest sense to indicate a mode that engages with otherness in various ways and that creates alternate fictional worlds. Therefore, I chose to focus on the novels that best demonstrate the postcolonial science fictional mode, although the case can be made for other Rushdie novels as well. The novels I discuss in this book span his body of work, from *The Antagonist* to his latest novel to date, *Luka and the Fire of Life*. I end the book with my reading of Rushdie's memoir *Joseph Anton*, a book that blends many fictional genres to create a hybrid form that best expresses Rushdie's conflicted subject position. It is here, no less so than in his more overtly fictional work, that we see Rushdie's unique brand of textuality at work.

This book outlines a different trajectory for a well known, highly controversial, and truly innovative author. Rushdie's claim to literary fame should be based on these enduring qualities of his work. I am confident he will not cease to pay that "one debt to history" owed by all artists, according to Wilde: Rewriting personal and national histories with a unique and always surprising Rushdean flair.

1
Rushdie's Peripheries: Imagined Histories of Nation

> "Over the Rainbow" is, or ought to be, the anthem of all the world's migrants.... It is a celebration of Escape, a grand paean to the Uprooted Self, a hymn — the Hymn — to Elsewhere.
>
> So Oz finally became home; the imagined world became the actual world ... the real secret of the ruby slippers is not that "there's no place like home," but rather that there is no longer any such place as home: except, of course, for the homes we make, or the homes that are made for us, in Oz: which is anywhere, and everywhere, except the place from which we began. — Salman Rushdie, The Wizard of Oz

My reading of Rushdie's work focuses on the science fictional dimensions of his later novels, *Fury, The Ground Beneath Her Feet, Shalimar the Clown* and *Luka and the Fire of Life*, his latest novel to date. I show how the author's oeuvre develops and moves towards a more consistent engagement with science fiction as a generic form and an ideological investment. I therefore discuss Rushdie's first unpublished novel, *The Antagonist* (1974), an earlier version of *Midnight's Children*. I look at both texts to show how the science fictional elements are transformed from the earlier, unpublished version into Rushdie's most successful novel (which was recently adapted to film). My analysis of the novels expands and reconsiders readings of Rushdie as a Magical Realist and poses his work in both form and thematics as SF. Following Wendy Faris' *Ordinary Enchantments*, where the author locates the links between Magical Realism and what she terms "postcolonial dynamics of alterity" (133), I suggest that although Rushdie's fictional project in the novels I examine does indeed "participate in these dynamics and [addresses] historical issues critically and thereby also [attempts] to heal historical wounds" (138), my critical framework locates Rushdie's work within a science fictional mode, his debt to Magical

Realists like Grass and Marquez notwithstanding. What Faris calls "magical historicity" (138) can also be applied to the texts I address here.

It is my contention, however, that Rushdie's oeuvre, as I chart it here, has evolved out of a science fictional framework and continues to enact it both formally and thematically. Rushdie's memoir *Joseph Anton* begins with a description of the young Rushdie in an English boarding school where he describes his alienation and alterity in science fictional terms:

> After Rugby School he never forgot the lesson he learned there: that there would always be people who didn't like you, to whom you seemed as alien as little green men or the Slime from Outer Space, and there was no point trying to change their mind. Alienation: it was a lesson he relearned in more dramatic circumstances later on [26].

Rushdie's sense of alienation, which he later revisits in his third person retelling of the events following the *fatwa*, is couched in science fictional terms. The young Rushdie, an avid reader of "yellow-jacketed science-fiction novels" who becomes "an expert on the so-called golden age of science-fiction" (31) defines this period in his life thus: "It might not have been the greatest revolution in history, this four-and-a-half year fall towards the fantastic fuelled by the truckshop snack foods"; but the young Rushdie, who managed to get out of "playing war games in the mud" by using his Indianness to justify this refusal to participate in an Imperialist project, realizes that "standing up for oneself could sometimes be well worth it" (31). It is this "fall into the fantastic" that Rushdie's work continues to chart in later years. Science fiction thus becomes, for the young alien in Britain, a way to escape the real world while simultaneously viewing it using science fictional tropes.

In my reading of Rushdie's novels, I therefore demonstrate how Rushdie recreates personal and national histories in a science fictional setting and mode, even if the novels do not openly announce themselves as belonging to the genre, as did Rushdie's first published novel *Grimus* (1975). Rushdie's choice of genre is by no means a departure from his earlier work. *Grimus*, which originated in a sci-fi writing competition, tells the story of Flapping Eagle, a migrant figure who leaves his place of origin and travels through the world in search of a new homeland. But unlike Rushdie's later novels, the political and social ramifications of this allegorical text about the immigrant experience remained vaguer and less politically committed than his later, successful works. Rushdie's first attempt at writing a postcolonial science fiction novel was not well received by critics. Rushdie himself comments on the failure of this first attempt, noting that he had not yet found his voice as a writer at this early stage.[1]

Postcolonial Science Fiction: How Rushdie's Novels Fit This Paradigm

Rushdie, however, remains an admirer of the genre, and his later novels are a reworking of the science fictional imaginary in a postcolonial setting. In recent years, much critical attention has been devoted to the inherent and almost paradigmatic links between the postcolonial and the science fictional imaginaries. In his seminal book *Colonialism and the Emergence of Science Fiction*, John Rieder outlines the ways in which "early science fiction lives and breathes in the atmosphere of colonial history and its discourses, how it reflects or contributes to ideological production of ideas about the shape of history, and how it might, in varying degrees, enact a struggle over humankind's ability to reshape it" (3). Reshaping history, then, is at the heart of early science fiction's vision of history, especially colonial history. This affinity between the (post)colonial and the science fictional imaginaries, where both discourses engage in some manner with "reshaping histories" of colonizer and colonized, is at the center of Rushdie's oeuvre from its (science fictional) inception with *Grimus*.

Following Reider's mapping of the links between colonialism and science fiction, other, more recent works engage with the links between postcolonial fiction and science fiction. In *Postcolonialism and Science Fiction*, Jessica Langer rightly notes that the "inherent instability of both categories, that of the 'postcolonial' and that of 'science fiction'" (2) is "not a weakness but rather a strength" (2). Both categories, "science fiction" and "postcolonial," are inclusive and flexible. Langer sees these traits as ensuring the "subversion, both generic and ideological that postcolonial science fiction represents" (3). Langer shows how the "classic oppositional SF tropes of the grotesque bug-eyed alien bent on Earthly domination and the beautiful but empty planet, ripe for colonization" are the "twin myths" (3) of both SF and colonialism: "The Stranger, or the Other, and the Strange Land—whether actually empty or filled with these Others—are at the very heart of the colonial project, and their dispelling is at the heart of the postcolonial one" (3–4). In other words, SF and postcolonial fiction and theory are both structured around the same tropes. As the example from *Joseph Anton* cited above shows, the alien (in this case the young Indian at a British boarding school) is imagined both as a postcolonial subject and as a creature from SF lore. This link between representations of the Other in postcolonial literature and SF is addressed in other recent works that locate the affinity between the two genres. I turn then to an examination of some of these studies that further demonstrate the links between the postcolonial and the science fictional.

In *Science Fiction, Imperialism and the Third World,* Hoegland and Sarwal point to the ways in which science fictional texts participate in an imperial project while simultaneously subverting it. Since "[the] days of empire are not over" (8), both science fiction and postcolonial theory and fiction acknowledge and deal with imperial rule in its many guises. Hoegland and Sarwal note, in a vein similar to Langer's discussion of the alien in SF and postcolonial fiction, that "[the] Other is one of the most well-known markers that science fiction and postcolonial literature share in common" (10). The role of the Other is similar in both genres:

> The "Other" consolidates difference as well as solidifies the norm; as both a theoretical concept and a tangible object, the "Other" is used to justify the exploitation and annihilation of people, whether red, black or green; it is used to explain how repulsion and desire can exist concurrently; and it signifies an ever-looming threat of contamination (by sex or disease) as well as violence [10].

The "alien other" can be "red, black or green"; the science fictional meets the postcolonial almost seamlessly, it would seem, suggesting that the two realms share more than just a superficial resemblance signified by the use of the same terms to describe both aliens from outer space and aliens in political or social terms.

In *Strange Encounters,* Sara Ahmed locates the figure of the alien in popular culture as both instantly recognizable and yet pushing the limits of representation: "The figure of the alien reminds us that what is 'beyond the limit' is subject to representation: indeed, what is beyond representation is also, at the same time, over-represented" (1). This "double and contradictory existence of aliens in and beyond representation invites us to ask questions about the very relationship between the categories of alien and human: What techniques are available to allow us to differentiate aliens from humans? How do such techniques of differentiation serve to constitute the very category of 'the human'?" (1). These questions reverberate in the SF imaginary but also in postcolonial literature's engagement with "history." Ahmed suggests we view postcoloniality "as *a failed historicity*; a historicity that admits of its own failure in grasping that which has been, as the impossibility of grasping the present" (10, italics in original). Ahmed locates the post-colonial project as being "about the complexity of the relationship between the past and present, between the histories of European colonization and contemporary forms of globalization" (11). Thus, "[history] can no longer be understood as that which determines each encounter. Rather, historicity involves the history of such encounters that are unavailable in the form of a totality" (11). Although Ahmed does not directly relate to SF texts, her discussion emerges out of the SF imaginary regarding the figure of the stranger and the alien.

Ahmed's rereading of postcoloniality as a site of failed historicity resonates with the ways in which I aim to read Rushdie's texts' engagement with imagined and reconstructed histories of India and the West. In that sense, Rushdie's novels enact this problematic of representing "alienness" in a postcolonial or science fictional mode. In my reading of specific texts, I therefore look at Rushdie's remaking of "history" into "histories" (both personal and national); I locate the SF/postcolonial imaginary in the texts' form and thematics. Although, as I have stated, the science fictional elements in some novels are more prominent than in others, I am interested in their function in Rushdie's creation of alternate fictional worlds. I shall therefore attempt to map how the term *science fiction* with all its attendant perils is used in this book. I shall show how the boundaries of this category, like the vexed boundaries of postcoloniality, make it possible to include Rushdie's oeuvre in the broad matrix of this mode.

Why SF? Why Rushdie?

John Rieder's genesis of the science fictional mode in the nineteenth century proves crucial in the mapping of what might be termed science fiction. Yet it is Rieder's refusal to define the parameters of the science fictional mode that will aid me in showing how even texts that are not seemingly science fictional in the narrow sense are nevertheless works of SF in the broadest possible sense. Rieder boldly states at the outset that he is "not going to define science fiction" (16). Following Paul Kincaid's thesis in "On the Origins of the Genre," Rieder adopts Kincaid's conclusion:

> Science fiction is not one thing. Rather it is any number of things—a future setting, a marvelous device, an ideal society, an alien creature, a twist in time, an interstellar journey, a satirical perspective, a particular approach to the matter of story, whatever we are looking for when we look for science fiction, here more overt, here more subtle—which are braided together in an endless variety of combinations [17, quoting Kincaid 416–417].

It is in this very broad arena in which what may be termed a science fictional text exists, that I wish to locate Rushdie's later novels and his early, unpublished novel, *The Antagonist*. All the novels I discuss and, as I shall claim in my conclusion, also Rushdie's memoir *Joseph Anton*, contain science fictional elements and view the world through a science fictional lens. At least two of Kincaid's examples of science fictional "things" are present in these texts: "a satirical perspective" and " a particular approach to the matter of story." In some of the novels, such as *Haroun and the Sea of Stories* and its "sequel" *Luka and the Fire of Life*, we can also locate a number of "marvelous devices" and "twists in time." A different form of twist in time is at the center of *The Ground Beneath Her Feet*. In *Fury*, we find an ideal society, or at least an imagined one, created in cyberspace. And the novel is Rushdie's most clear homage to the science fictional mode as "the best popular vehicle ever devised for the novel of ideas and metaphysics" (*Fury*, 169). In Rushdie's first unpublished work, *The Antagonist*, a satirical view of post–Imperial England is coupled with a number of "marvelous (and murderous) devices." Employing Kincaid's "particular approach to the matter of story" as a starting point, I suggest we view Rushdie's novels as embodying this approach.

In the second part of this chapter, I shall employ Wofgang Iser's model of the fictive and the imaginary realms in fiction, and especially the "as if" construction he posits as the condition of the fictional world(s) created by an author and accessed by the readers of the text, to show how this model can be read as a science fictional model or, in Kincaid's terms, how it embodies this approach to storytelling that can be termed science fictional. I first turn, however, to a closer examination of Rushdie's engagement with the science fictional imaginary.

If we return to Darko Suvin's classic definition of science fiction as "a literary mode or verbal construct whose necessary and sufficient conditions are the presence and interaction of estrangement and cognition and whose main device is an imaginative framework alternative to the author's empirical environment" (Suvin, 37), then we can see that Rushdie's work participates in this project because it offers an alternative imaginative framework to known reality. But, as some critics have shown, Suvin's definition remains limiting.

As Mark Bould puts it in *Science Fiction*, Suvin's definition of the genre is "so prescriptive as to exclude most of what is actually published as sf" (7). In a similar vein to Rieder, Bould offers a different approach to genres as "discursive phenomena, constantly defined and redefined by a host of different voices, with different degrees of influence, for many different reasons" (1). Science fiction is therefore not a "sleek Monolith, pristine, transcendent and unassailable, but a shape shifting Thing, constantly becoming and without fixed form" (2). This science fictional image of the SF genre also fits Rushdie's postcolonial thematics and aesthetics. The shape-shifter figure is also the migrant, forever becoming and never belonging, viewed as Other and at times as a threatening Thing. I would therefore suggest that Rushdie's project is science fictional in this broadest of terms. In these terms, SF is "less a genre ... than an ongoing conversation" (James and Mendelsohn 2003, 11). Rushdie's later novels are a major contribution to this conversation about the world or worlds we inhabit.

My work places Rushdie's novels as SF novels engaging in a re-imagination of both national and personal histories. The science fictional mode is the most appropriate vehicle for expressing these thematic and ideological concerns and is the organizing feature of Rushdie's oeuvre. I reevaluate and reread the later novels in light of recent critical engagement with SF as a vehicle for re-imagining national histories and as a potentially subversive tool for social and political engagement in a fictional realm.

Rushdie's choice of SF is highly political. His alternative histories and science fictional sites document the painful history of India, offering an even more disturbing version of historical events than is possible in a more realistic portrayal of the same events.

Rushdie's choice of the science fictional mode becomes a way of describing the violence done to his beloved Mother India and its dispersed children. This form allows Rushdie to distance himself from painful realities, employing a nonrealistic generic form, while at the same time it also offers access to these very painful sites of collective and personal memory.

I shall examine Rushdie's unpublished novel *The Antagonist* (first unpublished draft, May 12, 1974, and only recently made available to the public through the Salman Rushdie archive at Emory University), in which the young author imagines a parallel underworld—or what he calls the "New Empire"—that operates in clandestine ways and uses paranormal agents to continue the British Empire's rule in the world. This novel is in effect an early version of Rushdie's most successful work, *Midnight Children*. It offers a hitherto unexplored look into Rushdie's growth as an author and suggests that his science fictional imaginary was at work from the outset of his long and successful career.

As Fredric Jameson has noted in *Archaeologies of the Future*, postmodern science fiction creates "an imaginary enclave within real social space," with cyberspace offering a unique, new sort of enclave: "a subjectivity which is objective and which once more does away with the 'centered subject'" (Jameson, *Archaeologies of the Future*, 15, 21).

Jameson contends that unlike in fantasy, which remains a conservative and even reactionary form, in postmodern science fiction we may still find a revolutionary potential. I aim to locate Rushdie's later novels as the historicist project that Jameson finds in postmodern SF, a genre that returns to social, political and utopian imaginings within a fictional realm. The science fictionalizing of history becomes the focus of Rushdie's work, and, as Jameson notes, SF provides "an imaginary enclave in social space" (15).

This enclave entails a project of re-imagining society and rewriting history, which are Rushdie's main thematic and ideological concerns from his earlier novels to his latest works to date. As Jameson points out, "post modern SF shows a seemingly insatiable appetite for historicist visions," which, as I have mentioned, are Rushdie's main concerns from his earlier novels on. These enclaves are "something of a foreign body within the social" and "testify to its political powerlessness, at the same time that they offer a space in which new wish images of the social can be elaborated and experimented on" (16). Rushdie's later novels provide such imaginative enclaves and explore these "wish images" while questioning the possibility of their realization.

Rushdie's later novels enact Jameson's "objective subjectivity," which he explores in his ever-growing focus on the world of the Web. In *Fury*, the interaction of the enclave created in cyberspace and the real world ends badly and influences the protagonist's escapist fantasies of life "inside the electricity"; *Luka and the Fire of Life* adopts the form of a computer game and engages with the issues of (techno) immortality.

Fredric Jameson's model of postmodern SF as a historicist project and a genre that returns to social, political and utopian imaginings within a fictional realm fits with my rereading of Rushdie as a SF author. I shall, however, focus, as stated above, on the meeting points between the postcolonial and the science fictional in Rushdie's oeuvre. To that end, I shall examine what I call *imagined cosmopolitan* sites in Rushdie's work. This term, I suggest, provides a way of locating the unique textual spaces created in Rushdie's oeuvre; these spaces are science fictional in the broadest sense of the term, as I suggested above. I employ Appiah's rereading of cosmopolitan encounters as possibly redemptive options as a basis for this discussion. My textual example is a novel I shall not discuss in full in the book but which provides me with the clearest example of Rushdie's poetics, *The Moor's Last Sigh*.

Imagined Cosmopolitanisms: The Moor's Last Sigh *and Appiah's Cosmopolitan Ethics*

In Rushdie's 1995 novel *The Moor's Last Sigh*, he introduces the readers to one of his many fictional alter egos, Aurora Zogoiby, a controversial painter and overwhelmingly dominant mother to the eponymous Moor and an embodiment of Rushdie's vexed position as both a local artist and a citizen of the world. Aurora declares her strong resistance to ideologically motivated art and claims, "Throughout history, efforts to make artists socially accountable had resulted in nullity: tractor art, court art, chocolate-box junk" (*TMLS*, 234). She rebels against the public's demand to "speak profoundly of 'underlying motives' when she had only whims, to make moral statements where there had been only ('only'!) play, and feeling, and the unfolding inexorable logic of brush and light" (234). Aurora's demands seem to echo Rushdie's own wish to be spared the need to provide grand motives for his art and reflects his call for the importance of play in his work. It also echoes his conflicted position when it comes to making moral statements regarding his work.

Rushdie chooses Aurora to embody his artistic, personal and national dilemmas. What I offer is a reading of Rushdie's oeuvre that is political in the broadest sense of the term.[2] Rushdie, like his fictional Aurora, shies away from ideologically motivated art. Yet, like Aurora, he expresses his engagement with the conflicted state of his home country in the unfolding of his narrative brush and in his (word) play. *The Moor's Last Sigh* explores the cosmopolitan options, both in and out of India, through the exilic figure of its protagonist Moares Zogoiby or the Moor, a "high-born crossbreed" (*TMLS*, 5) of a Jewish father (Abraham) and a Christian artist mother (Aurora). The Moor is banished from his mother country by his enraged mother Aurora, and this banishment from the (mother) country occupies the center of the novel. Moraes, as well as Aurora, joins the set of Rushdie's fictional alter egos.

Like other migrant figures in Rushdie's fiction, Moraes is forever in the conflicted position of ultimate longing for a lost mother country and engaged in a constant search for the ultimate "elsewhere." This "elsewhere," as Rushdie tells us, may become the migrant's only true home. The novel uses this search for possibly redemptive locales as a way of dealing with this conflicted state of the migrant. This endeavor characterizes Rushdie's fictional project, which he attempts to construct as a possibly redemptive site where the conflicted state of constant longing without belonging may be mitigated. Rushdie explores possible locales where a cosmopolitan option may be imagined: In his re-imagined Bombay, he locates one such cosmopolitan space. Although Rushdie is not unaware of the possibly negative versions of the cosmopolitan ideal, as I shall show in my reading of *The Moor's Last Sigh*, he nevertheless presents this option as an *imagined* site where his protagonists may find hope for a better future.

Labeling Rushdie a "cosmopolitan" writer, Timothy Brennan included Rushdie (alongside Derek Walcott, Isabel Allende and Mario Vargas Llosa) as a representative figure, a writer who acts as both an interpreter and a public voice for the Third World. This labeling (or rather branding) also calls forth the negative implications of the terms *cosmopolitan* or *citizen of the world*. It conjures up the image of an affluent and glorified migrant who chooses not to reside in his home country and yet is considered to be its representative voice. In Rushdie's case, the issue is complicated by his choice to write in English and his rejection of the indigenous languages of India as a literary vehicle. As a possible corrective to this (mis)conception of Rushdie as a "cosmopolitan" writer, a recent book places him within another group of "cosmopolitical" South Asian writers. In her book *When Borne Across*, Bishnupriya Ghosh locates a "literary cosmopolitics" or what she calls "a distinctive South Asian cosmopolitical discursive formation," which shares "fundamental political and ethical commitments" (4). Ghosh identifies a group of commercially successful South Asian writers or IWEs (Indian writers in English) who participate in this "discursive formation": "Those writers to whom I attach the moniker 'cosmopolitical' are part of this South Asian progressive discursive formation, challenging both the forms of nationalism reinforced by global flows and the pernicious globalism surfacing in dispersed local contexts" (5). This formation shares a "social imaginary of sorts: of democratic self-rule and of contingent cosmopolitics." The writers Ghosh includes in this group (Salman Rushdie, Vikram Chandra, Amitav Ghosh, Upamanyu Chatterjee and Arundhati Roy) "exemplify the cosmopolitical writing ... both in their direct political overtures (in interviews, manifestos, nonfiction), and in their indirect literary expressions" (5). This group of South Asian writers becomes, then, the chosen representatives of this literary cosmopolitics outlined by Ghosh. Unlike the "elite varieties" of cosmopolitanism or the "fetishized cosmopolitanism of liberal individualism" (21), the cosmopolitical writer has "an unflinching commitment to the local struggles and the subsequent ethical stance" (22).

Ghosh constructs a model for ethical and political activism in the literary sphere. She attempts to rescue cosmopolitanism from its possibly negative implication as a strategy of avoiding political activity in the public sphere. In her reinvented grouping of cosmopolitical writers headed by Rushdie, she locates the possibility for "global progressive ethiopolitical transformations" (22). Ghosh examines the direct political (or nonfictional) production of these writers and their indirect literary productions as sites of these possible transformations.

In my engagement with Rushdie's work, I offer a different hierarchy. My focus is on the *poetics* more than on the *ethics* of Rushdie's brand of cosmopolitanism. I argue that Rushdie's fiction may be examining ethicopolitical dilemmas *within* the fictional space. Rushdie's novels are not *outside* the political arena. They are, however, located *aside* or *beside* the actual political events that he narrates. In reinventing historical and political events in his nation's history as science fictional sites, Rushdie invests in a different kind of investigation. Rushdie's investigation employs the fictional realm as a site for possible transformation without offering political solutions or cures. It is within this fictional realm that I locate Rushdie's ideological and artistic investment in his imaginary spaces of cosmopolitan sensibility.

Rushdie's fiction engages in constructing such cosmopolitan sites as a way of engaging with the author's own vexed position both personally and nationally. Rushdie's imagined, constructed sites where history meets science fiction are the fictional grounds in which these dilemmas are played out. As suggested above, science fictional thematics feature in Rushdie's later novels discussed in this book. Rushdie chooses science fiction as a vehicle most suited for his project of re-imagined worlds and alternative histories.[3] This choice indicates his belief in the power of the (science) fictional text as a way of reinventing national and personal realities in literary form. Borrowing both the narrative and thematic tools of the science fictional text, Rushdie creates imagined locales that function as though reflected from and refracting like a broken mirror, the sad and joyous realities of the quintessential migrant: always longing for home while being "elsewhere."

It is important to note here that Rushdie's use of the term *migrant* (and my consequent use of the term) is different from the more overtly political usages. While Rushdie does not ignore the political ramifications of the term, he seems to locate migration as a state of mind as well as a sociopolitical state. As I shall later show in more detail, Rushdie hints that the *reasons* for the migrant's loss of his or her homeland concern him less than their *effects* on migrant psychology. This is the place where he locates his engagement with imagined locales, which in turn become possible homes for the migrant. As I have claimed, Rushdie posits the cosmopolitan option as a possible cure for the migrant's traumatized state. But this does not mean he considers migrant existence to be a purely negative experience.

In *The Moor's Last Sigh*, Rushdie examines the cosmopolitan ideal as a possible venue for this exilic sensibility in which to find a home. He explores cosmopolitan sites as imagined locales, which are always and forever "elsewhere." Aurora's cry against "nullity art" occurs in "one of these dark years of the mid–Seventies"—namely the infamous Emergency, the ultimate dark age in Rushdie's fiction. Aurora's response to this crisis is to provide her son Moraes with a Spanish passport and exhort him to keep the passport valid so that he may leave India when the need arises. Aurora tells her son not to "go to the English. We have had enough of them. Go find Palimpstine; go see Mooristan" (235). Spain is transformed into an imaginary land (Mooristan), a magical nowhere land, where the Moor may find his home. But as he indeed flees India and goes to Spain in search of his mother's lost painting, "The Moor's Last Sigh," this Edenic, imagined locale turns out to be a nightmarish prison from which he barely escapes alive.

One of the most prominent options of a local (Indian) space that transcends locality to become a cosmopolitan option is the city of Bombay. Moraes describes his mother city Bombay as follows: "Bombay was central, had been so since the moment of its creation: the bastard child of a Portuguese-English wedding, and yet the most Indian of Indian cities" (350). In this "hybrid" city "all–India met what-was-not India, what came across the black water to flow into our veins" (ibid.). And this Bombay, the city that is at once India and not-India, also provides the magical option of avoiding, at least to some extent, the nation's other bloody struggles: "[On] the way to Bombay the rivers of blood were usually diluted, other rivers poured into them, so that by the time they reached the city's streets the disfigurations were relatively slight" (359). Bombay represents a different type of Indianness, which Rushdie's narrator (and the author) seems to favor over the Delhi brand of national Indian identity. The Moor describes the two opposing factions:

> Between Delhi-folk and Bombay types there has always been a measure of mutual contempt; Bombay-wallahs have tended to dismiss Delhiites as the fawning lackeys of power, as greasy-pole-climbers and placemen, while the capital's citizens have sneered at the superficiality, the bitchiness, the cosmopolitan "Westoxication" of my home town's business babus and lacquered, high-gloss femmes [178].

This "Westoxication" is one of the many charges laid at Rushdie's feet. He has been accused, time and again, of pandering to Western tastes and providing the West with an exotic version of India.[4] I maintain, rather, that in the imagined version of Bombay (or as he calls it in *The Ground Beneath Her Feet*, "Wombay"), and in Aurora's "Mooristan"/"Palimpstine" vision, Rushdie offers an imagined locale that is a hybrid construction or a "bastard child" like Moraes (who comes to suspect he is not his father's child but Nehru's offspring). This site is then both Indian and non–Indian. This option will perhaps dilute if not stop the rivers of blood that pour into this Indian Sea, or as Rushdie calls it in describing Bombay's mixture of languages and peoples, that "insaan-soup" (350). But Rushdie's vision does not remain wholly optimistic. While celebrating the possible power of hybridity and the redemptive options inherent in the cosmopolitan/Bombayite option, he also sees its perils.

In the figures of Aurora and her son Moraes, Rushdie provides us with two options of imagining a cosmopolitan sensibility. Aurora creates paintings that move away from realistic and socially responsible art into an imagined depiction of India as a dream or nightmare land; she reimagines Moorish Spain as India and vice versa to paint her own vision of "Mooristan." This vision at times celebrates the possibilities inherent in breaking down and melting boundaries of all kinds (most notably of land and sea), but at other times it becomes an apocalyptic version of what India may become: Into such apocalyptic works, Aurora had poured "her larger, prophetic, even Cassandran fears for the nation, her fierce grief at the sourness of what had once, at least in an India of dreams, been as sweet as sugar-cane-juice" (236).[5]

This description of Aurora's art reflects Rushdie's own endeavor as artist in the novels I discuss. Rushdie veers between his optimistic vision of the power of hybridity and border crossing and his bleak, apocalyptic, "Cassandran" visions of India's future. Aurora's "India of dreams" is also Rushdie's imagined India. In the figure of Aurora's son, a man who finally becomes a cosmopolitan by leaving his (mother) India, Rushdie presents us with the darker option of the "Palimpstine" dream. The Moor becomes a nowhere man in nowhere land. Like the international, zombie-like community of foreigners in the strange village of Benengali in Spain, the Moor is also detached from his homeland and lost in a hellish transit zone. As he first encounters this odd group of expatriates, the Moor reflects: "Perhaps these expatriates are the new Moors ... and I am one of them, after all, arriving here in search of something that matters to nobody but myself, and staying, perhaps, to die" (390). Here the cosmopolitans are presented as invaders, only to be driven out by the "true" inhabitants—the "real" Spaniards.[6]

In what follows, I would like to chart a way of reading Rushdie's oeuvre in light of this conflict between cosmopolitanism as an imagined option of freedom from all national, social and religious boundaries and its counter-vision as a nightmarish transit-zone or zombie-like existence of a nowhere man in nowhere land. I therefore turn to an ethical investigation of the cosmopolitan option in Anthony Appiah's work to examine where and how his project meets Rushdie's reinvention of the cosmopolitan option.

In his reflection on cosmopolitan ethics and moral responsibilities, Kwame Anthony Appiah discusses the ways in which cosmopolitans, and cosmopolitanism, may offer us a way of engaging with the problematics of globalization. Appiah sees the challenge of modern day cosmopolitan as "[taking] minds and hearts formed over the long millennia of living in local troops and [equipping] them with ideas and institutions that will allow us to live together as the global tribe we have become." (xii) To that end, Appiah offers ways of rescuing the term *cosmopolitanism* from its perception as "an unpleasant posture of superiority toward the putative provincial" (xii). What Appiah offers is in effect a compromise between the nationalist position that "abandons all foreigners" and what he calls the "hard-core" cosmopolitan position or the "imperialist" version, which maintains that as a "citizen of the world" you are "supposed to abjure all local allegiances and partialities in the name of ... humanity" and that "the boundaries of nations are morally irrelevant — accidents of history with no rightful claim to our conscience" (xvi).

Appiah believes the "position worth defending might be called (in both senses) a partial cosmopolitanism" (xvii), offering a model that he calls "conversation": "[In] national communities, we need to develop habits of coexistence: conversation in its oldest meaning, of living together, association" (xix). This conversation also involves the kind of cross-cultural and cross-lingual encounters Appiah experienced in his childhood in Ghana: "Conversations across boundaries can be fraught, all the more so as the world grows smaller and the stakes grow larger. It's therefore worth remembering that they can also be a pleasure" (xx). In the post–9/11 world, which increasingly stresses the divide between "us" and "them," Appiah's model "will make it harder to think of the world as divided between the West and the Rest; between locals and moderns; between a bloodless ethics of profit and a bloody ethic of identity; between 'us' and 'them'" (xxi).

In this call for conversation across and between cultural boundaries, Appiah seems to meet Rushdie's vision of hybridity.[7] Appiah draws on the Roman playwright Terence, whose "own mode of writing — his free incorporation of earlier Greek plays into a single Latin drama — was known to Roman litterateurs as 'contamination'" (111). Appiah locates in Terence's comedy *The Self-Tormentor* what "has proved something like the golden rule of cosmopolitanism: ... 'I am human: nothing human is alien to me'" (110). Appiah shows how, in the play's humorous context, this rejoinder is not "an ordinance from on high; it's just the cause for gossip" (112). And it is this gossipy element that Appiah links to literature:

Certainly the ideal of contamination has no more eloquent exponent than Salman Rushdie, who has insisted that the novel that occasions his fatwa "celebrates hybridity, impurity, intermingling, the transformation that comes of new and unexpected combination of human beings, cultures, ideas, politics, movies, songs" [112].

Appiah points out that it "didn't take modern mass migration" to create this possibility of cultural contamination: "The early Cynics and Stoics took their contamination from the places they were born to the Greek cities where they taught. Many were strangers in those places; cosmopolitanism was invented by contaminators whose migrations were solitary" [112].

Appiah celebrates this notion of contamination, claiming that "the larger side of human truth is on the side of Terence's contamination" and that "[cultural] purity is an oxymoron" (113). He states that most of us "already live a cosmopolitan life, enriched by literature, art, and film that come from many places, and that contains influences from many more" (113). But this cultural influence is not one-sided. It is not just the West that influences the rest. In Appiah's formulation, "people in each place make their own uses even of the most famous global commodities" (113). Appiah concludes: "A tenable cosmopolitanism tempers a respect for difference with a respect for actual human beings—and with a sentiment best captured in the credo, once comic, now commonplace, penned by that former slave from North Africa (Terrence)" (113).

Appiah's celebratory position is not without its perils. He seems to paint an almost idyllic world picture where cultural religious and ethnic differences can be resolved by a plea for conversation and "respect for difference"; it would seem that these cultural differences, for one, cannot be resolved as easily as Appiah seems to believe. I would like, however, to use one of his historical examples of a figure that he claims embodies both cosmopolitanism and anti-cosmopolitanism as a way of addressing Rushdie's vexed position as a writer.

Appiah begins his contemplation on the cosmopolitan ideal in a chapter entitled "The Shattered Mirror," centering on the figure of the Victorian adventurer Sir Richard Francis Burton. Appiah chooses Burton as an embodiment of the ultimate cosmopolitan and shows how this option can be both liberating and dangerous at the same time. The very choice of title already leads us to Rushdie's constant use of the mirror and the shattered mirror trope as ways of dealing with identity dilemmas faced by his migrant characters. In *The Ground Beneath Her Feet*, for example, the narrator describes his life as "living on a broken mirror," thereby indicating his confusion as to the reality of his world when faced by options of other, alternate worlds. Appiah chooses Sir Richard Francis Burton, "a Victorian adventurer whose life lent credence to that dubious adage about truth being stranger than fiction" (1), as an example of a character combining elements of both cosmopolitanism and anti-cosmopolitanism. Burton, a traveler, an expert linguist and translator, also tested the boundaries between truth and fiction much in the way Rushdie does more than a century later. Appiah tells of Burton's 1880 poem, which he claimed was a translation of a *qasida* written by Haji Abdu El-Yezdi, a native of central Persia. This poem, as it turns out, was not written by this fictitious character but rather by Burton himself. Burton hints as much by telling his readers that Abdu preferred to call himself a man of "No-hall, Nowhere": This nowhere man leads me again to Rushdie's Moor and also, by implication, to Rushdie himself, who, like Burton's fictitious character, can be said to come of "No-hall, Nowhere" when he creates imagined locales in his fiction.

The shattered mirror image comes from Burton's poem: "Burton's poet, too, seems mostly to speak for Burton: himself an agnostic of a scientific bent, with a vast store of knowledge of the world's religions and an evenhanded assessment of them all" (5). This assessment is expressed in Burton's lines, quoted by Appiah, which echo Rushdie's narrator's sentiments in *The Moor's Last Sigh* to a very large extent. Burton's "Abdu" describes faith and religion in these striking terms: "All Faith is false, all Faith is true: Truth is the shattered mirror strown [*sic*] / in myriad bits; while each believes / His little bit the whole to own" (5). The Moor speaks of his parents' religious beliefs (or lack thereof) thus:

> I watched Epifania praying and gave thanks that somehow, by some great fluke ... my parents had been cured of religion. (Where's their medicine, their priest-poison-beating anti-venene? Bottle it, for pity's sake, and send it round the world!) [55].[8]

Appiah describes both Burton's "cosmopolitan openness to the world" and his racial prejudices and contempt for the "darker races" and the not-so-dark: "He was an odd sort of mélange of cosmopolitan and misanthrope" (7), says Appiah of Burton. Though Appiah seems to be fascinated by Burton's "voracious assimilation of religions, literatures, and customs from around the world" (5), he is nonetheless wary of Burton's moral relativism expressed in the shattered mirror image: "Life would be easier if we could stop with that thought. We can grant that there's some insight everywhere else and some error *chez nous*. But that doesn't help us when we are trying to decide exactly where the truth lies *this* time" (8).

Appiah sees this as "one of these cases where our obligations depend on our positions. You should be faithful to your spouse, we can agree, but *I* don't need to be faithful to your spouse" (9). This choice of example is telling. Appiah then claims that "[someone] might say in the same spirit 'Muslims should go to Mecca, and if you *are* a Muslim, you don't think that anyone, not even a Catholic, has a duty to go to Mass" (9). Appiah finds fault with Burton's shattered mirror: "Burton, with his mastery of thirty-nine languages was something of a freak of nature in his ability to penetrate different cultures—to 'go native,' as we say, and do so time and time again" (11). Although most of us don't share Burton's gift (or freakish nature), we still

> have that ability to some lesser degree: we can often experience the appeal of values that aren't, exactly, our own. So perhaps when it comes to morality, there is no singular truth. In that case, there's no one shattered mirror; there are lots of mirrors, lots of moral truths, and we can at best agree to differ [11].

Hence, Haji Abdu's words—"There is no good, there is no bad; / these be the whims of mortal will" (11)—do not express a position Appiah cares to endorse. Clearly, Appiah believes there *are* some values—of Good and Bad—while granting the possibility there is no *one* moral truth. I would try to reclaim Burton's fiction, his invented man of "No-hall, Nowhere," as espousing an *artistic and authorial* position. Appiah's concerns are more *ethical and social*. Even when he discusses Burton's literary work, he relates to it merely as a marker of Burton's lack of moral concerns and his extreme cosmopolitan/anti-cosmopolitan blend of "going native" paired with racism. Appiah's call for "partial cosmopolitanism," which allows for cross-cultural conversation, indeed meets Rushdie's ideological and thematic concerns. Rushdie's espousal of hybridity as a possibly redemptive option reflects Appiah's model in many ways. But whereas Appiah attempts to rescue the term *cosmopolitanism* from its possibly negative ramifications by making it a positive tool for social and political change, Rushdie's concerns are with the literary and artistic ways in which the cosmopolitan option is imagined and re-imagined *within* the space of the literary work. I am not claiming that Rushdie shares Burton's stance, which seems to refuse the possibility of any moral evaluation. I assert rather that Rushdie, like Burton and his alias Haji Abdu, create imagined locales, questioning the boundaries that separate truth from fiction. The shattered mirror image hints at the possibility of fictional realms meeting real ones—where the boundaries between the two are no longer that obvious. In order to explore this literary or textual aspect of Rushdie's imagined cosmopolitan locales, I turn to a theoretical model that delineates the uniqueness of the literary text as an autonomous site. Employing this model helps demonstrate how Rushdie's fictions come to function as independent locales for boundary crossings between the fictive and the real. It is in these sites, I would claim, that Rushdie performs his artistic and ideological work of recreating our known world(s) as alternate sites of meaning.

As I suggested, Rushdie's imagined sites form part of his science fictional imaginary. Returning to Rieder's formulation of science fiction as a "web of resemblances" (17) that can "be extended in an unpredictable number of new and different ways" (17), I suggest a reading of Wolfgang Iser's model of textuality as science fictional. As Rieder claims, the "fluid boundaries" of science fiction "have been defended and contested in many ways for many reasons, but the existence of the category as a condition of literary and cultural production and reception is incontrovertible" (17). It is this condition of literary and cultural production that Iser outlines and that Rushdie's novels embody.

The "As If" Mode: Iser and Rushdie

I thus turn to Wolfgang Iser's model in *The Fictive and the Imaginary* as a point of departure for addressing this dynamic between the fictive and the real that informs Rushdie's project. Iser claims, "[T]here is little point in clinging to the old distinction between fiction and reality as a frame of reference." This duality should be replaced, according to Iser, with "a triad: the real, the fictive, and ... the imaginary." Iser claims, "[It] is out of this triad that the text arises" (Iser, 1). The focus should then be shifted to what Iser calls "the fictionalizing act" (2). This act already entails "a crossing of boundaries" (3).

This act of transgression, or boundary crossing, is where Iser locates the all-important function of the imaginary and the ways in which the literary imaginary functions: "Reproduced reality is made to point to a 'reality' beyond itself, while the imaginary is lured into form.... Consequently, extratextual reality merges into the imaginary and the imaginary merges into reality" (3). In other words, this interplay between the three elements of Iser's triad recasts the ways we read the literary text as a unique category. The science fictional text manifests this quality of the literary text in a highly marked way as its very nature depends on this merging of the imaginary and the real.

Iser offers a corrective to the binary opposition of real and the fictive that has an important influence on the ways we read literary texts. He concludes that "[given] this reformulation of the situation, the old antithesis between fiction and reality is revealed as inadequate and even misleading ... there is no longer any need to assume the transcendental stance that was necessary whenever the opposition between fiction and reality had to be explained" (4). Getting rid of the "transcendental stance" will, according to Iser, also rid us of the "latter-day fate of epistemology, which, in its struggle to grasp the nature of fictionality, has ended up having to recognize its own premises as fictions and, in the face of its ever increasing implication in the fictiveness it is attempting to define, has had to forfeit its claims to being a foundational principle" (4). In other words, if we look at the fictive *quality* of the literary text, we will be able to read it on its own terms and have a better understanding of the ways it operates in the world without confusing it with real events. This fictionality can be read, I suggest, as science fictionality; the science fictional text may be one of the clearest examples of Iser's more general model.

Iser claims that the act of fictionalizing itself involves boundary crossing. The literary text, as "the product of an author," reflects "a particular attitude by which the author directs himself ... to the world" (4). The author, however, *selects* which elements from the real world are included in his fictional text. This very act of selection, claims Iser, must involve "a stepping beyond boundaries, in that the elements selected are lifted out of the systems in which they fulfill their specific function" (5). These acts of selection "in turn reveal the attitude adopted by the author to the given world" (5). Iser points out that these "operations point to a purpose, although this purpose is not verbalized in the fictional text itself. Thus selection as a fictionalizing act reveals the intentionality of the text" (6). He urges the readers to turn to the *text* and not to the "author's life, dreams, and beliefs" in order to discover the "manifestations of intentionality expressed in the fictional text itself through its selection of and from extratextual systems" (6). Let us examine what the text *does* rather than focus on "what the text is meant to mean" (6). Although my reading of Rushdie's novels does take into account the author's "life, dreams and beliefs," I would like to employ as a way of re-approaching Rushdie's textual universe Iser's distinction between the fictive, the real and the imaginary and also his insistence on the autonomous nature of the fictional work as a site that generates meaning and, as he puts it, has a purpose.

Rushdie's novels to be later examined are such autonomous sites. His selection of elements from the real world mixes in with a host of extratextual elements: from literary allusions to inverted and reinvented historical events and figures and a recasting of national histories in a science fictional mode. Rushdie's imagined sites and transformed locales create a fictional universe with a purpose and a meaning of its own: It is not divorced from the real world; rather, by selecting and rearranging historical facts and retelling national and cultural tales, Rushdie creates his own versions or alternate fictive realms. His novels participate in what Iser calls the "'as-if' construction" (Iser, 13). Iser claims:

> [As] the world of the text is to be taken only *as if* it were real, it becomes part of a comparison that — according to the "as-if" construction has to be related to something "impossible" or "unreal" (i.e., in either case to something other than itself) [15–16].

This move highlights the status of the fictional world as fiction and demands the reader's response to the "world represented in brackets" (16): the fictional world as it encounters the actual world outside the fiction. If the fictionality of the text is thus made observable by the reader, it may "also instigate the reader to extend beyond habitual dispositions" (16). We, as readers, now have "to imagine what has been stimulated by the 'as-if,'" which entails "[placing] our faculties at the disposal of an unreality and [bestowing] upon it a semblance of reality in proportion to a reduction of our own reality" (17). This description of the relationship between reader and text is surely most at work when readers are confronted with a text that contains science fictional elements. It is in such texts that readers have to give in to the unreality of the text while still "bestowing a semblance of reality" on the text at the time of reading in order to access its meaning.

This is what Rushdie's fiction compels us to perform: We are drawn into Rushdie's "as-if"' worlds. We have to extend our habitual dispositions and willingly place our faculties at the disposal of an unreality. Rushdie's science fictional sites lead us to this imaginative activity. They lead us to "recognize the multiplicity of possible interpretations as a sign of the multiplicitous availability of the imaginary" (Iser, 19).

Rushdie's creation of alternate and imagined spaces in his fiction may prove to be his way of working out the many conflicts of his authorial and personal positions. In an essay devoted to Terry Gilliam's movie *Brazil*, Rushdie describes the ways in which the migrant sensibility always dwells in such imagined locales: "Migrants must, of necessity, make a new imaginative relationship with the world, because of the loss of familiar habitats" (125). Rushdie chooses the cinema as the ultimate imaginative site where the "plural, hybrid, metropolitan result of such imaginings" takes place. It is this location, the cinema, "in which peculiar fusions have always been legitimate," which may prove to be the "ideal location" (125) for such imaginative forays. But for the migrant, this is also the kind of dream land (or nightmarish vision) he or she inhabits. Rushdie extends his ruminations on Gilliam's film to include the migrant state as a place/no place — a land that is imagined as the Brazil of the film's title. This Brazil, Rushdie reminds us, is not in South America. It is located in an old tune that creates Brazil as an idyllic, romantic and futuristic space. If "the location of *Brazil* is the cinema itself," where "the dream is the norm," then this imaginative locale is where the migrant finds his true home: "[This] cinematic *Brazil* is a land of make-believe which all of us, who have, for whatever reason, lost a country and ended up elsewhere, are the true citizens" (125). In other words, the migrant can only ever find a home in an imagined or alternative space; and his own homeland, like Rushdie's "India of dreams," has in turn also been transformed into such an imagined locale. Thus the ultimate migrant anthem, as Rushdie has stated in his meditation of his favorite film, may be "Somewhere Over the Rainbow."[9] As in the romantic song that gave *Brazil* its name, this land has an indeterminate status: It is neither here nor there but always "elsewhere."

If we return to Appiah's sociopolitical "partial cosmopolitanism" model and link it to Iser's textual model that centers on the fictive text as an alternate site of meaning and, as I have suggested, locates the fictionality of the text as science fictional in nature, we may arrive at what I call Rushdie's model of "imagined cosmopolitanism." In this hybrid Rushdean model, the text *itself* acts as a site for boundary crossings and offers multiple versions or imaginary options. The conflicts of exilic existence, carried over from Appiah's real-world dilemmas into Rushdie's (science) fictional worlds, are encountered in a new form in the fictive work. They are not resolved but rather explored and interrogated within the science fictional space.

Rushdie creates alternative textual worlds, employing the science fictional mode. He conjures up different, slightly skewed versions of the world we live in and thereby manages to unsettle his reader. Rushdie chooses science fiction as a vehicle for imagining alternative worlds and for reassessing personal and national histories. Since my focus is on this science fictional aspect of Rushdie's fiction, my choice of texts is based on the extent to which they best demonstrate the unique Rushdean mode of employing the genre. I chose to focus on novels that reintroduce familiar science fictional tropes in a new way and reinvent them in fictional settings that are not traditionally considered science fictional. The novels effectively explore and employ the science fictional mode as a vehicle for reinvention of self and nation and engage with the possibilities of the genre in an unusual fictional terrain. Rushdie chooses to transpose science fictional themes and tropes into a postcolonial setting, thereby offering a comment on the genre's philosophical and ideological implications as a narrative of becoming. The novels I discuss in detail (*Fury, The Ground Beneath Her Feet, Midnight's Children* and *The Antagonist, Shalimar the Clown, Haroun and the Sea of Stories* and its sequel *Luka and the Fire of Life*) offer different versions of Indian and migrant histories. By creating these alternate (hi)stories in SF mode, Rushdie attempts to make sense of a troubled, at times incomprehensible, tale of the birth, growth and possible future of the new Indian nation.

In the chapter entitled "Rage Against the Machine?" I focus on the rewriting of postcolonial narratives of identity in the New World — the United States of America — but also in the Brave New World of the World Wide Web. Malik Solanka, the novel's protagonist, a philosopher turned puppet (and world) maker, engages in a failed attempt to escape reality and "live in the electricity." I examine the Web-based world in the novel as a possibly utopian space and examine the consequent breakdown of this imagined world as it interacts with real political events in the world of the novel. Solanka's alternate virtual world becomes the inspiration for a deadly postcolonial revolution on an "Indo-Lilliputian" island that serves to mitigate his dreams of the ultimate "elsewhere." The novel ends with his vexed homecoming but leaves him suspended, both literally and figuratively, in the novel's final scene.

The chapter on *The Ground Beneath Her Feet*, entitled "The World Is (Not) What It Is," focuses on the notions of history and cultural memory as they come together in the novel. Rushdie's novel, an alternative history of rock 'n' roll, which tells the story of the mythological pair of Indian-born pop icons Ormus Cama and Vina Apsara, offers a rewriting of historical narratives as science fictional tales. The novel reinvents and re-imagines Eastern and Western mythologies as loci of self(re)formation in a postmodern age. It performs a dual function: reaffirming the possibility of selfhood and individuality while paradoxically locating this option at the site of fissures of postmodern subjectivity as copy or version. In this novel, Rushdie imagines alternative versions of historical narratives. He chooses memory's truth over the truth of the historical chronicle, and his pop icon protagonists become emblems not only of what we choose to remember but also of what we choose to forget or misremember. The novel's narrator and photographer, Rai, is forever dominated by the shadow of the mythological pair. Although the novel ends with Rai's seemingly peaceful domestic bliss with his new lover Mira and her young daughter Tara, the destabilizing elements still hover over this scene in the forms of Ormus and Vina's dead but all-too-present figures.

In the chapter entitled "*The Year of the Reverse*," I read Rushdie's most successful text alongside a previously little-discussed earlier version of the same novel that Rushdie did not publish, called *The Antagonist*. This version of *Midnight's Children* features a very different Saleem Sinai as the protagonist, or rather the "antagonist," as Rushdie names him. The early novel also introduces Saleem's alter ego, Black Saleem, who reappears as Shiva in *Midnight's Children*. In this earlier piece, the science fictional elements that appear as a faint echo in the later novel are the most prominent feature of the young author's reimagining of England's and India's intertwined histories. In this early work, the focus is on England in 1974 and the dystopian aftereffects of empire. The backdrop is India's nuclear experiment in May 1974, a topic that would later resurface in *The Ground Beneath Her Feet*, in which earthquakes come to metonymically signal India and Pakistan's nuclear experiments and the way these may shake the world.

In light of this early unpublished piece, I reexamine *Midnight's Chil-*

dren as a science fictional attempt at charting the role of imaginary locales at the very heart of nation making. Rushdie provides "hallucinatory recreations of the past," to borrow Pierre Nora's term, thereby recasting India's history in a unique science fictional space. Saleem Sinai, the often deluded and "forgetful" narrator, a "midnight's child," who communicates telepathically with his fellow midnight children, becomes the skewed reflection of Rushdie's own attempts to tell his nation's story. I read Rushdie's most famous and successful work as his attempt to chart the role of imaginary spaces and locales at the very heart of nation making. Rushdie (un)tells the story of India's coming into being by erecting a place of memory in his text. Rushdie's narrator gets the historical facts wrong or misremembers them (what Rushdie calls in another context "forgeterry").[10] This device allows Rushdie to retell India's history as an always-already-imagined construct. Saleem Sinai, Rushdie's narrator, has apocalyptic visions of the young nation's future. His son, aptly named Adam, who represents this new generation, appears as a character in *The Moor's Last Sigh* and becomes a symbol of the new and corrupt India of the 1990s. Although *Midnight's Children* maintains the Indian locale, we still have glimpses of migrant characters and some foreign (American) ones; and the very vision of Mother India offered by the (unhinged) narrator is always already "elsewhere."

My fifth chapter is entitled "*Haroun* and *Shalimar*: Kashmir and Koshmar: Rushdie's Dreamscapes." Although my focus is on Rushdie's later novels, I locate *Haroun and the Sea of Stories* (1990) as a template for the unique science fictional spaces created by Rushdie in later novels. In *Haroun* we find what I would suggest calling the "science of fiction" as SF. One of the characters in the novel, the Walrus, a figure of a benevolent scientist, or an "Egghead," synthesizes a happy ending for the novel, in potion form. Thus the "science/magic" of creating fictions and finding fictional resolutions to life's travails becomes a trope both for Rushdie's endeavor as a writer and for the inherent failing to provide magical solutions to "real" problems. The Walrus's happy ending only cheers up things for a little while. It is not meant to be a solution or a recipe for solving personal and national problems.

Haroun also serves as a marker of Rushdie's different brand of fantasy. This is not "Magic Realism," where fantastic events and miraculous occurrences interpose into the realism of the novel's surface. In *Haroun* there is no such distinction. The world of Rashid and Haroun is always already a fictionalized version of India or at least of certain aspects of Indian life. The magical world of the Walrus and the other fantastic beings in the novel is just another version of this fantastic world, another alternative universe, one of many, all existing at the same time. Rushdie's alternative histories and science fictional sites do not avoid the inherently violent nature of his nation's coming into being and the never-ending bloodshed unmitigated even in the imagined versions of true historical events. Thus, in *Shalimar the Clown*, the bloody history of Kashmir, although imagined by employing science fictional tropes, is no less violent and painful than a more realistic rendering of the same tale. I show how the earlier novel and the later one signal a change in Rushdie's treatment of the magical locale that appears in his novels time and again as the ultimate locus of longing and hope. Kashmir, which appears as the "Valley of K." in *Haroun*, becomes more real in *Shalimar*, as Rushdie laments the bloody history of this paradise-like piece of land. The novel, however, does imagine a future with the next generation, although, as in *Fury*, this is only an option. The novel remains open-ended; it ends in a possible future.

My final chapter centers on Rushdie's latest novel and is entitled "Immortality Now: *Luka and the Fire of Life*." Rushdie's latest novel (2010) adopts the form of a computer game and engages with the issues of (techno-)immortality. The novel, a sequel to *Haroun* and dedicated to Rushdie's younger son, mimics a computer game in both form and content. It thus becomes the template for a SF tale for the new generation, in the image of Rushdie's younger son, who grew up with this technology at his fingertips. Rushdie imagines his alternate worlds in terms of the game console as he taps in to the notion of a new narrativity both inspired and shaped by the world of computer games.

In my rereading of Rushdie's work as SF, I show how Rushdie's "broken mirrors" reflect past, present and possibly future worlds. In the shards of this mirror, we may find our own reflection staring back at us. And if we are indeed living "on a broken mirror," as Rai says, we may glimpse bits of reality mingled with the fiction that shapes our personal and collective histories. These Rushdean tales end up re-imagining history and story, but they also reshape our own experience of ourselves as personal and historical beings.

I trace Rushdie's engagement with SF as an organizing feature not only of his fiction but also of his life. To that end, my conclusion reads Rushdie's memoir *Joseph Anton* as an attempt to retell the events of the *fatwa* as a tale of a man whose "world was exploding around him" and is beset by "lethal blackbirds" (3): a nightmarish vision that enacts the real life drama as a horror story, a fantastic retelling of the real in a science fictional mode. Rushdie's memoir is not a first person recounting of events. He chooses the third person narrator, a distancing device, which allows him to retell and rethink his own life through a fictive lens. Joseph Anton was Rushdie's alias during the years he was in hiding following the *fatwa*. But the act of (re)naming, in fiction as well as in real life, becomes a gesture of reinvention. The shape-shifting nature of migrant existence is at the core of the Rushdean text, as I have shown above. It is this state of becoming that he documents, in science fictional terms, even in his most personal account of his own life.

2

Rage Against the Machine: Cyberspace Narratives in Rushdie's *Fury*

In *Fury,* published in 2002, Salman Rushdie employs science fictional narrative devices and themes as a means of engagement with the redemptive nature of cyberspace. Set in a New York of the new millennium, the novel explores cyberspace as a possible locus for utopian imaginings. The protagonist, Malik Solanka, a philosopher-turned-puppet-maker, is caught up in this new world, creating a narrative of cyborgs and their puppet master entitled "Let the Fittest Survive." Not only does this cyber-tale become a great commercial success, it eventually influences the real world as it inspires a bloody postcolonial revolution in the fictive island of Lilliput-Blefuscu. Solanka's virtual world infringes on the real world, creating a site of multiple boundary confusions. The novel questions the artistic newness offered by cyberspace narrativity. Solanka becomes increasingly disillusioned by the Internet, which he initially believed might have the potential for the reinvention and reinvigoration of creativity. The novel's ending offers a bizarre return to the real world, culminating in Solanka's attempt to reunite with his abandoned son, Asmaan.

This chapter argues that Rushdie represents the new form of narrativity offered by cyberspace, a form seemingly free from the shackles of linearity, as unable to avoid the real world, because it is shaped by events in the world and shapes them in turn. Although Solanka first sees the boundless possibilities of this new narrativity, with "its formal preference for lateral leaps and its relative uninterest in linear progression" (*Fury,* 186) and its electronic instead of narrative links allowing for "omniscience ... at the merest click of a mouse" (*Fury,* 187), the narrative is nevertheless unable to avoid being implicated in the world that it seemingly transcends.

Rushdie presents the allures of cyberspace narrativity as a seductive but ultimately dangerous means of artistic escape rather than as enabling artistic freedom. Solanka's disillusionment thus mirrors Rushdie's skeptical stance towards cyberspace's possibly redemptive potential.

Fury enacts the problematics of the science-fictional imaginings of a future that is also very much a past and a history. Contemporary New York, likened to the decadent Roman Empire and reflected in Solanka's imagined Rijk civilization, is envisioned as a possible refuge from Solanka's personal fury, but this imagined civilization is also a reflection of its creator's rage as he incorporates the minute details of his life in New York into this cyber-fantasy. Rushdie's novel examines the postcolonial condition in its intersection with cyberspace. The intervention of the real in the form of a postcolonial rebellion in Solanka's cyber-narrative entails the breakdown of the cyber-world and of the real world, which it both mirrors and inspires. Thus, the disillusionment from the dream of an ultimate elsewhere, a subject Rushdie revisits in his novels time and again, becomes even more pronounced. The migrant protagonist's return home to London is an attempt to recapture the elusive presence of a real place, one that would replace the realm of virtuality. However, this return home is also problematic as the Indian-born Solanka returns to the former colonial capital of the British Empire, attempting to reunite with his son Aaasman, the hybrid product of a mixed marriage.

The novel's main locale is New York, an ideal setting for Solanka's engagement with the virtual world. As Gonzalez points out in her astute reading of the novel:

> What better place than New York to tell the story of postmodern culture, a vampire metropolis, based on obsessive consumption and tragically devoid of substance. The epitome of ersatz, New York is the perfect setting of the self conscious politics of the novel and the anti hero's solipsism [Gonzalez, 769].

The science-fictional scenario in *Fury* pays homage to one of Rushdie's favored genres. But this choice of genre is also an ideological statement: Science fiction is not only popular but also has ethical, philosophical and ontological implications;[1] it is therefore the genre most suited for Rushdie's project of disorienting notions of subjecthood and querying the possibility of transcendence through technology. Science fiction is "a term that resists easy definition," as Adam Roberts (1) reminds us in his study of the genre. However, if we follow Darko Suvin's definition of science fiction as "a literary mode or verbal construct whose necessary and sufficient conditions are the presence and interaction of estrangement and cognition and whose main device is an imaginative framework alternative to the author's empirical environment" (Suvin, 37), then we can see *Fury*'s cyberspace narrative as fulfilling these requirements of the mode.

If we choose to look at science fiction, a mode that provides this alternative imaginative framework, as "less a genre ... than an ongoing conversation" (James and Mendelsohn, 1) then we shall find that *Fury* takes part in this ongoing conversation about the limits of the genre in its cyberspace mode. *Fury*'s cyberspace narrative provides an alternative to the empirical environment, which it both mirrors and estranges, while engaging with science fiction's imaginative possibilities and its construction of alternate worlds that critique existing social and political realities. The conversation that *Fury* enacts is, as I shall show, about the very nature of reality and its interaction with the fictive. As Madelena Gonzalez points out:

> the information age throws down a specific challenge to literature and thus forces it to engage with its order. *Fury* adopts the oxymoronic stance of troubled celebration of technology, the "strange euphoria" experienced by the protagonists of cyberpunk novels such as Gibson's *Neuromancer* (1984: 9), undercut by a desperate scepticism [Gonzalez, 766].

Rushdie's novel engages with the political and ideological role of the science-fictional imaginary as a liberating site, concurrently offering and deconstructing a version of cyber transcendence.

Rushdie's choice of genre is by no means a departure from his earlier work. As I have shown in the preface, *Grimus* (1975), Rushdie's first SF novel, was not well received by critics. Rushdie claimed that he had not yet found his voice as a writer at this early stage. In my exploration of Rushdie's unpublished novel of the same time, *The Antagonist*, I show how this piece creates a science fictional universe that reflects the current political situation at the time of writing. Although Rushdie chose not to publish it, it is, as I will show, a text that reflects a very clear Rushdean voice. However, Rushdie remains an admirer of the genre and his later works, like *Fury*, contain many science fictional elements and engage with the genre's imaginary in various ways. Rushdie's love for this fantastic genre is voiced by Malik Solanka, the protagonist (and Rushdie's alter ego in

2. Rage Against the Machine

many ways), as he thinks back to his days as a young man in the sixties.[2] Solanka reflects on his attraction to the genre: "In flight from his own life's ugly reality, he found in the fantastic — its parables and allegories, but also its flights of pure invention, its loopy, spiraling conceits—a ceaselessly metamorphosing alternative world in which he felt instinctively at home" (*Fury*, 169).[3] This escape into the fantastic recurs later in his life as he creates his alternative world in cyberspace. Solanka's early love of the genre's golden age, a term coined to describe the (mostly American) science fiction novels of the late forties and fifties,[4] however, is more than a youthful fascination. The older Solanka considers the genre to be much more than a mere escapist venture: "Golden-age science fiction and science fantasy was the best popular vehicle ever devised for the novel of ideas and metaphysics" (169).

Solanka's view of the philosophical and ideological implications of writing science fiction is shared by Salman Rushdie's fictional project in *Fury*. The novel tells the story of Solanka's entanglement in the tale he had created and his eventual disillusionment. Rushdie engages with science fiction's narrative, thematic and ideological possibilities as a means of investigating the problematics of selfhood: Can one escape the shackles of a unified self through an imaginative engagement in the realm of the fantastic? Will the new options for transcending time and place opened up by cyberspace offer such an escape? What are the dangers that such a route poses?

Rushdie explores these issues by devising a unique intersection between three different, yet related, worlds: the postcolonial arena outside the U.S. (in the fictive island of Lilliput-Blefuscu); the postcolonial scene in the U.S. (in the stories of immigrants and other Others) and cyberspace (Solanka's creation of an alternative world). The three worlds mirror each other, affect each other and finally merge, thereby questioning their "fictive" or "real" status. I shall focus on the way in which the novel enacts the destructive clash between the fictive (cyberspace) and the real (the postcolonial arena). *Fury* dramatizes this conflict between worlds, both fictional and real, using cyberspace as the ultimate elsewhere, the arena where these conflicts are played out and also the site of their final (and ultimately bloody) resolution.

As the above overview of the novel's concerns suggests, Rushdie is reenacting Baudrillardian notions of simulation in the virtual realm. In *The Transparency of Evil*, Jean Baudrillard presents the notion of simulation as a state of endless repetition, which he names "the epidemic of simulation," eliminating the possibility for revolution and redemption. In this state, "[nothing] (not even God) now disappears by coming to an end, by dying. Instead, things disappear through proliferation or contamination" (Baudrillard, 4). Baudrillard situates this epidemic in the linguistic realm as it reflects the shift in our experience of the world: "the possibility of metaphor is disappearing in every sphere," leaving us with metonymic relationships "replacing the whole as well as the components" (8). The loss in language is in turn reflected in a collective mental state Baudrillard names "melancholy," which he sees as one of the defining features of our age. This state is the outcome of the only law "imposed on us," namely "the law of the confusion of categories. Everything is sexual. Everything is political. Everything is aesthetic. All at once" (9).

This collective melancholy is conspicuous in *Fury* as the protagonist ruminates upon his mental state. After wandering around New York, enjoying one of its many parades and finding comfort in the "satisfying anonymity of the crowds" (7), Solanka returns home and is seized by "melancholy, his usual secret sadness, which he sublimated into the public sphere" (7).[5] This state of melancholy, both private and public, is also reflected in Solanka's lament, again closely echoing Baudrillard's sentiments about the loss of metaphoric language: "In these days when the age of pulse was giving way to the age of tone. When the epoch of analogue (which was to say also of the richness of language, of analogy) was giving way to the digital era, the final victory of the numerate over the literate" (8). Thus, Solanka's attempt at self-rejuvenation through cyberspace ends up being confounded by the same logic of Baudrillardian simulation or endless copies without originals.

The Metaphysical Laboratory of Cyberspace

In reflecting on Rushdie's depiction of his protagonist's experience, I first turn to investigate a number of theoretical paradigms that explore the genesis of cyberspace as a way of understanding its allure and perils.

In "The Erotic Ontology of Cyberspace" Michael Heim rethinks the role of cyberspace as a way of engaging with reality. He locates the allures and perils of cyberspace in the realm of the erotic: "Rightly perceived, the atmosphere of cyberspace carries the scent that once surrounded Wisdom.

The world rendered as pure information not only fascinates our eyes and minds, it captures our hearts" (Heim, 61). Heim considers virtual reality to be a realm where the erotic becomes disembodied. This cyber-erotics is reflected in *Fury*'s depiction of the Web as providing a substitute to libidinal pursuits.

A similar view is expressed by Slavoj Žižek's meditation on fantasy in cyberspace. Žižek's post–Lacanian reading of cyberspace investigates the "artistic potential of the new digital media" (Žižek, 110). Žižek sees the possibilities inherent in this new media for liberating the subject by offering potential fulfillment of fantasy. Cyberspace play entails total immersion and leads to a dismantling of subjecthood, which paradoxically becomes a form of liberation. However, like Heim, Žižek also sees the terrifying ramifications of this total immersion in cyberspace.

The erotic appeal of cyberspace activity may lead us away from our physical bodies toward a realm of simulated bodies. This loss of subjectivity is both alluring and dangerous. Heim claims that "when on line, we break free, like the monads, from bodily existence" (Heim, 73). While recognizing the possible benefits of such freedom, Hcim chooses to focus on the dark side of computer technology. It is this loss of subjectivity that Žižek sees as the possibly redemptive potential of cyberspace as well as having potentially terrifying and violent implications when "the consistency of our (self) experience can perhaps be undermined" (Žižek, 123). This dark side of the alluring, potentially liberating freedom from bodily restraints is examined in *Fury* as Solanka is finally disillusioned from his vision of total creative freedom in the brave new world of the Web.

Heim warns against the loss of the erotic thrill of discovery in the cyber-world: "Computerized reality synthesizes everything through calculation, and nothing exists in the synthetic world that is not literally numbered and counted" (Heim, 79). In such a "synthetic" world, asks Heim, "can we be touched or surprised ... or will it always remain a magic trick, an illusory prestidigitation?" (79) — and he concludes with an impassioned call to the "fleshly world" with its "hidden horizons" (80). Žižek casts cyberspace play as an act of dismantling coherent selfhood, an "authentic act" (Žižek, 122) that liberates the subject from the shackles of subjectivity while also risking total disintegration to the point of no return. Žižek leaves these contradictory options open, claiming that the possible influence of cyberspace technology ultimately "hinges on the network of socio-symbolic relations (of power and domination, etc.) which always-already determine the way cyberspace affects us" (Žižek, 123). These relations of power and domination are very much at play in *Fury* as Solanka discovers that his venture into cyberspace play has deep ties with the political, economic and social systems it both describes and influences. The eruption of the real into cyber-fantasy no longer allows it to remain a solipsistic and solitary realm where play takes over from reality.

These concerns with the possibility of true creativity in a digital world are one of *Fury*'s main themes. As Rushdie's protagonist enters this cyberworld, he encounters the dilemmas that Heim describes: Solanka has to choose between this numbered (or digital) world and its literary (or analogue) counterpart. Rushdie's twin tales of postcolonial revolution and a cyberspace revolt become absurd copies of each other, thus reflecting the ways in which Solanka is implicated in his own tale. His authorial position becomes no more than a hollow mask rather than what he first perceives as god-like omniscience. This conflict between the numbered and the digital is enacted in the tale of the Web-inspired postcolonial revolution on Lilliput-Blefuscu. The revolutionary impulse at the heart of both tales (the cyberspace saga and the revolt on the island of Lilliput-Blefuscu) is critiqued by the protagonist as he witnesses the bloody outcome of the wish for independence and freedom from (colonial) oppression.

Laptop as Lapdancer: The Allures of Cyberspace

Rushdie's protagonist is in many ways the monad of Heim's narrative of the genesis of cyberspace. Solanka is introduced to this exciting new realm by Mila Milo, a young woman who models herself after his most famous creation and his first commercial success: the philosophical doll, Little Brain. Malik and Mila become entangled in an (unconsummated) erotic relationship that enacts Mila's own (possibly incestuous) relationship with her dead father. It is only after the breakdown of this illicit relationship that the scorned Mila offers Solanka the opportunity to encounter the exciting new world of the Web. Mila's offer of "something else" (176), then, is the way she chooses to describe the proffered Internet venture, and this offer comes only after Solanka abandons Mila for another woman — Neela Mahendra. Therefore what Mila offers is an erotic replacement for the illicit pleasures in which they had previously engaged. Mila describes cyberspace in sexual terms: "This new world is my life, Malik, it's the thing of my time, growing as I grow, learning as I learn, becoming as I become. It's where I feel most alive. There, inside the electricity" (179). Mila promises Solanka a thrill that would rival their past tryst: "Well, baby, for me that's better than what was waiting under the cushion on your lap" (179). Solanka's excited response mirrors Mila's erotic enthusiasm as he envisions the computer screen "[bursting] into life" and becoming sexually charged: "This was technology as hustler, or, as if in a darkened nightclub, gyrating for him. Laptop as lapdancer. The auxiliary sound system poured high-definition noise over him like golden rain" (179). Thus computer technology is envisioned, even before Solanka becomes actively involved with it, as a potential site of erotic pleasure.

Living "inside the electricity" promises unimagined delights, causing the previously skeptical Solanka to be immediately tempted. His venture into the "brave new electronic world" (186) is described as no less than regeneration: "The blood seemed to pump harder through his veins. This, he thought, was renewal" (186). The *bodily, sensual* impact of the *disembodied* computer world is described, again, in erotic terms. Though Solanka is "intoxicated" (187) by his self-created world, the dangers of his complete absorption in this imagined world are already apparent. As Heim observes, with the "thrill of free access to unlimited corridors of information comes the threat of total organization" (Heim, 79).[6] The threat of totality is never far away. Cyberspace offers putative freedom from the constraints of the physical body and offers seemingly endless artistic freedom, but this independence may entail another form of enslavement.

Solanka first becomes enraptured by "the possibilities offered by the new technology, with its formal preference for lateral leaps and its relative uninterest in linear progression" (186). He marvels at the move away from previous narrative forms to this new medium: "Links were electronic now, not narrative. This was ... an exact mirror of the divine experience of time. Until the advent of hyperlinks, only God had been able to see simultaneously into past, present and future alike" (187). But as Gonzalez points out, "[this] creative omniscience ... is no more than a delusion, for the omniscient artist has been superseded by the technology of the counterfeit" (773).

This "omniscience" at "the merest click of a mouse" (*Fury*, 187) is an exhilarating prospect.[7] However, it also becomes a site of moral and ethical dilemmas that come into play as Solanka plots his cyber-saga — "Let the Fittest Survive"—finally entailing his change of heart and eventual disillusionment. But even at this early stage, Solanka comes to realize the dangers of his new pursuit:

> He found himself inhabiting a world he greatly preferred to the one outside his window, and came to understand what Mila Milo had meant when she said that this was where she felt most alive. Here, inside the electricity, Malik Solanka emerged from the half-life of his Manhattan exile, traveled daily to Galileo-1, and began, once more, to live [187–8].

The dangers of this immersion in cyberspace become most evident (or real) when the story of Solanka's imagined planet Galileo-1 and the cyborg revolt inspire a postcolonial coup in Neela Mahendra's home island of Lilliput-Blefuscu. This event forces Solanka to become aware of the many ways in which his fictional creation is both implicated in reality and influences it and finally leads not only to Neela's death but also to the demise of his artistic-virtual project. Solanka's cyberspace narrative thus merges with a real postcolonial revolt in the novel's imagined version of ethnic conflict on a (fictive) island. Rushdie alerts us to the many ways in which both his fictional creation and Solanka's cyber-narrative are implicated and influenced by real and imagined historical events, entailing a confusion of boundaries between the fictitious and the real. The postcolonial arena becomes another space for Rushdie's engagement with these multiple sites of the fictive and the real. The violent outcome of both cyber-revolt and postcolonial revolution reflects Rushdie's critique of grand national causes and of the pursuit of power and domination, whether in a fictional cyber-tale or very bloody fact.

Revisiting Swift: Rushdie's Postcolonial Gulliver

The story of Lilliput-Blefuscu as a site of postcolonial struggle is a retelling of an episode in Jonathan Swift's *Gulliver's Travels*. Rushdie casts the tale that depicted the Anglo-French war in North America as a postcolonial site of ethnic conflict between two groups living on the island: the Elbees and the Indo-Lilliputians. As John C. Hawley points out, Swift's narrative engages in "imaginings of places that are pointedly *Not Here* thus providing a "unique angle of vision on the society against which they are 'placed'" (17). This changed vision affects the returning traveler who, once returning "home," feels both estranged and strangely enlightened. Solanka, much like Gulliver, experiences this change of heart and mind when he returns to London at the end of the novel. Solanka's journey into the "not here" takes place in cyberspace, which in some sense is the ultimate site of such nowhere-ness. It may thus be argued that his venture indeed transforms him in ways he only begins to fathom in wake of his homecoming.

Moreover, Rushdie complicates the relationship between real and imagined worlds by presenting Lilliput-Blefuscu, the inspiration for "Let the Fittest Survive," as always already implicated by its own fictional status. The choice of Swift as an intertext causes the reader to pause and question the fictional status of a tale within a novel replete with constant references to real historical events and persons (George Bush and Al Gore, Monica Lewinsky, Ridley Scott's *Gladiator*, and Hillary Clinton, to name but a few). Thus, Rushdie alerts his readers to the elaborate game of boundary confusions he unfolds in *Fury*.

As Neela, Solanka's new lover, recounts her ancestors' rise from slavery to domination of the island, she refers to Swift jokingly, employing his terms of describing the Anglo-French conflict in her own story. The two warring ethnic groups are described as representing polar options: the indigenous Elbees are meat eaters whereas the Indo-Lilliputians are vegetarians; the Elbees are collectivists while the Indo-Lilliputians represent "good business practice ... free market mercantilism and profit mentality" (158). Neela refers to *Gulliver's Travels* as she describes this rivalry: "The Elbees ... say that the only end of a soft-boiled egg to break is the little one. Whereas we — or at least those of us who eat eggs — are the Big Endians, from big Endia" (157).

The Indo-Lillys (or Indians) thus take over the island with their good business practices and their computer know-how. Rushdie's joke here hinges on the alternate meanings of Big Endian, which has become a technological term denoting the order in which a sequence of bytes is stored in a computer's memory; this term is therefore associated with the notions of the Indo-Lillys as representing the numerical or digital aspect of the conflict.

Neela comments on this reversal of former subject positions when the Indo-Lilliputians ascend to power: "[The] world speaks our language now, not theirs," says Neela, "It is the age of numbers, isn't it? So we are the numbers and the Elbees are the words" (158). She then comments on the nature of this conflict: "[The] battle between the Indo-Lillys and the Elbees is also the battle of the human spirit ... between what's mechanical and utilitarian in us and the part that loves and dreams." Neela admits that "with my heart I'm probably on the other side" (158).

Her commitment to the national cause, however, overrides such sentimental concerns: "But my people are my people and justice is justice and after you've worked your butts off for four generations and you're still treated like second-class citizens, you've got a right to be angry" (158). The battle of the human spirit, then, gives way to loyalty for a national cause.

Rushdie posits the national sentiment as a destructive force — another aspect of the fury that pervades the novel. The impulse to "right a grave injustice, to be a servant of the Good" (*Fury*, 246), ends up in disaster. Neela's death seems futile: although she sacrifices herself to save Solanka and her film crew, the national cause takes on horrific manifestations in the form of Babur, the leader of the Indo-Lillian rebels.[8] Choosing to name the rebel leader after the famous emperor of the Mughal Empire provides an ironic comment on the nature of leadership.[9] While the historical (and mythological) Babur has come to represent a leader who is very much aware of his own vices, a learned man, who despite his overwhelming cruelty, can still provide ironic comments on his own debauchery, Rushdie's Babur retains the physical attributes and the cruelty of his namesake with none of the mitigating virtues of humor and sharp wit. Babur is transformed into a deranged and grotesque mirror of Solanka's own quest for (artistic) godlike power.

The futility that underlies grand national causes is a recurrent theme in the novel.[10] The revolt in Lilliput-Blefuscu is at least as ridiculous as Swift's Little/Big Endian dispute, but its consequences are very real. This defining moment, when "fictional characters [begin] to burst out of their cages and take to the streets" (225), marks "the intervention of the living dolls from the imaginary planet Galileo-1 in the public affairs of actually existing Earth" (226).

The revolutionaries identify with the "Puppet Kings" in Solanka's tale, the cyborg slaves fighting for liberation, entailing, as Solanka realizes, "no less than a third 'revolt of the living dolls'" (227). The cyber-world, previously viewed by Solanka as a refuge from reality, is contaminated by this intervention of the fictional in the real.

It commences with an Elbee merchant's attempt to thwart the liberal president's plan to give Indo-Lilliputians equal electoral and property rights.

2. Rage Against the Machine

In the counter-coup that ensues, the role of Solanka's cyber world becomes central. The revolutionaries (known as FRM or Fremen) steal masks and costumes of Solanka's cyber-characters and don them in "their co-ordinated armed assaults on Lilliput-Blefuscu's key installations" (226). The cyber-world—viewed as a site of escape from reality—is contaminated by the intervention of the fictional in "actual existing Earth." The revolution claims a heavy toll: "[Hundreds] dead, hundreds more seriously injured.... The noise of pain and fear filled the little nation's hospital doors" (227). This bloody outcome and ultimately Neela's death questions the easy boundary between fictionality and reality. As his tale of the "Puppet Kings" queries the notion of "life" in the form of all too human cyborgs, the real revolution on Lilliput-Blefuscu that mimics the cyber-story becomes another version of the tale. If it is indeed another "revolt of the living dolls," only this time with real casualties, where can we locate the boundaries between real and artificial life or between a real revolution and one in cyberspace? I believe that Rushdie does not share in the postmodern project that views this site of boundary confusion as a liberating/redemptive option.[11] His vision is bleaker, offering his readers a warning against the dangers of indulging in the seeming pleasures of transgressing boundaries.

The danger in such transgression becomes evident as Solanka witnesses his fictive character announce his victory on television: "[The] leader of the FRM uprising who was dressed from head to foot in a Kronos/Dollmaker costume and who referred to himself only as Commander Akasz, went briefly on LBTV to announce his operation's success" (227). Solanka is troubled by the "old problem of ends and means again. 'Commander Aksaz' didn't sound to him like the servant of a just cause" (227–228). But Neela is "elated": "The incredible thing is that's it's so unlike Indo-Lillys to be like this: militarized, disciplined, taking action in their own defence instead of just weeping and wringing their hands" (228).

Neela delights in what she had previously abhorred. She is excited by the prospect of making a film about the revolution: "This coup makes my film really sexy" (228), says Neela, hinting at the erotic excitement induced both by the prospect of military action and by the figure of Akasz, ironically Solanka's alter ego in "Let the Fittest Survive." Solanka's reaction is quite different: "Malik Solanka, standing at one of the high peaks of his life, feeling, like Gulliver or Alice, like a giant among pygmies, invincible, invulnerable, suddenly felt tiny invisible fingers tugging at his garment, as if a horde of little goblins were trying to drag him down to Hell" (228).

The Swift allusion takes us back to the Lilliput-Blefuscu tale, recasting Solanka as a fallen Gulliver. The goblins/pygmies may then be his creations, leading him once again (as in his first commercial success as "Doll-maker") to Hell. Ironically, this descent into Hell, or Lilliput-Blefuscu, and the ensuing confrontation with Commander Akasz, or Babur, will end up being the means of an unlikely salvation. His decision to go to Lilliput-Blefuscu in search of Neela becomes a turning point (or point of no return) in the conflict between the creator and his creations, the Doll Maker and his living dolls.

Solanka finds that he cannot disengage himself from his creations. He is troubled by the "strange piece of mask theatre played out on this remote island stage" (235), a theatre act in which he becomes both main actor and director. Babur's decision to don the Akasz Kronos mask becomes a locus of further confusion: The creator becomes his creation. Solanka ponders the role he plays in this piece: "[As] time passed, he had come to resemble his creation more and more. The long silver hair, the eyes made mad by loss" (235). This conflation of creator and creation is one of the recurring motifs in *Fury*. As a doll maker, Solanka is continually confronted by his creations in the flesh (Mila as "Little Brain," Neela Mahendra recreated as Zameen of Rijk or Goddess of Victory and finally dying as a living embodiment of this fictional creation, Solanka's son as another "Little Brain"). He is engaged in a futile attempt to disengage himself from the moral and ethical consequences of being a "Doll-Maker" only to find himself facing them over and over again. Solanka finds he cannot renounce his responsibility for the events on the island, however.

Despite his wish to convince himself that he is "not a party to these events" (234), he comes to realize that "the action intimately concerned him, that the great or perhaps trivial matter of his perhaps significant, more probably rather pitiful life — but still, his life! — was arriving, here in the South-Pacific, at its final act" (235). The ensuing meeting with Akasz Kronos and Zameen of Rijk (or Babur and Neela) proves to be the novel's decisive moment.

Upon arriving at the scene of conflict, Solanka is already its main actor. When Babur appears in public as Akasz Kronos, Solanka's face is the "dominant image" (239) on the island. Therefore, he is viewed ironically as a look-alike or imitation of the original leader:

> Here in the Theatre of Masks the original, the man with no mask, was perceived as the mask's imitator: the creation was real while the creator was the counterfeit! It was as though he were present at the death of God and the god who had died was himself [239].

Solanka arrives at a place where his identity, the tenuous link between name and self, is finally broken down: "Here 'Professor Malik Solanka' had no existence as a self, as a man with a past and future and people who cared about his fate" (240). And his god-like status ("Doll-Maker") becomes no more than a mere "dollmaker" (242), "an inconvenient nobody with a face that everyone knew" (240). Solanka is taken into custody and meets "Commander Akasz" and "a woman wearing camouflage fatigues and a 'Zameen of Rijk' mask: concealing her face behind an imitation of itself" (243). The Theatre of Masks continues as Babur/Commander Akasz stages his mastery over Solanka and Neela in a scene at once comic and ominous. The new, confident leader who had "already acquired the royal we" (243) parades his mastery by forcing Neela to agree to his ridiculous propositions: The moon is made of cheese, the earth is flat and the sun never sets in the newly named Filibistan. Neela, an errant Galileo, assents. The imprisoned Solanka, surrounded by the masked versions of his fictional creations, reevaluates his life in a telling passage:

> Lilliput-Blefuscu had reinvented itself in his image. Its streets were his biography, patrolled by figments of his imagination and altered versions of the people he had known. The masks of his life circled him sternly, judging him. He bowed his head before their verdict. He had wished to be a good man, to lead a good man's life, but the truth is he hadn't been able to hack it.... When he had attempted to retreat from his darker self, the self of his dangerous fury, hoping to overcome his faults by a process of renunciation, of *giving up*, he had only fallen into new, more grievous error. Seeking his redemption in creation, offering up an imagined world, he had seen its denizens move out into the world and grow monstrous; and the greatest monster of them all wore his own guilty face [246].

Solnaka's disillusionment is expressed in this passage in the most certain terms imaginable. Yet more than expressing a merely personal realization of past misdeeds and a recanting of his misguided faith in the imagined world he had created in cyberspace, this quote also seems to indicate Rushdie's own authorial intent, perhaps of casting *Fury* as a cautionary tale: a reevaluation of the postmodern celebration of boundary confusion and blurring of fact and fiction. The mini-utopia that Solanka stages, "Let the Fittest Survive," is, however, an open-ended narrative providing no closure and offering a scene of moral ambiguity, reflecting a very postmodern project.

Let the Fittest Survive? Rushdie's Dystopian Imaginary

The Darwinian overtones of the subtitle foreshadow the tale's engagement with the battle for survival in a hostile, otherworldly environment in which the nature of humanity is put to the test. This tale within a tale acts as a subversive counter-text in the novel. As Fredric Jameson has noted in *Archaeologies of the Future*, postmodern science fiction creates "an imaginary enclave within real social space," with cyberspace offering a unique, new sort of enclave: "a subjectivity which is objective and which once more does away with the 'centered subject'" (15, 21).

"Let the Fittest Survive" is Rushdie's own such imagined space. Significantly, this enclave is located in cyberspace, which, as Jameson observes, provides a space for postmodern re-imaginings of subjectivity. Jameson contends that unlike in fantasy, which remains a conservative and even a reactionary form, it is in postmodern science fiction that we may still find a revolutionary potential. I propose that Rushdie's cyber- tale enacts the idea of revolution, showing both its perils and potential for change. Revolution, meant to be the vehicle of liberation and redemption, is thus transformed into a bloody cycle of relentless violence.

Solanka's cyber-saga appears midway through the novel in italicized typeface, thus signaling a story within a story that is set apart both graphically and thematically from the rest of the novel. It is only in the next chapter that the readers are told of Solanka's love of science fiction and that explanations for some of the characters' names and the story's events are provided. This miniature science fiction tale within the text incorporates elements from works of Rushdie's admired authors, engaging with core metaphysical dilemmas of the genre. The story centers on Akasz Kronos, a puppet-maker who created figures he calls the Puppet Kings, only to find out that they have turned against him — their maker. Kronos is clearly, then, Solanka's mirror image or evil doppelganger. Solanka's own conflicted status as doll-maker provides the impulse for writing the tale and is ultimately the reason for his change of heart in the wake of the tragic consequences of the realization of his fiction.

Solanka's tale is self-reflexive from the outset, as it casts the events of his life in a science-fictional setting. The tale appears to be an odd pastiche of generic tropes ("The Prime Directive," for one),[12] utopian elements, and the theme of golem/Frankenstein's rebellion against its creator, as well as a parodic retelling of events taking place in contemporary New York.

Solanka finds out that it "wasn't necessary to end the story—indeed it was vital to the project's long-term prospects that the tale be capable of almost indefinite prolongation, with new adventures and themes being grafted on to it at regular intervals and new characters to sell in doll, toy and robot form" (190). Although the commercial potential of this cyber-venture is stated as the reason for this "indefinite prolongation," it nonetheless offers new and exciting ways of exploring the nature of narrative.

The tale is metaphorically described as a living being, a "many-armed, multi-media beast" (190), symbolic of the dangers of this commercial venture and its monstrous consequences. But Solanka's tale also has ethical and philosophical implications, raising dilemmas without solutions: "[I]t was not necessary to answer questions; far better to find interesting ways of rephrasing them" (190). Solanka's engagement with his characters' moral choices is described as an addiction: "Professor Solanka was intoxicated for hours on end by the Puppet-Kings' six-pack of ethical dilemmas" (187). He is at once "fascinated," "revolted" and

> deliriously entranced by the shadow play possibilities (intellectual, symbolic, confrontational, mystificational, even sexual) of the two sets of doubles, the encounters between "real" and "real," "real" and "double," "double" and "double," which blissfully demonstrated the dissolution of frontiers between the categories [*Fury*, 187].

Again, we see Baudrillardian language replicated almost verbatim. This fascination with endless doubling and mirroring masquerades as artistic freedom but, as Gonzalez points out, is merely "a parody of creativity that produces only clones; ... complicit with the recuperation of difference and the mechanization of the human, ... the dead aesthetic which is the by-product of the conditioning of marketing" (Gonzalez, 774).

The action takes place on "Galileo-1," the "Rijk's home planet" (161). This imagined space is a close echo of millennial New York as Solanka experiences it. "Boom America" (188) is "in a golden age": "Outside his window a long, humid summer, the first hot season of the third millennium baked and perspired. The city boiled with money" (4). Solanka recreates this urban space in his cyber-tale — it indeed becomes an extension of New York as well as prophesying its imminent (imagined) fall as the Roman Empire of our times.

This new narrative and urban space can find its ultimate expression in science fiction. Cyberspace becomes the realm for narrative engagement with the very issues that have been occupying the genre from its earliest manifestations. "Let the Fittest Survive" explores the limits of human perception, comprehension and possible intervention in the world, suggesting that the seemingly liberating site of cyberspace creativity ends up in the collapsible real. Both in New York and in Lilliput-Blefuscu, the real invades what Solanka identifies at the very beginning of the novel as "phoney":[13] "Something was amiss with the world. The optimistic peace-and-love philosophy of his youth having given him up, he no longer knew how to reconcile himself to the increasingly 'phoney' (he loathed, in this context, the otherwise excellent word 'virtual') reality" (7). In the novel's final scene, we find Solanka returning to the real in a conflicted attempt to do away with the phoney nature of the world.

Asmaan's Heath, or: Can the Weary Traveler Return Home?

Michael Heim's cyberspace erotics become its neurotics. As cyber-rebellion becomes bloody fact, there is no longer any room for indulgence in a reassessment of philosophical and metaphysical quandaries. The novel's final scene can therefore be seen as a return from the isolated cyber-world to the real, though a very bizarre homecoming it is. As Gonzalez points out:

> Closing with an image of infantile regression, the tale leaves Solnaka jumping up and down on a bouncy castle, in a parody of Gatsby, that "gold hatted" bouncer and self made man. Literally reaching for the sky, the ending falls (intentionally?) flat, an ironic judgment on the American dream, fuelled by the flows of fast capitalism [Gonzalez, 778].

While she accurately reads the ending's ironic references, Gonzalez does not refer to Solanka's genuine wish to reach for the "Sky," which is also his son's name. She concedes rightly that "the novel's nostalgia, not so much for realism as for the real emotion expressed in its title, is a surgical strike against our world of simulacra while also being complicit with it, as both its tone and form, and indeed, its post-realist aesthetics suggest (Gonzalez, 778). She fails, however, to recognize the protagonist's real emotions expressed in the novel's very moving last scene.

In my own reading of the final scene, I suggest rather that Rushdie's playfulness, though conspicuous, finally gives way to the expression of emotion: not of fury but of love. Although Rushdie leaves us bouncing with Solanka as he attempts to make his son notice him, we nevertheless feel that this closing scene signals a return to life and to real emotion, after a long hiatus in the Web's simulated life, in the novel's very last lines:

> But grand and high was his bouncing; and he was damned if he was going to stop leaping or desist from yelling until that little boy looked around, until he made Asmaan Solanka hear him ... until Asmaan turned and saw his father up there, his only true father flying against the sky, *asmaan*, the sky, conjuring up all his lost love and hurling it up high into the sky like a white bird plucked from his sleeve. His only true father taking flight like a bird, to live in the great blue vault of the only heaven in which he had ever been able to believe. "Look at me!" shrieked Professor Malik Solanka, his leather coat-tails flapping like wings, "Look at me, Asmaan! I'm bouncing very well! I'm bouncing higher and higher!" [259].

The entire paragraph is cast linguistically, as well as thematically, in the mode of possibility. We will never know if Asmaan does indeed hear his father. We are left, much like Solanka, to ponder the possible instead of realizing the actual. Although he has abandoned his dreams of the ultimate space "inside the electricity," Solanka is yet unsure of what the future may hold. In this last cinematic scene, we see the protagonist in a "freeze frame moment." If this is a happy ending, then it is a qualified and limited one. It is only in this frozen moment in time within the space of the novel that a glimmer of hope for a better future remains.

Fury thus ends in a realm of prospects. While the novel has offered us the possibility of a liberating utopian option in cyberspace, only to deconstruct it and demonstrate its inherent perils, its final scene brings us back to London, Solanka's former home. Leaving the decadent New York for London, the capital of a former empire, a city facing its post-imperial and postcolonial reality, may signal a move towards a different engagement with futurity. Solanka returns home, but like Gulliver and the "antique traveller" in Shelley's Ozymandias, he finds that "nothing beside remains" (*Fury*, 257). Nevertheless, Solanka is drawn to the one place in the heart of the metropolis that he renames after his son: "Asmaan's Heath — or at least Kenwood" (*Fury*, 257). This place is "studded with magical trees" and with the magic of artistic creation: "[t]he Hepworth sculpture was a sacred spot" (257). Returning to this hallowed ground then, on a "perfect April day" (257), offers a vision of a possibly better future for Solanka who longs to reconnect with his "only true son." Instead of disembodied space, we find a real place: a manmade garden in the midst of a different urban space. Rushdie's choice to end the novel in that particular spot envisages a possibly different future for both father and son.

This possibility of futurity may also lie in the promise inherent in the next generation: Asmaan, the son/sky/heaven is projected unto Solanka. As Solanka bounces up, he becomes Asmaan if only for a split second. Futurity becomes an embodied rather than a science-fictional option. Cyberspace gives way to a literal and figurative sky.

We may say then that in *Fury*, Rushdie's science fictional spaces collapse into the real: The science fictional option seems to be discarded, if only for a second, for an engagement with the real world with all its attendant joys and perils. The promise of futurity emerging in the next generation is a recurrent theme in Rushdie's oeuvre. We see it again in *Shalimar the Clown*, where the possibility of a better future is projected onto the figure of India/Kashmira, the hybrid daughter of a Jewish man and a Kashmiri woman. But Rushdie's engagement with possible futures is also an imagining of alternative histories, and this is where I locate his most ambitious retelling of the histories of East and West. In *The Ground Beneath Her Feet*, which I discuss next, this reimagining of a possible past, one only slightly different than our own, and yet significantly so, may be one of Rushdie's most clearly science fictional texts.

In this imagined history, music takes center stage. Rushdie takes on the icons of popular music and reinvents them in his image. In typical Rushdean manner, fiction meets reality. Rushdie's imagined pop duo's song "The Ground Beneath Her Feet," which gives the novel its name, ends up as a real pop song, performed by the mega band U2. In *Joseph Anton*, Rushdie recalls this momentous moment thus: "What happens next was entirely unexpected. Bono telephoned to say that he had taken some of the lyrics from the text of *The Ground Beneath Her Feet* and written 'a couple of melodies'"(553). Rushdie comments on the meeting of the imaginary and the real: "This was a novel about the permeable borderlines between the imaginary and the real worlds, and here was one of its imaginary songs crossing that borderline and becoming real" (553). These permeable boundaries are explored in the novel but are also part of the author's life. Rushdie's awareness of these boundary crossings is evident throughout his work. In my reading of the novels, I aim to show how Rushdie's work both celebrates the possibility of boundary crossings of all kinds, while being keenly aware of the attendant dangers. *The Ground Beneath Her Feet*, much like *Fury*, is a case in point.

3
"The World Is (Not) What It Is": *The Ground Beneath Her Feet*

> *Migrants must, of necessity, make a new imaginative relationship with the world, because of the loss of familiar habitats. The cinematic Brazil is a land of make-believe of which all of us who have, for whatever reason, lost a country and ended up elsewhere, are the true citizens.*—Salman Rushdie, *Imaginary Homelands*
>
> *"Where is Kansas?" asked the man with surprise. "I don't know," replied Dorothy sorrowfully, "but it is my home and I'm sure it's somewhere."*—L. Frank Baum, *The Wonderful Wizard of Oz*

In the cult BBC television show *Goodness Gracious Me*, a cast of recurring characters offer their parodic insights on the lives of Indians in England. One of the most hilarious characters is Mr. "Everything Is Indian" who insists that everything originates in India. Thus for example: "The royal family? Indian! Have arranged marriages, live in the same house and all work for the family business. Indian!" In Salman Rushdie's novel *The Ground Beneath Her Feet* (*TGBHF*), this comic notion of India as point of origin is reworked in the retelling of the history of both East and West.

It is a tale of a romantic triangle: Ormus, Vina and Umeed (or Rai), the narrator/photographer who tells the story of the two larger-than-life rock star lovers. Rai describes the three as "kings of Disorient," who choose not to belong to family, nation or race. "Disorientation is loss of the East," or so the common (navigational) wisdom tells us, says Rai, but "what if the whole deal—orientation, knowing who you are and so on—what if it's all a scam? What if all of it—home, kinship, the whole enchilada—is just the biggest, most truly global, and centuries-old piece of brainwashing?" (*TGBHF*, 193). If this is indeed the case, in order to become truly free you have to "go through the feeling of being lost, into the chaos and beyond; you've got to accept the loneliness, the wild panic of losing your

3. "The World Is (Not) What It Is"

moorings, the vertiginous terror of spinning round and round like edge of a coin tossed in the air" (193). Most people do not give up their moorings, however. Only the unique individuals who dare to "[step] off the edge of the earth" or "go through the fatal waterfall," like Ormus, Vina and Rai, find the "magic valley at the end of the universe"(194). This magical place (which is in effect no-place) in turn becomes their "element" and "feels better than belonging." Of the three "Kings" only Rai lives to "tell the tale" (194), and it is through his eyes (and lens) that the mythical tale of the two rock 'n' roll gods is recounted. But Rai is not merely a spectator; he is also a part of this love triangle and his narrational position is made more complex. He is by no means only a "wry" observer and is thus as implicated in the tale as the protagonists.

The novel tells the story of Ormus and Vina's rise to stardom, their ultimate separation and Vina's tragic end as she is literally swallowed up by a Mexican earthquake. A devastated Ormus spends the rest of his life looking for Vina replacements both in life and on stage. Ironically, it is Rai, the third party to this love triangle, who ends up finding Mira Celano, an Italian American woman who seems to be the living incarnation of the young Vina. Mira refuses the role of a Vina clone, however, and becomes a performer in her own right. The novel ends with Rai, Mira and her little daughter Tara in a scene of domestic bliss, seemingly free from the mythic shadows cast over them by Ormus and Vina. Ormus meets a bizarre end as he is killed by a Vina-like apparition who seems to have risen from the dead to claim his soul. The novel becomes a rock 'n' roll legend for a postmodern age, a retelling of the Orpheus myth, but even more so, a re-imagining of both Eastern and Western (hi)stories.

The Ground Beneath Her Feet rewrites historical narratives as fantastic and science fictional tales while re-imagining Eastern and Western mythologies as loci of self (re)formation in a postmodern age. The novel performs a dual function: reaffirming the possibility of selfhood and individuality while paradoxically locating this option at the site of fissures of postmodern subjectivity as copy or version. The novel's larger than life lovers, Ormus and Vina, are thus versions of Orpheus and Eurydice but are also imagined as Elvis and Marilyn Monroe, or David Bowie and Madonna, to name but a few of the cultural icons evoked in the novel. In all their incarnations, however, there is a decidedly Rushdean twist. They are the *Eastern* version of Western classical and popular myths set in a text that deconstructs notions of East and West as polar opposites. They both subvert and reaffirm the West's power in shaping images of personal and cultural selves. When Ormus and Vina become the king and queen of America, they do so at America's peril. The brown Elvis and the dark Marilyn can only ever be a refracted mirror of the original, further complicating notions of origin and questioning the foundational myths that structure both Eastern and Western cultures. Ormus and Vina (who are both members of diasporic cultures that are always-already hybridized) provide an alternative version that undermines Western culture's imaginary history of centrality. Rushdie disorients the mythological (hi)story of rock 'n' roll by constructing its Eastern mirror image in the form of a "Dark Diva" and a "Brown Elvis," thereby providing us with an alternative history of Western popular music. Conjuring up an alternative universe where rock 'n' roll's origin is in fact *Indian* (among many other disorientations of known historical events, the most significant musical one being the birth of "Jesse Garon Parker," Elvis's dead twin brother, instead of Elvis), Rushdie rattles and shakes our known world. By exploring our fascination with our immortally ephemeral corpses, while singing a hymn to the redeeming power of the pop icon, he provides us with one of many alternative (hi)stories.

As I have argued above, this re-imagining of alternative worlds employs science fictional narrative modes and thematics. Rushdie conjures up a different, slightly skewed version of the world in which we live, thereby managing to unsettle his readers. This choice of science fiction as a vehicle for re-imagining alternative versions of a known universe offers, as in other Rushdie novels, a way of reassessing personal and national histories. *The Ground Beneath Her Feet* is a novel that constructs variants of a known world but does not, I would claim, offer a corrective vision; Rushdie does not offer a cautionary or moralistic tale. He rather opens up possibilities of different worlds but does not provide utopian or dystopian scenarios. Science fiction offers him the best vehicle for re-imagining alternative universes, and he employs it both to baffle and implicate his readers in the project of disengaging them from the version of the world they have come to know as real.

As Brian McHale famously noted, postmodernist fiction is characterized by an ontological dominant rather than an epistemological one. The postmodernist text raises questions that "bear either on the ontology of the literary text itself or on the ontology of the world which it projects" (McHale, 10). The text raises questions such as these:

3. "The World Is (Not) What It Is"

> What is a world? What kinds of worlds are there, how are they constituted, and how do they differ?; What happens when different kinds of world [*sic*] are placed in confrontation, or when boundaries between worlds are violated?; What is the mode of existence of a text, and what is the mode of existence of the world (or worlds) it projects? [10].

The Ground Beneath Her Feet raises these kinds of questions in its erection of multiple worlds. The novel questions these worlds' ontological status and examines the implication of boundary violation and confrontation between textual worlds. The novel's world, which seems at first to be quite similar to our world, gradually reveals itself to be a slightly skewed variation of our known world. In this world, John F. Kennedy escapes the first attempt to assassinate him, Elvis's twin brother survives and becomes "Elvis," Lou Reed is a woman, Carly Simon and Guinevere Garfunkel are a famous musical duo and the *Watergate Affair* is a work of fiction. These are only a few examples of the many literary, historical, musical and cultural variants that Rushdie envisions. In another twist, Ormus, the novel's Orpheus/artist has visions of another world. In his visions, historical events as we know them have indeed occurred. But ironically enough they are considered to be an effect of his double vision or madness in the world of the novel. To further complicate the notion of multiple worlds, Rushdie introduces another science fictional trope: the existence of parallel dimensions or "universes like parallel bars or tv channels" (*TGBHF*, 384). Ormus and Rai encounter two visitors from one such parallel dimension on the verge of extinction. The two travelers—Maria, a beautiful and deranged Indian girl and her caretaker—introduce another option of plurality. The coexistence of parallel worlds contributes to the notion of instability in the novel as their presence evokes the possibility of rips or holes that allow movement from one dimension to another. The "ground beneath our feet" is never safe. Earthquakes are present in the novel throughout, and their presence conjures up a symbolic as well as a very real threat to the stability of a precarious universe.[1]

Given this (over-)abundance of science fictional tropes and thematics, it is interesting to note that critical readings of the novel have not addressed this aspect at length. Judith Leggatt addresses the novel's engagement with science fictional tropes and states that Rushdie "uses these speculative fiction techniques for postcolonial as well as postmodern purposes" (106). She finally claims that the meeting of the two cosmic worlds serves "to emphasize both the creative possibilities and the dangers inherent in all cross-cultural encounters" (107). Although I agree that the novel does employ the science fictional technique as a way of commenting on post-colonial and postmodern thematics, I believe more attention should be paid to the very choice of the genre and its implications. Elsa Linguanti's collection of essays devoted to the novel, *The Great Work of Making Real*, discusses many aspects of this multi-thematic text—ranging from biblical allusions, to mythological aspects, the role of popular music, the narrator's dual role and other narratological concerns—but the science fictional aspect is never mentioned. In an essay dealing with the different worlds in the novel, Linguanti reads the multiplicity of worlds employing the "possible worlds" model. This model offers a semiotic/rhetorical/philosophic analysis of the different worlds existing in literary fiction. According to the model:

> [Literary] fiction is an active experimental laboratory ... the huge, open, fascinating fictional world must not be reduced to the model of a single world, that of actual human experience, as in discourses about realism, even if poetic imagination operates on "material" borrowed from actuality.... The laws of the actual world ... are just one example of the many possible "general orders"; there are many alternative universes [154].

Therefore, "the ontological status assigned to fictional worlds and their components is that of possible things that have not been actualized (Hamlet is a possible individualized person who lives in an alternative world)" (Linguanti, 154). This model, then, applies to *every* fictional work, insomuch as that work, by virtue of being fictional, deviates from the rules of other discourses committed to reporting "actual human experience." I claim that although it is possible to utilize this model to read the different alternative universes in *The Ground Beneath Her Feet*, it may prove too broad for a novel that draws on a number of genres, among them science fiction, to present its vision of these alternative worlds.[2] I therefore turn to Richard Saint-Gelais' discussion of temporal modes in science fiction narratives in which he outlines the ways contemporary science fiction texts continually invent and reinvent time (34). His delineation of the ways science fiction narratives perform this manipulation of time and concepts of history proves a useful vehicle for reading Rushdie's unique text.

Saint-Gelais describes a subgenre in science fiction that he names "uchronia." In this type of narrative, the underlining principle is the same (despite variations in form): "It proposes a fictional world that implies a history whose course has deviated from the course of real history" (28). He states that usually this entails "a bifurcation in the framework of real historical events at any given point deemed to be decisive" (28). Although *The Ground Beneath Her Feet* does not focus on a specific historical event but rather offers us dents in the historical story as we know it, Saint-Gelais' model of uchronic narratives fits the novel's stylistic and ideological underpinnings, as I shall show.

Saint-Gelais comments on the effect this kind of text has on the (unsuspecting) readers:

> If uchronia has shock value, it is because it disrupts the "peaceful coexistence" ordinarily maintained between reality and the imaginary. With uchronia, the imaginary is not located in an obscure zone of reality (a distant land or an unrealized future era); the imaginary hits reality head-on, confronting us with an irrevocable shift from coexistence to open contradictions [28].

This "shock value" can definitely be said to be one of the effects that Rushdie's manipulation of historical facts has on the readers. These "open contradictions" come to play in the various worlds introduced in the text and in the different reactions of the characters in the fictional world, as well as the reader's experience when facing them.

But uchronia does more than just shock its readers. Its uniqueness as a fictional mode has more crucial implications. Saint-Gelais points out that while "all fiction triggers this kind of interference between reality and imaginary," because all fictional works involve "fictional characters having fictional adventures within a framework that appears to coincide with reality," the effect on the readers is not the same as in other genres. In most fictional works, "this insertion of the imaginary into a supposed reality is conventional enough to be neutralized by the reader." Therefore, "the reader does not ask whether the novel's world had been fictionalized by the presence of fictional individuals." This is not the case with uchronia, claims Saint-Gelais: "Uchronia disrupts this delicate balance: It is the entire fictional world that tips over into the imaginary" (28). In other words, uchronia is a unique narrative mode that implies category confusion or a tipping over of one fictional realm into another. The reader is then faced with the problematic task of reassessing his or her place in relation to the fictional world, the real world and the imagined space created in the uchronic text.

In *The Ground Beneath Her Feet,* this tipping over into the imaginary takes place as the readers begin to grasp that the novel's world is not what they thought it was. But, as Saint-Gelais notes, uchronia may take different forms according to the writer's attitude towards the world he or she had created. This attitude may

> vary between nostalgia (for a state of affairs that the real course of history has interrupted) and fear (of a disturbing event that has not in fact occurred but that is developed by the narrative in a more or less masochistic manner). Uchronia overlaps with utopia and dystopia; It may also be located beyond these two genres when it explores historical alternatives *in a humorous mode, neither valuing nor devaluing the historical possibilities* [28–9, my emphasis].

This is exactly the kind of narrative Rushdie provides in *The Ground Beneath Her Feet.* The novel is not a utopian or dystopian text but rather an exploration of historical alternatives in a humorous mode, or perhaps one should say a very Rushdean mode.[3]

I propose a reading of Rushdie's text, in Saint-Gelais' terms, as a "uchronic novel," that is, as

> a narrative that presupposes, rather than exposing—a deviation from history; the deviation is not the object of the text, but a background against which a novelistic plot stands out, a plot that sometimes is not intrinsically science-fictional except for its insertion into a curiously unfamiliar world [Saint-Gelais, 29].

In Rushdie's novel, this "deviation from history" indeed proves to be the background to the novel's main plot: the Rai-Vina-Ormus triangle with its many twists and tribulations. Rushdie employs the uchronic device in order to introduce the historical confusion as a backdrop to the very personal history of his narrator. In other words, Rai's personal story does follow a linear, coherent storyline: We are not asked to question his life story in the fictional world of the text. The readers are introduced into Rai's world where this "deviation from history" has already occurred.[4] Their confusion stems from having to reconstruct this world. Saint-Gelais compares this reading process to reading a detective novel: "Science fiction reading resembles detective-novel reading except that instead of seeking to reconstruct an isolated fact (a murder), the reader seeks an imaginary frame of reference" (30). The text becomes "an enigmatic device ... a mechanism that, especially in contemporary science fiction, abandons didacticism and situates itself in a context taken for granted and therefore all the more disorienting" (30). In *The Ground Beneath Her Feet*, this disorientation is both a thematic device and an effect achieved by the narrative's confusion tactics. And although, as I have demonstrated, Rushdie's text indeed employs this science fictional device in a text that may not be overtly science-fictional, it nevertheless participates in the project that Saint-Gelais identifies as the project of the contemporary science fiction narrative, which "while not turning its back on reality, has ultimately constructed a considerably extensive and complex field of fictional explorations, capable of evolving according to its own logic and thereby continually inventing and reinventing time" (34). I claim that Rushdie's text does indeed reinvent time, doing so in a playful, humorous way. This reinvention of time has both ideological and thematic implications. *The Ground Beneath Her Feet* does not then turn its back on reality but rather reconstructs it *within* the fictional text. As in the other novels I discuss, this constitutes Rushdie's unique mode of reassessing both national and personal histories in a fictional frame.

I aim in my reading of the novel to show how its imagining of alternative pasts and futures, its reinvention of time if you will, opens up, rather than forecloses, the possibilities of imagining different worlds. I shall focus on the twin plots of what I call Vina's "postmortem stardom" and Rai's necrophiliac obsession with her posthumous existence. I shall relate to the concepts of mortality and immortality in postmodernity and show how the novel both queries and at times embraces this variant of postmodernity. I shall relate to the trope of the dead (and returning) woman as revenant as a possible reading of Vina's postmortem existence in relation to both Rai and Ormus, and as a way of rereading her mythological status as a modern-day Eurydice. Finally, I shall try to assess whether the novel's ending functions as a healing device for both its narrator and readers. In other words, I shall question whether Rushdie offers us a happy ending by replacing one problematic triad (Rai-Ormus-Vina) with a better one (Rai-Mira-Tara) or whether we have another version of the same story. Is Rushdie claiming that there may be a more mature existence, both culturally and personally, which can only come about after the loss of collective gods and goddesses? Or is he offering us a rather more sobering reflection on the nature of our (post-)modern existence?

The novel opens with the dramatic death of Vina Apsara, an Indian diva who takes America by storm and dies in a Mexican earthquake only to remain a mythological figure inspiring a multitude of impersonators (both male and female) and becoming immortal. This dramatic opening thus sets the scene for Vina's canonization as a postmortem diva. Rai, who took Vina's last photograph at the scene of the earthquake, describes his beloved as a fallen icon at a moment when her career (and her life) seems to be careening toward destruction. Her posthumous existence, however, is quite a success: "[By] then Vina was already passing into myth, becoming a vessel into which any moron could pour his stupidities, or let us say a mirror of our culture, and we can best understand the nature of this culture if we say it found its truest mirror in a corpse" (*TGBHF*, 4). Vina, the "plastered Unvirgin," however, may also provide a redemptive option for this moronic culture: "Seeing ourselves in Vina's mirror, and forgiving her, we also forgave ourselves. She redeemed us by her sins" (20). Vina performs an inverted Jesus role: She redeems mankind through *her* sins. This dual function is also linked to Vina's role as a fallen figure.

Vina's role as a female martyr is complicated by her race. Being both dark and sexually alluring, she hardly fits the role of the conventional Madonna. Vina is a simultaneous gender-bender and race-bender, a role she plays in life and after death. The many Vina look-alikes who perform her role are men and women, young and old, black, white and Asian. Vina's status as a postmortem diva is then a comment on the centrality of (Christian) icons in our contemporary culture; Rushdie points to the cultural role played by the pop star as modern day saint/sinner. But as Vina is by no means Christian, the role of a Jesus-like redeemer that she plays becomes even more ironic. She can never fit this role either, in much the same way she can never be a Marilyn or a Madonna. But her canonized posthumous existence nevertheless offers the possibility of a new kind of icon. Neither white nor black, neither saint nor sinner, neither Western nor Eastern, but a curious hybrid construction: a flayed icon for a moronic culture, on the one hand, but a redeeming figure for the same wounded and ailing society, on the other. It is Vina as postmortem diva/goddess/rock star, then, who will perform this dual role — allowing the overabundance of meanings to make her the ultimate icon for her age.[5]

In a move that is at once parodic and reverent, the last image of Vina — captured on film by her adoring fan Rai — becomes another museum piece offering vicarious pleasures to the crowds avidly watching it. Vina will forever remain the frozen image of death in midlife. Her iconicity is both an effect of the culture she lived in and a tribute to her power to go beyond the limits this culture imposes on its iconic figures. Vina as a posthumous goddess is by no means only a repeated version of other cultural icons made immortal by their untimely death. She is also an emblem of this culture as a celebrator of death in life. And it is this obsession with death and immortality as markers of an era to which I turn, employing Zygmunt Bauman's discussion of postmodernity's tactics for grappling with mortality and immortality.

Bauman claims that, unlike modernity, which had sought to deconstruct mortality by making death visible and manageable, postmodernity's aim is to deconstruct immortality. His analysis hinges on the ways postmodern culture, social mores and thought patterns, or what he calls "life strategies," are at work to manage the unmanageable fact of one's mortality. He argues that postmodernity's insistence on the "now" as its central project leads it to the deconstruction of immortality, a concept that hinges on the idea of futurity. Immortality is therefore no longer at the center of our existence: "The sting of finality has been pulled out from mortality, all mortality, including the mortality of immortality: things disappear from view for a time only; that time may last long, but the odds are that it will not last forever" (Bauman, 173). Death is now "but a suspension, a transitional state" (173).

If death is replaced with disappearance (that is followed by a return), then all we are left with is repetition: "In the world in which *disappearing* has replaced the dying, immortality dissolves into the melancholy of presence, in the monotony of endless *repetition*" (Bauman, 175). In *The Ground Beneath Her Feet*, as I shall later show, the notion of endless repetition or immortality as an endless loop is played out in the novel's ambivalent ending. At this point, however, I look at how Bauman's concept of repetition and originality chimes in with Rushdie's concept of the immortal icon as a cultural commodity. As I have shown, the posthumous Vina becomes the ultimate iconic figure for her culture. And as Bauman shows us, this culture is based on a rejection of death, on the one hand, and a celebration of its repeated posthumous traces, on the other.

Rai, the admiring fan and sometime lover of the dead Vina, reflects on the ways his beloved had been appropriated by the masses, used for capital gain, revered and scorned and finally how she ended up "changing the world" (530) after no longer being a living part of it. In a chapter aptly entitled "Vina Divina," Rushdie celebrates the redeeming power of Vina as pop icon, as I have shown, while also warning against the perils of manipulation and exploitation at work on the admirable corpse. Rai comments thus on Vina's post-life power:

> This posthumous goddess, this underground post–Vina, queen of the Underworld, supplanting dead Persephone on her throne, grew into something simply overwhelming.... Dying when the world shook, by her death she shook the world, and was quickly raised, like a fallen Caesar, to the ranks of the divine [528].

The mythological and historical allusions merge. Vina is both Caesar and Persephone — a male emperor and a queen of the mythical underworld. In a rewriting of the Orpheus myth, Vina/Eurydice is a ruler of the underworld, not a victim; and by turning her into an emperor, Rushdie recasts gender and power roles as he continually does throughout the novel. In his rewriting of the Orpheus and Eurydice myth, Rushdie reverses the conventional reading of the tale as the ultimate triumph of love over death. Rai reflects on the Orpheus myth: "Love is more than death, or is it. There are those who say that the songsmith Orpheus was a coward because he refused to die for love, because instead of joining Eurydice in the afterlife he tried to drag her back to the life before; which was against nature, and so failed" (225). Ironically, the novel's Orpheus, Ormus, finally *does* join his Eurydice in the afterlife. But as Rushdie offers this alternative reading of the myth, he also questions the female/male and active/passive roles at the heart of this mythological tale. Casting Vina/Eurydice as the winner of the tale, or as the strong counterpart to Ormus/Orpheus's cowardice, questions our concepts of mythologies as a kind of shorthand for structuring our worldview. If the Orpheus/Eurydice tale is not what we think it is, maybe all our other certainties should be put into question.

Rereading the Orpheus/Eurydice myth as it is re-embodied in the Ormus/Vina story, Rushdie shows how it may be a tale of love's failure to conquer death rather than its ultimate triumph over death. Rai, who comments on the enduring power of music after death, will also be the one whose own mortal tale will finally win; he may end up offering a corrective version to the failed yet immortal love of the mythological pair. As this comment on the post–Vina musical performances shows, Rai is aware of both the enduring power of Vina and Ormus's music and his own role as the third party to this love triangle: "Music — Vina's voice, singing Ormus's melodies — surges round the world, crossing all frontiers, belonging everywhere and nowhere and its rhythm is the rhythm of life" (531). Ironically, it is also the emblem of *death*: "Disembodied, or rather embodied in song, their love hangs in the air, its story no longer by corporeal or temporal constraints. This love is music now" (531). Vina and Ormus's mythology is "immortal": "Their immortal story, in which my own love's mortal tale is nowhere to be heard" (531), laments Rai. But, of course, it is Rai we hear. He is the one telling the tale. He also ends up casting himself in the main role while he is seemingly only a marginal character in the lovers' tale. Rai offers yet another version of the Orpheus/Eurydice myth at the very beginning of the novel. He casts himself as Aristaeus, the beekeeper in Virgil's rendition of the tale. Aristaeus, the first beekeeper in world literature, made unwelcome advances to the dryad Eurydice, leading her to step on a snake, whereupon the wood nymph perished and mountains wept. In this version, claims Rai, there is "no more need to worry about those foolish doomed lovers," since "[the] real hero of the poem is the keeper of bees" (21). Or in other words, Rai is a stand-in for Aristaeus; like Aristaeus — who can perform the miracle of generating bees from the carcass of a cow — Rai, the photographer, "can spontaneously generate meaning from the putrefying carcass of what is the case" (22). Rai then becomes the hero of the tale, and the "doomed lovers" are relegated to the margins. But if Rai can generate life from death, as he does in capturing Vina's last death-in-life image and in his subsequent exhibit of "Post-Vina" photos, he is also fascinated by Vina's corpse and finds himself drawn to interpreting the meanings of her post-death power.[6]

After Vina's death, her power to enthrall and engage her audience is not diminished but rather becomes even more significant. She performs another miracle in drawing the grieving masses together, Vina creates, if only for a moment, a sense of community in an age that seems to have lost this sense. According to Bauman, postmodernity "is the age of *communities*"; these communities, however, are "works of the imagination, and they derive all their confidence — donating power from the stamina and devotion of those who imagine them" (197). Vina's "community" of mourners imagines it knows Vina. The crowds mourn her death, not the "myriad Mexican dead" in the earthquake. Vina's (imagined) familiarity becomes also the catalyst for change: "Dead Vina is changing the world." The crowds gather to commemorate her death in what becomes a collective and universal experience: "In all the world, or so it seems, there is only this single, uniting event: the miracle of the stadiums, the people gathered to share their loss" (530). Or what Bauman, following Baudrillard, calls "the time of the orgy": "After the modern orgy of liberation came the postmodern age of community chasing; of tribalism, of rock-festivals and football crowds" (Bauman, 199). The crowds perform a ritual of imagined sharing; they come together to mourn an emblem of death. They do not mourn the faceless, nameless dead in the earthquake but the iconic representative of the ultimate death — the death of a celebrity. And although this celebration of death has some positive effects (there are some positive political and social changes as a result of this communal feeling), Vina's death ends up being exploited for financial and ideological gains.

One example is when Vina appears in a cartoon alongside "Jesse Garon Parker," Elvis's twin who survives in Rushdie's alternative universe, and becomes a figure of the undead in a parodied version of the commercialized aspect of rock stardom.

In this instance, the alternate Elvis of Rushdie's novel meets the fictive Vina in a cartoon by Gary Larson, a real figure in our actual world.[7] This blurring of boundaries — between the historical allusion, pop lore as always-already represented as a clichéd image and an entirely fictive pop diva — demonstrates how in this novel of cultural memory, the blurring of boundaries is no longer queried. It becomes part and parcel of this postmodern loop. If Vina is Jesse's mate, then she too is part of the zombie existence of the dead rock star. Rushdie positions Vina as the "queen of America" or "Elvis's" mate; she becomes both the butt of the joke and proof of the overwhelming power extended by the dead icon over her living fans. Her immortality is presented here in a more parodic light; yet as the cartoon shows, the dead Vina is as much a commodity as the Elvis figure; she is suspended in this transit zone, doomed to a shadowy existence. Like Elvis, she will never really die.

Dead Vina's legacy becomes a matter of cultural controversy. The meaning of her life and death becomes a subject for debate that is at once a struggle for meaning and a full-blown commercial enterprise. One reading of Vina's death, however, seems to chime in with Rai (and the implied author's) sentiments: "Of all the things said and written about her, the comments that made most sense to me were the ones about death being just death, the arguments against interpretation. Don't make her a metaphor. Just let her die in peace" (538). Ironically, the work of *interpreting* Vina's life and death is a task Rai cannot escape. He tries in vain to fight the "meanings like amorphous aliens, putting out pseudopods like suction pads and sucking at her corpse" (538). The necrophiliac engagement with the beloved's dead body continues. Rai finds himself looking at Vina's photos and calling her home to hear her voice, left as a trace on her answering machine.

Like Ormus, Rai cannot let go of Vina. He ends up re-membering her by assembling a photo exhibit called "After Vina."

The mysterious appearance of a shadow woman in the photographs further enhances the notion of mystery and introduces the idea of the dead woman as having a double and thus doubly haunting presence.

I turn now to Elisabeth Bronfen's reading of the links between death, representation and the process of mourning as a way of assessing Rai's and Ormus's different responses in their efforts to re-member and reclaim Vina. Bronfen argues that there is a paradox at the heart of the process of mourning a dead beloved. Lovers "choose a desired object because they discover the resemblance to an earlier one, but they also mourn the old in the new.... To recover a lost love object in the embodiment of another entails acknowledging precisely the loss that one is reinvesting libidinal energy to deny" (103). But this process of repetition is paradoxical as the "second term"; the other woman in Rai's photograph, for example, is never identical to the first — Vina. In this case:

> The repeated event, action, or term always contradicts its predecessor because, though similar, they are never identical; and though recalling the unique, singular, and original quality of the former event, the second emphasizes that is *more than one*, a multiple duplicate, occurring at more than one site [103–104].

Or, as Rai puts it, "now there are two" (539). Bronfen claims that the very process of mourning a loved one entails this paradoxical relationship between loss and repetition:

> Love is based on loss and repetition, suggesting a conjunction between the two terms. Repetition is inscribed by the death drive; in fact, it serves one of its forms of articulation. At the same time, repetition can be seen as an attempt to counteract absence, loss, and death. Repetition suggests that, as a double of the lost object, the first object can return in a new form, thus questioning the uniqueness of the first term and implying that the loss is not irrevocable [Bronfen, 105–6].

The Vina shadow double in the photograph — later discovered to be the disturbed Maria from Ormus's visions of an alternative universe —

reveals her to Rai as he encounters a slew of Vina impersonators and is finally made aware of Ormus's manic search for the living embodiment of his dead lover. The links between the process of mourning and remembering become then even more striking. Rai discovers that "Ormus Cama, the notorious recluse, has added to his list of bizarre obsessions the growing imitation–Vina industry" (545). This obsession makes Ormus feel he is losing his grip on the "real" Vina.

Vina, buried under the "avalanche of versions (550)," endlessly multiplied, copied, acquiring different shapes and forms, can no longer be the original love object for both Ormus and Rai. Rai realizes that he shares Ormus's agony: "O Ormus, my brother, my self. When you scream, the noise bursts from my throat. When I weep, the tears seep from your eyes" (551); the effort to recover (or reinvent) Vina is shared by both. But while Ormus insists on finding a Vina clone to replace the dead object of his affections by another "body"— that of Mira Celano, Vina's "mira" on the wall — Rai finally realizes that he cannot objectify his new found love. Mira demands and receives her own agency and voice.

Bronfen describes the psychic process of mourning as entailing a redefinition of the lost lover in the body of a second woman. In a discussion of Poe's "Ligeia" and Hitchcock's *Vertigo*, she claims both texts "revolve around the protagonist's loss of a first beloved and his refinding her in the body of a second woman" (106). In both texts, the protagonist's "initial response to the loss of his beloved is a form of melancholy; he withdraws from the world, his desire is invested in the dead. The world of the living regains his interest only when he sees that he can retrieve his *lost* love object by falling in love with a second woman who resembles the first" (106).

Thus, both Ormus and Rai first respond to Vina's death by withdrawing from the world. Both emerge only when their interest is sparked by a vision of her double.[8] But whereas Rai recognizes Mira Celano for who she is, Ormus wishes to make her into his young Vina. He uses Mira as "the embodiment of the first beloved, as the object through which the lost woman is refound or resurrected." And it follows, therefore, that

> the second woman's body also functions as the site for a dialogue with the dead, for a preservation and a calling forth of the first woman's ghost, and thus for the articulation of necrophiliac desire. Yet the reciprocity of original and copy is such that the second beloved can disappear within the process of repetition, subsumed under the representation of the first wife, who in turn may be just a copy of an original absent female body [106].

3. "The World Is (Not) What It Is"

It is this vexed relationship between original and copy that is played out in the Mira-Ormus-Rai triangle. In this triad, which is a stand in for the original love triangle, it is Mira who finally declares her independence from the original Vina and confronts Ormus with the fact of her death: "No more Vina.... Nobody comes back from the underground. Nobody did return. Vina Apsara's gone" (608–9). Significantly, however, this confrontation only occurs after Mira (as a Vina clone on stage) is almost killed by an angry audience that refuses to accept "a girl in a Vina costume" (307); the Vina version will not do. As a Vina copy, Mira comes close to death. As Mira Celano, she lives. If we return to Bronfen, the mourner who tries to re-member his beloved by finding (and at times killing) her living double, may be, like Ormus, also drawn by the dead woman into her own underworld. Bronfen claims that the dead woman in the texts she reads may be understood as "a revenant, returning to feed on the living man's memory to preserve her own existence in the world." The dead woman "[draws] him into her sphere of death and away from the world, making it impossible for him reinvest his libido in another, living woman" (116). In the culmination of Rushdie's novel, Ormus is murdered by a Vina look-alike. Rai comments: "If you ask me, I think it was Vina, the real Vina ... I think she came and got him because she knew how much he wanted to die. Because he couldn't bring her back from the dead she took him down with her, to be with her, where he belonged" (630). Or, returning to Bronfen's reading, this may be a "form of mourning that prefers a preservation of the dead object, even if it means self-mummification or suicide over an acknowledgment of loss" (116).

Vina is then both literally and figuratively a femme fatale. Bronfen claims that the femme fatale figure may be in fact fatal, not because she is the cause of death for the male but rather as she achieves her own subjectivity by revisiting the male's construction of her as object: "[What] is menacing about the femme fatal is not that she could be fatal for men but that she presents a 'subject fully assuming her fate' [quoting Žižek's analysis of *Vertigo*]" (126). If the real Vina, as Rai sees it, returns to save Ormus by granting him his death wish, she can only do so as a corpse. Mira, like Vina before her, brings Ormus back to life (Vina wakes her "sleeping beauty" after his near-fatal accident, and Mira wakes him from his drug-induced stupor and gets him back on stage), but she rejects the Vina model and the implied femme fatal role. In the figure of Mira, then, Rushdie reverses this lethal game of multiple murders or deaths; although Mira is at first a "mira"(or mirror) of the dead Vina, she nevertheless manages to break free from this deadly role.

This disparity between model and modeled, or original and copy, is first demonstrated as the male voyeurs spy the perfect Vina clone. Ormus's frantic search for the new Vina leads him finally to the one girl he deems perfect for the role, and he shares his discovery with Rai. Although Rai's first amazed reaction to seeing Mira is: "Vina. It's Vina returned from the dead" (571), he soon comes to note the differences rather than the striking similarity between original and copy. He notices the disparity in skin color: "This girl had actually been blacking up to play dark Vina" and then goes on to describe Mira Celano as "a beautiful if kind of slutty young girl, more Latin-American than Indian looking ... and really pretty unlike her meal ticket, barren Vina, Mrs. Ormus Cama, my dead love" (576). The ironic twists here are numerous: Mira has to become blacker to play Vina (who is not really black either); she is a young and slutty mother whereas Vina is barren; and she is not Indian but rather Latin-American. In other words, she does not fit the role although she seems at first to be the perfect match. It is her *body*, however, that proves a dead ringer for Vina: "On the monitor, Mira Celano is taking off her kimono. Underneath it is Vina's naked body" (576). It is as body (or, if you will, as corpse) that Mira is Vina. As a living woman, she is "pretty unlike" her.

This necrophiliac desire for a dead woman's body stems, according to Bronfen, from a wish to return to what is perceived as the primary state of wholeness with the maternal element — the mirror stage:

> The position of the mourner ... also proves to be the position in which images are born and materialized. As such it serves as a recuperation of the mirror stage where, supported by the security of wholeness with the maternal body, the child experiences its first jubilation at recognizing its own integrity over the images it has psychically formed [127].

And the mourning Ormus indeed finds this wholeness in his dying moments cradled in the arms of a maternal figure — or surrogate mother. Ormus's devoted servant Clea Singh rushes to the scene upon hearing the fatal gunshots. Ormus "died there in the snow ... with his head in Clea's lap" (629). Clea cradles him in her arms and adopts the role (and the language) of Ormus's (dead) mother, Spenta Cama: "Ormus, she said, sobbing, and he opened his eyes and looked at her. Oh, my Ormie, she mourned, my little shrimpy boy, what to do for you? Do you know what you want? What you need?" Ormus does not respond at first but ends up answering Clea's last frantic plea: "Do you know who you are?" with "Yes ... Yes, mother, I know" (629). It is at this moment of death, then, that Ormus re-finds the mother figure he had lost a long time before her actual demise. The dying moment becomes a moment of recognition. And if Ormus is to be united with his beloved Vina in her underworld, he is also, at the moment of death, at one with his mother. In a moving scene that reads almost like a pieta, the dying Ormus, a larger than life mythical figure, becomes a little shrimpy boy, rejected by his mother and his lover.

Ormus is the ultimate migrant figure in the novel. He is a shape-shifter, a transformer, eliding boundaries of nationality and race and traversing time zones, only to be finally vanquished by his own obsession. Ormus becomes the emblem of music's power to traverse boundaries and to re-imagine alternative histories.[9] Rai comments on Ormus's alternative version of rock music's origin, beginning not in America, but rather in Bombay:

> So according to Ormus and Vina's variant version of history, their alternative reality, we Bombayites can claim that it was in truth our music, born in Bombay like Ormus and me, not "goods from foreign" but made in India, and maybe it was the foreigners who stole it from us [104].

In this ironic twist, it is not the West but India that takes center stage as the origin of rock music.[10] Yet this is by no means intended only as a joke or another Rushdean twist. As Shaul Bassi points out, Ormus's role in the novel is more complex.[11] Bassi states, comparing the fictitious Ormus to Freddie Mercury,

> [Like] Freddie Mercury, Ormus Cama, Rushdie's Orpheus is no herald of some politically correct message. He cannot be criticized for not being a perfectly accomplished mix between East and West (a naïve Western fantasy). His story rather embodies all the contradictions of the globalization of culture, extolled by some, demonized by others [113].

Bassi argues that both Mercury and Ormus, in their function as pop stars, are "exemplary agents,"

> embodying roles that are translatable in dialectic pairs: they are nomadic/insecure subjects; they make utopias/dystopias; they are popular creators/vainglorious; make changes/invent fads; play a part in the public sphere/fail to represent social movements and subaltern identities [113].

Bassi further comments on Rushdie's ideological position regarding his character's role as a modern day Orpheus:

> *The Ground Beneath Her Feet* is an original contribution to the Orpheus myth insofar as it is a narrative inquiry into the mythmaking (hence ideological *and* utopian) power of pop music in the full recognition of its embeddedness in the system of late capitalism. Rushdie harbours no illusion of music's authenticity or innocence [113].

Ormus's dual roles in the novel, as an "exemplary agent" according to Bassi's formulation, make him subject to the critique both of Indian purists and music critics who blame Ormus for "selling out," becoming too commercial. Rushdie documents the changing fortunes in Ormus's musical career, parodying both the claim for authentic music and the fickle nature of stardom.[12]

But Rushdie also presents Ormus as more than just a mythical pop icon and Orpheus figure. Ormus is also a visionary: His visions of an alternative universe and his encounter with the disturbed and seductive Maria and her guardian perform a dual function in the text. They cast Ormus in the role of a disturbed visionary but also show that he may be the only true seer after all. In one of the conversations Ormus has with Rai, he tells him of this "other world." The skeptic Rai ponders Ormus's "sudden possession of the idea that, like a runaway freight train, the world has veered sideways off its proper track and was now banging about out of control, upon a great iron web of twisted points" (201). Rai is terrified by the possibility: "[F]or if the world itself were metamorphosing unpredictably, then nothing could be relied upon anymore. What could one trust? How to find moorings, foundations, fixed points, in a broken, altered time?" (201). And although Rai comforts himself with the thought "The world is what it is" (201), he later comes to doubt his certainty as he too encounters Maria and hears of the parallel dimension. Rushdie winks at his readers by showing that Ormus's "access to some other plane of existence, some parallel, 'right' universe" (201), is a hallucination only in the world of the novel. Rai tells Ormus: "You'll be telling me next there's no Jesse Garon Parker" (203); we, the readers, know there *isn't*. Not in *our* world, anyway.

In this narrative and thematic twist, then, Rushdie seems to toy with the possibility that our world may be veering off its proper track or that it is *not* what it is or seems to be. In his rewriting of mythical tales—

3. "The World Is (Not) What It Is"

recasting them in the figures of iconic pop culture "gods"—Rushdie subverts the inherent meaning of classical mythological tales and parodies (post)modern star worship: Ormus and Vina may indeed be "living myths," but they are also, as I have shown, both commodities and at times unwilling participants in this commercialization process of their mythical status. As Rai points out, however, Ormus and Vina were also "consummate mythologisers of themselves" (99); they wittingly participate in the process of molding themselves as living myths by telling their love story as a mythological story that is larger than life. Their version of the Ormus-Vina tale may also be compromised. What Rushdie provides us with, then, are *versions*—of the mythological tales we have taken for granted, of known historical events, dates and public personas that seem so clear and understandable to us and structure our everyday lives—and asks us to question these givens in a world that seems to have lost its moorings or is about to veer off its proper track. In my reading of the novel's enigmatic ending, I examine how Rushdie's vision of this postmodern existence differs from Bauman's rather bleak view; I claim that Rushdie may in fact be offering us a glimpse of hope—with a postmodern twist, or loop, rather.

The novel ends in what appears to be a blissful domestic scene. We encounter another triangle consisting of Rai, Mira and Mira's young daughter, Tara, in their newfound home in America. This triad seems to offer a corrective to the troubled Rai-Ormus-Vina relationship. There is a reestablishment of a family unit (father-mother-daughter) in what seems to be a stable, known and safe setting. This surrogate family offers Rai the element of stability—or, if you will, solid ground—previously missing in his life. Having lost both his parents in tragic circumstances, Rai longs for a family of his own. It would seem, then, that Rai can finally become a true adult—responsible not only for his own life and wellbeing but also for the lives of his lover and her child.

This reading of the novel's ending as a moment of newly found peace of mind and adult existence, however, may only be part of the complex tale Rushdie offers us. Rai reflects on his personal tale and compares it to the endings of the mythological tales: "In the old stories, in different ways, the point is always reached after which the gods no longer share their lives with mortal men and women, they die or wither away or retire. They vacate the stage and leave us alone upon it, stumbling over our lines" (633–634). In this analogy, the mortal Rai no longer has the shadow of the mythological Ormus and Vina hovering over him; they have left the stage. But the following lines as well as the notion of "stumbling" show that this may not be entirely the case:

> This, the myths hint, may be what a mature civilization is: a place where the gods stop jostling and shoving us ... a time when they move back, still leering ... still whimsical, from the realm of the actual to the land of the so-to speak ... leaving us free to do our best or worst without their autocratic meddling [634].

As the novel constantly moves between the twin realms of the actual and the "so-to speak," choosing not to determine whether reality is indeed what we make of it, the vision of a mature society may be a bit more problematic than it seems at first.

The novel engages with possible versions, histories and alternative worlds and continually ponders the possibility of solid ground or mature stability. Thus, on the personal level, there may be a momentary space of calm and stable existence. On the collective level, however, or where cultural memory becomes confused, this is not the case, as the continually hovering figures of Vina and Ormus haunting the scene of Rai's domestic bliss demonstrate. The meaning and significance of Ormus and Vina's legacy is constantly questioned in the novel. They are remembered as sinners and saints, traitors to their homeland and its saviors, commercial artists who sold their soul to the mighty dollar, and true artists forever faithful to their music. Their legacy is eternally subject to (historical) change. But as places of memory they remain, haunting Rai's newly found safe haven.

Rai reflects on this domestic bliss: "I'm looking at Mira and Tara, my islands in the storm, and I feel like arguing with the angry earth's decision to wipe us out, if indeed such a decision has been made" (634). The tenuous nature of ordinary human life is never forgotten. Rai longs to believe in the possibility of goodness, however ordinary and clichéd it may seem: "Here's goodness, right? The mayhem continues, I don't deny it, but we're also capable of this. Goodness drinking o.j. and munching muffins" (634). But the mayhem lurks, the ground is not stable, and Rai, who had found (momentary) peace at last, proclaims: "Here's ordinary human love beneath my feet. Fall away, if you must, contemptuous earth, melt, rocks, and shiver, stones. I'll stand my ground, right here" (634).

With its biblical undertones, this statement reads like an admonition to the forces about to undermine it. Rai's call for the possibility of ordinary, banal goodness is couched in very grand terms; he becomes the admonishing prophet — raging against God's intent to wipe out the earth's inhabitants. Rai seems to direct this admonition to the figure of an avenging or biblical God. Mythological gods and goddesses, however, are another matter.[13] As Rai declares, his only true legacy is the mythological one:

> The old religions' legacy of living stories—the Ash Yggdrasil, the Cow Audumla ... the vain Olympians, the fabulous monsters, the legion of ruined, sacrificed women, the metamorphoses—continues to hold my attention; whereas Judaism, Christianity, Islam, the Market, utterly fail to enthrall. These are faiths for the front pages, for CNN, not for me. Let them struggle over their old and new Jerusalems! It's Prometheus and the Nibelungs, Indra and Cadmus, who bring me my kind of news [555].

This true legacy is indeed what Rai has to hold on to in an unstable world. But at the same time, his own "living myths," Ormus and Vina, the ultimate god and goddess for a (post)modern age, still hover above him. They reappear at the novel's end, in the very midst of this scene of domestic mirth, and complicate the vision of a cozy, optimistic happy ending.

In the novel's final scene, we see and hear Tara,[14] Mira's daughter, acting in typical childlike fashion. Rai comments with more than a hint of fatherly pride: "Tara's got the hold of the zapper. I've never gotten used to having the tv on at breakfast, but this is an American kid. She is unstoppable." Rai continues: "And today by some fluke, wherever she travels in the cable multiverse she comes up with Ormus and Vina" (634). There is no escaping the mythological pair, then. And although Rai offers a logical explanation ("[maybe] this was some sort of VTO weekend"), this does not seem too convincing. It is Tara who provides the answer: "I don't believe it, Tara says, zapping again and again. I don't *buh-leeve* it. Oh, *puh-leeze*. Is this what's going to happen now, for ever and *ever*? I thought they were supposed to be *dead*, but in real life they're just going to go on singing" (634). This short and hilarious passage both sums up and opens up Rushdie's "multiverse" novel. Tara poses the question of immortality and stardom as she significantly conflates real life with life on screen. In Tara's formulation, Ormus and Vina are only supposed to be dead. In fact, here they are in real life — namely on TV — singing forever. And furthermore, their singing constitutes an endless loop: The gods have not left the stage. They have never really left it and never will. In this postmodern, multi-channeled universe, we can never really get rid of our dead icons. Their immortality on air is just one more sign of the times we live in. The postmodern/postmortem god and goddess are the ultimate "living dead": They haunt the living in an endless, repetitive performance. And their insistent presence seems at once ominous and comforting. As Tara's question (Is this going to go on now, for ever and *ever?*) points out, we may be facing a different kind of immortality, one that our culture seems to have created and cannot now get rid of, try as we might.

This concept of life in death leads us back to Bauman's notion of deconstructing immortality in postmodernity. Bauman claims we have arrived at a paradoxical moment when "[death] is back ... un-deconstructed, unreconstructed. Even immortality has now come under its spell and rule. The price of exorcising the spectre of mortality proved to be a collective incapacity to construct life as reality, to take life seriously" (199). This incapacity to "take life seriously" or to gauge what is real life and what is, to borrow Rushdie's phrase — the "so-to speak"— is at the crux of the novel. The ending only serves to intensify the paradoxical nature of precarious human existence in uncertain and unstable times.

This does not mean Rushdie's novel ends on a bleak note. His essential optimism and belief in the redemptive potential of human love are still very much apparent. The final domestic scene offers the possibility for a happy ending, but it is just that, a possibility. It can ever only be one of many options. Rai, like Dorothy in *The Wonderful Wizard of Oz* (Rushdie's favorite film and one he sees as a metaphor for the life of migrants), may not know exactly where home is, but he knows it is "somewhere." In Rushdie's novel, this "somewhere" is transformed into a "nowhere" that is also "everywhere." Ormus and Vina live forever in the multiverse universe of cable TV. Rai, Mira and Tara live in what seems to be a stable version of our known world but really isn't. The ground shakes beneath their feet (and ours). The only certainty in this world is its uncertainties.

This sense of doubt is repeatedly expressed in the novel. Rai is constantly confused and baffled by the news he hears and by the overwhelming speed of global and national events. If Rai has some modicum of order and stability in his personal life, collective life is more confusing than ever. Rushdie demonstrates that our collective memory may be faulty. Like the alternative histories and multiple time dimensions in the text, this comment attests to the ways we (mis)understand the times we live in. Rai's playful description of the times he lives in sounds like Bauman's description of postmodern existence as a sphere of "[making] history in a world without history" (170). Bauman claims that since "making history" means becoming immortal, in the postmodern world — or in "the universe lived as a series of episodes, every event and every actor can 'make history'" (170). Rai's following remarks on the nature of historical infamy echo Bauman's comments on the nature of "historical events" in a postmodern age: "That woman powdered the president's Johnson! In her dreams—she's a celebrated fantasist! You're a sex god! You're a sex pest! She's to die for! She's a slut!" (387). The list goes on. In this age of the now, nothing remains the same. And we can never be sure of anything. But the humorous tone of this (and other) passages in the novel leads us to believe, that, unlike Bauman, Rushdie sees the humor as well as the potential perils in the postmodern condition.

Returning then to the second part of Bauman's formulation, we see that the inability to "construct reality" also entails not being able to "take life seriously." Bauman seems to be lamenting this state of affairs. His tone here sounds admonitory, almost preacher-like, as he warns against the perils of living too much in the postmodern now. If one cannot take life seriously anymore, then this loss may be the cause of our collective downfall. In the process of deconstructing immortality, we have "[subverted] the meaning and [denied] the need of a pattern" (199). Bauman argues that we are in need of such "pattern" and "meaning" in our lives. And he may also be claiming we have *lost* more than we gained by our addiction to the "now."

But Rushdie's novel does not participate, I would claim, in this admonitory practice. His reinvention of time is an attempt at deconstructing the ways we view personal and collective histories. Throughout the novel, Rushdie repeatedly toys with versions and possibilities. He continually rewrites historical tales and casts doubt on what we have come to hold dear. He urges us to "break the rules, deny the frame story, smash the frame" (384). He repeatedly invites us to revel in the stories "with No Entry signs on them" (217), the rejected versions rather than the accepted truths that structure our world. This project of re-imagining cultural and personal narratives thus may end up offering hope for a baffled and confused existence in a world that seems to have "lost the ground beneath its feet." By questioning these truths we hold so dear, and that structure our existence, Rushdie may be offering us a healing option: His belief in the power of stories and storytelling to create and reinvent reality within the space of a fictional text remains an option to be embraced. Rushdie's novel then may function as a healing device for author and readers alike. The questioning of cultural and historical memory thus provides us with a possible "way-out" or (to use Rushdie's metaphor) an "Entry sign" into different worlds.

I believe that *The Ground Beneath Her Feet* ends up celebrating life rather than mourning it. Rushdie offers us slanted versions of received truths and asks us to embrace them or at least to live at peace with the options they offer us. The novel opens up, rather than forecloses, our ability to re-imagine our world. If we return to McHale's formulation of postmodernist poetics, we see Rushdie sharing this postmodernist project of inquiry, the ontological quandary rather than the epistemological will to knowledge. The vision of different and alternate worlds as possible versions reinforces Rushdie's commitment to the open-ended and elusive textual space. The novel does not offer a solution or a resolution to the questions posed within the space of the literary text. As I have claimed, this is not a utopian or dystopian text. Rushdie remains, to the end, a celebrator of doubt and possibility rather than a preacher at the gates of a new (or old) Jerusalem. *The Ground Beneath Her Feet* remains one of his most convincing hymns to the power of doubt and uncertainty as vehicles of re-imagining our world(s).

This more optimistic vein in Rushdie's work comes perhaps as a result of the changes in his personal life. Although the *fatwa* on his life had not been lifted, he nevertheless enjoyed relative freedom of movement. The novel, as I have suggested above, takes the ominous year of the *fatwa* as its starting point, but it ends, as does *Fury*, in a more optimistic imagining of futurity. The young author, however, was not so optimistic. Rushdie's first unpublished novel, which I examine next, paints a very bleak picture of post–Imperial England. Its science fictional imaginings of a dark underbelly to the known world and its engagement with plots, counterplots and supernatural agents of destruction leave little hope for a better future. Rushdie dismisses this early text in *Joseph Anton*: "After that there was another novel-length text, *The Antagonist*, so bad, in a sub–Pynchon kind of manner, that he never showed it to anyone" (50). I would suggest, rather, that this early text foreshadows many of Rushdie's later writing. Not only is it an early blueprint for his most successful work, *Midnight's Children*, but it is also a work that can be read for its own merits. It may be a glorious failure in Rushdie's path to authorial acclaim, but it nevertheless manifests both the science fictional direction of his literary imagination and the exuberance and spirit which make his writing so uniquely his own, literary borrowings notwithstanding.

4

The Year of the Reverse: *The Antagonist* and *Midnight's Children*

> *I knew a man once whose thing is was to wreck the toilets in office buildings and write a slogan on the ruined walls: "if the cistern cannot be changed, it must be destroyed." I'm beginning to understand how he felt. And to remember how, in a younger, hairier, angrier, phase of life, I often used to feel.* — Salman Rushdie, Step Across This Line
>
> *I had spent my entire life in opposition, and had indeed conceived the writer's role as including the function of antagonist to the state.* — Salman Rushdie, The Jaguar Smile
>
> *If the modern state is a fantasy — if it relies on fantasy for an authority it can ultimately neither secure nor justify — than fantasy will always be there to one side of it.* — Jacqueline Rose, States of Fantasy

Rushdie's most successful novel to date, *Midnight's Children*, locates the birth of the Indian nation in 1947 as a founding moment that is also a moment of undoing. The protagonist, Saleem Sinai, is "handcuffed to history" and his life, as he sees it, is dictated by the life of his emerging nation. The vexed ties between personal and national "fissures" are presented in the novel employing science fictional tropes: Saleem has telepathic abilities and is able to commune with the Midnight Children, children born, like him, on the fateful night in 1947 when India too was born. This science fictionalizing of the historical is, as in the other Rushdie novels I discuss, a way of accessing personal and historical trauma through retelling and re-imagining key events in a nation's history by indirection: The science fictional mode becomes a vehicle for retelling a painful (hi)story as a fantastic site, thus both enhancing the horrific elements as the heart of the national tale while also allowing for the (artistic) distance needed to relate to such simultaneously traumatic and euphoric events in the new nation's birth.

As Jacqueline Rose points out in the epigraph above, the existence of the modern state *is* a fantasy in some sense. Rose links Freud's psychoanalytic notion of "phantasy" to the notion of the state as a "state of mind." Following Freud, Rose locates the role of fantasy in "the real world of the unconscious dreams of nations" (3). Fantasy, then, "far from being the antagonist of public, social, being — plays a central constitutive role in the modern world of states and nations" (4). This role of fantasy in the "dreams of nations" has been at the center of Rushdie's oeuvre from its earliest, unpublished work. Rushdie links the personal state of mind to the collective State. As Rose points out, it is this inextricable link between states of mind and the modern state that drives both the personal and the collective wills of nations and individuals: "[the] terrifying fragility and intransigence of the modern statehood can be illuminated by placing it into this dialogue with Freud.... Psychoanalysis can help us to understand the symptom of statehood, why there is something inside the very process upholding the state as a reality which threatens and exceeds it" (10). Rushdie's novel exposes this symptom at the heart of the national and private imagination.

I shall explore the fantasy aspect of Rushdie's early, unpublished novel as a *science fictional* element — fantasy as an exploration of a mode of alternative reality or speculative fiction — but also in Rose's psychoanalytical sense: The state of mind of Rushdie's protagonist, Saleem Sinai, the hero of both the earlier piece and *Midnight's Children,* is a perfect example of the links between the states that Freud recognizes in both the individual and the collective psyche.

In this chapter, I shall look at Rushdie's unpublished, early version of *Midnight's Children, The Antagonist.* I aim to show how Rushdie's engagement with the science fictional mode of telling a national tale is at work in this early novel. This version of *Midnight's Children* features a different Saleem Sinai. He is younger, sexually potent, married to a white British woman, the daughter of a former Imperial official who seems to epitomize the evils of empire. In this early version, Saleem is in a state of becoming. His sexual romps and his unwitting role in the conspiracies that seem to surround him at every turn pose his as an antagonist figure. As in the Rushdie quote above, Saleem too is an "antagonist of the state," but it is also his state of mind that is antagonized. The novel ends with his complete unhinging upon returning to India. The notion of antagonism is central to the novel's re-imagining of England and India in the "Year of

4. The Year of the Reverse

the Reverse," namely 1974. In it, the "younger, hairier and angrier" Rushdie, as the quote above from *Step Across This Line* playfully demonstrates, lashes out at the "System." But as the epigraph demonstrates, the "System" becomes a "cistern" in Rushdie's playful manipulation of language. There is certainly rage in the early novel, but this rage is manifested via playful language and punning, which somewhat masks the more sinister undertones of the text. This Rushdean trait is apparent throughout his writing career. It is interesting to note here that even a "younger, hairier and angrier" Rushdie is nevertheless, like the Rushdie we have come to know, very much a manipulator of language and a playful celebrant of its many punning possibilities as well as a very politically minded author. The title also gestures to what Rushdie would later define (in *The Jaguar Smile*) as the writer's main role: to be an antagonist of the state. Rushdie's role as an antagonist, then, has been a defining feature of his work, from its earliest, unpublished, first novel.

In that way, the early, unpublished piece, is not only a version of what would become Rushdie's most successful novel, *Midnight's Children,* but also a comment on the writer's antagonistic role, a role of which Rushdie would become the living embodiment following the *fatwa* in 1989. *The Antagonist*, then, provides us with an uncanny instance of the ways in which the young author prefigures his destiny as a writer whose antagonistic quality becomes his most defining feature. "The Antagonist," then, is not only a clever title, playing with the notion of the reversal of fictional roles: protagonist and antagonist, self and other, the State and the Individual who vies against it. The antagonist in the novel may also be Saleem's alter ego, Black Saleem, who becomes Shiva in *Midnight's Children*. On the plot level, at least, this seems to be the case as the narrative moves towards the final confrontation between the two Saleems in India. But this fateful encounter never happens. Saleem is too late, and the murderous Black Saleem had already killed his target. The principle of antagonism that structures the novel, however, refers to a wider perception of antagonism as a way of being in the world, one that both author and character seem to share. The young Saleem in *The Antagonist* seems to be a reflection, in some sense, of his young, angry and hairy creator.

It would seem, then, looking at the novel in retrospect, that the title, and the novel, encapsulate Rushdie's artistic credo. If the writer is an antagonist, albeit a playful one at times, then the explosive potential of writing, and its role as a (time) bomb, is very evident in this early novel.

The novel revolves around explosive events of different kinds, both literal and metaphorical. The many subplots and characters, all vying against each other, are a reflection and an enactment of this principle of antagonism.

The Antagonist uses for its main plot the device that structures the plot in the later novel. As I have suggested above, on the plot level, the antagonists in the novel are the two Saleems: Saleem's alter ego, Black Saleem, who reappears as Shiva in *Midnight's Children,* signaling his metaphoric role as the destructive element in Indian history, and Saleem Sinai, whose name hints at the Sinai desert and the prophets who dwell in and come out of the desert. In a typically Rushdean twist, the "desert" becomes a "deserter." Saleem is not a faithful husband, for one, but he is also a man who is always on the run: leaving women, affiliations, professions and countries behind him in search of a self that is always shifting. Black Saleem is the antagonist in the title as his rivalry with Saleem, his doppelganger and the person who took his "rightful place" as a baby when the two were swapped in their cradles, comes to signal, as he does later in *Midnight's Children*, the negative, murderous aspect of Indian national identity.

It becomes clear, however, that this rivalry, which may be read as rivaling aspects of one personal and national entity, is only one of the many antagonistic principles structuring the novel. In this earlier piece, the science fictional elements, which appear in *Midnight's Children* in the form of the telepathic Saleem who converses with his fellow Midnight Children, become the most prominent feature of the young author's re-imagining of England and India's intertwined histories. Rushdie imagines a world in which counter-forces are at work, vying for control of post–Imperial England. In this world, the supernatural powers of telepaths and witches are used to control an explosive political situation. As in *MC*, the occult plays a significant role in establishing the climate of fear and paranoid suspicion. But, whereas in *MC* the main science fictional device in the novel centers on Saleem Sinai's telepathic powers, in this early work the focus is on England in 1974 and the dystopian aftereffects of empire.

The backdrop is India's nuclear experiment on May 18, 1974. In this test, India detonated a nuclear device in an underground facility. The device had been built using material supplied for its ostensibly peaceful nuclear program by its allies, the United States, France and Canada.

4. The Year of the Reverse

Rushdie reinvents this "peaceful nuclear explosion"—as India chose to call it, naming the operation "The Smiling Buddha"—as an explosion with more dire consequences, which happens on a fake frontier in a simulated film set. The reinvention of this historical event as a literal "sex-bomb" is one of the ways in which the young author embarks on what would later become a defining feature of his oeuvre: the blurring between real and fictional events to create a site of fantastic or science fictional alternate reality. I shall relate in detail to this major scene in the novel, as it encapsulates Rushdie's main thematic and aesthetic concerns.

In light of this early unpublished piece, I re-examine *MC* as a science fictional attempt at charting the role of imaginary locales at the very heart of nation making. Rushdie provides "hallucinatory re-creations of the past," to borrow Pierre Nora's term, thereby recasting India's history in a unique science fictional space. Saleem Sinai, the often deluded and forgetful narrator, a "midnight's child" who communicates telepathically with his fellow Midnight Children, becomes the skewed reflection of Rushdie's own attempts to tell his nation's story. In the earlier, unpublished piece, a young Rushdie provides us with an intricate, multiple, at times confusing, array of plots (in both senses of the word), a plethora of characters who dabble with the occult, and an outrageous re-imagining of a nuclear test as a (literal) "sex bomb": Rushdie's Ahorgans are human bombs, who activate the nuclear device attached to their "organ." This is only one of the many imaginative twists in *The Antagonist*, where the historical becomes science fictional at every turn.

In *The Antagonist*, the young Rushdie presents the core ideas that would later resurface in his fiction. Not only is this early unpublished piece the "blueprint" for *MC*, it also provides us with the blueprint for the whole Rushdean oeuvre. For it is in this early piece that the young author first forms what would later become his defining trademarks: linguistic brilliance, multiple allusions to high and low culture, an interest in the cinematic as a way of accessing reality, the migrant condition as a fraught, yet potentially exuberant space, the longing for Mother India—and the realization that this longing can never become belonging—the insistent, obsessive parallels between the national story and the personal one, and the dismantling of the fiction of a coherent self in favor of multiple, at times warring selves on both the national and personal levels. I would suggest, therefore, that this early piece provides us with an invaluable tool for reading the later works. This unpublished piece is not an early exercise gone wrong and therefore unpublished. I would claim rather that the unchecked Rushdean spirit that emerges in the later novels is very apparent in this early work. This piece encapsulates both the thematic and stylistic aspects of the author we have come to know as Rushdie.

At this early stage, Rushdie is still finding his artistic way. However, it is heartening to realize that he has remained true to his vision, from this early novel to his last novel to date. My interpretation of *The Antagonist* cannot be read without acknowledging that Rushdie later reinvents both the main character, Saleem Sinai, and some of the major events in the plot, namely the switching at birth of the two midnight's children, Saleem and Shiva (Black Saleem in *The Antagonist*), to create the core narrative in *MC*. The inextricable links between personal history and national events are first given a (science fictional) form in the unpublished piece.

As I have suggested, however, *The Antagonist* should be read for its own merits, not merely as a precursor of a later work. Therefore, I believe that the major differences between Saleem Sinai in *MC* and the earlier version of the character bearing the same name in *The Antagonist* are of greater interest than the similar narrative device that Rushdie playfully adopts in both novels to provide what he calls in *MC* "melodrama piling upon melodrama." The Saleem character in *The Antagonist* is not only a more youthful version; his sexual prowess, for one, is sharply contrasted with the later, run-down Saleem. But both characters are marked by a physical condition that symbolizes their mental breakdown. In *MC*, Saleem imagines he is literally falling apart, while in *The Antagonist* Saleem is plagued by worms in his intestines, which both explain his insatiable hunger and become a symbol of the fear of the "Worm," a monstrous creature who circles the globe but is also an emblem of decay and death. Interestingly, Rushdie chooses the baby swapping theme, a staple of melodrama, in this earlier novel as well as in the later one, to signal the ways in which India, like Britain, is affected and shaped by class warfare. The affluent baby is swapped for the pauper baby, thus signifying how an accident of birth can change the fate of a child and, by extension, also of a nation. I shall discuss at greater length the two different Saleems—the earlier version in *The Antagonist* and the Saleem of *Midnight's Children* fame. But the first part of this chapter will be devoted to examining *The Antagonist* as a text that centers on "The Year of the Reverse," 1974, and the disastrous aftereffects of empire.

4. The Year of the Reverse

Time Bomb: The Aftereffects of Empire

Both the early and the later novel highlight time — both historical and mythical — as a fundamental feature in the personal and the national stories of the protagonists. Historical time (the birth of the Indian nation in 1947) becomes mythical time in *MC*. The birth of the nation is presented as a magical moment, fraught with danger and potential, symbolized by the Midnight Children, born at the same time as their new nation. Midnight, the witching hour, a liminal time, then becomes an apt metaphor for both the perils and the potential of the new nation and its newborn sons and daughters. This idea of time as magical, dangerous but also potentially redeeming reoccurs in Rushdie's novels. But in his earliest work, he chooses to focus on a year that becomes a symbol of the reverse of the birth of the Indian nation. Beginning his tale in England in 1974 signals the ways in which the two dates (1947 and 1974) are mirror images of each other. The mythical importance of numbers and dates is highlighted in the very first pages of the novel. *The Antagonist* takes place in the "year of the Reverse," 1974:

> It is February 1974. The Prime Minister has just inquired, curiously, who governs Britain; the miners have stopped digging coals and started digging in their heels; the week is three days long. The Year of the Reverse ... is upon us, the first great culmination of the nation's shift into contraction which began in 1947. Film Britain today and you should leave the film in the negative [TA, 3].

Employing a filmic metaphor (film in the negative) and a geographic and geological metaphor (the nation's shift into contraction), Rushdie overlays the date with symbolic meanings. The political tensions (miners' strike and loss of control indicated by the prime minister's wry question) are interwoven with the symbolic elements that make this description of political unease a more general, even metaphysical comment on the nature of time as an agent of change or, more likely, destruction. The significance of dates and their magical implication are highlighted at the beginning of the novel, as the description of the ominous year, 1974, indicates. Rushdie literalizes the film metaphor: The novel opens with a film set, and there is another film set to come later on, which proves to be literally explosive. In this way, Rushdie uses film and the cinema as representations of the "real" as "reel": The movie set is a place where the events of everyday life become the place of inverted reality.

Trevor Gutte, the young director, is at work filming a documentary about a London neighborhood, ironically named "Bliss Grove." But this place, at the time before a fateful election that Rushdie describes as a "pre-electoral arabesque" (4), is also the place where "the fragments of a story, a secret history waiting to be woven into its invisible tapestry," where "[reality] had been inverted" (4). This inversion of reality is at the center of the novel as it imagines secret histories underneath the seeming reality of Bliss Grove, a metonymic stand-in for immigrant Britain. The wry description of the fate of the immigrant, which Rushdie later describes with great force in *The Satanic Verses*, highlights the idea of the reverse: the immigrants to Britain are colonizing it in reverse, creating a new England that is no longer insular and elitist. Gutte, the filmmaker who (perhaps like Rushdie) "speaks English too well, with the over-rounder vowels of the arriviste" (*TA*, 11) tells Vanilla Icequeen, another half-breed, a very bewitching witch and Saleem's Sinai's partner in a "live show," that his visit to New York has shown him that "the multinational community ... is a source of infinite richness" (11). What Gutte ignores, Rushdie tells us, is "the encyclopaedia [sic] of unspoken words ... the other side of the multinational community," which contains "a wealth of submerged folklore, suppressed history and aspirations without a channel" and is "written in the passionate rhetoric of separatism" (11). It is this other side, or underbelly, of the immigrant condition that Rushdie begins exploring here and will return to in his later novels, most famously in *The Satanic Verses*. The secret history of England, interwoven as it must always be with the fate of its former colonies, is envisioned in the novel as a battle between two secret organizations.

Rushdie's novel imagines a clandestine organization called the New Empire, which seeks to continue Britain's colonial rule using covert means, plots, spies and atomic bombs. Against this clandestine organization there is Index, the anarchist cell that has destructive plans of its own. The novel imagines various underworlds operating beneath the surface of the real world. Things (and people) are never what they seem: almost every character in the novel has an alias, a false name and a falser identity. The principle of antagonism between different worldviews that vie for domination is at the heart of the novel. The many subplots all tie together and all lead to (what should have been) the final confrontation between Saleem Sinai and his doppelganger, Black Saleem. But this final encounter never takes place. Rushdie ends the novel in India, where Saleem finally breaks under

4. The Year of the Reverse

the pressure of warring selves and falls into an autistic state. In this way, the return home to India signals a final undoing rather than a resolution.

The struggle over Britain's image is at the heart of the novel. Rushdie locates its origins in Britain's colonial rule in India and its aftereffects. The narrator comments on the immigrant condition as an alien one, in both senses of the word. If the novel is to be about the "year of the Reverse" or "the second civil war, the True War," then "[other] aliens are involved" like "Sinai, whose story this will probably turn out to be" (3). Trevor Gutte gets his chance to film Bliss Grove and the upcoming municipal elections since, as he is told by one of his bosses, he can provide "the outsider's view of the election. Men from Mars we can't have, but Pakistanis we've got. You're half–Indian, Gutte. You'll fit in" (3). The link between the alien from outer space and the alien immigrant is no more than a racist joke here. But Rushdie plays with the science fictional aspects of this pun throughout the novel, suggesting that Gutte, Sinai and Vanilla Icequeen, the woman who is both Sinai's and Gutte's lover, are aliens. This alienness is the bond between them as well as the cause of their possible undoing. Rushdie presents this erotic triangle as the basis for his novel and provides many reflecting or parallel triangles throughout. This is a theme he will return to in *The Ground Beneath Her Feet*, where, as I have previously shown, the erotic triangle and the obsession with doubling and reflections is at the center of the novel. In *The Antagonist* Rushdie explores the erotica of triangles as well as their more sinister side.

The novel imagines Bliss Grove as the stage on which the immigrant nation acts out its (post)colonial fantasies: the street is the scene of a carnivalesque performance of difference. One of its manifestations is the erotic performance of Vanilla Icequeen and Saleem Sinai: a live show that mimics the sexual act without ever really performing it. The erotic aspect of the quest for selfhood is a repeated theme in the novel. Gutte, Saleem and Vanilla are one of the many erotic triangles in a text that dwells on both the redeeming and the destructive aspects of Eros. Saleem's impotence, and later his unending sexual powers, are central in Rushdie's depiction of selfhood in erotic terms, in a very detailed manner, one to which he will not return in his more sober later novels.

In that way, Rushdie creates an "explosion of difference": The sexual becomes explosive, both literally and figuratively. One of Rushdie's most ingenious science fictional inventions is a living "sex bomb," a suicide bomber with an atomic bomb attached to his sexual organ, going off at the same time he does. The nuclear tensions between India and Pakistan are the backdrop for Rushdie's invention. In this way, the political tensions are eroticized: in Rushdie's novel, the sexual is always political. His characters engage in sexual acts as ways of expressing their conflicting and warring selves. There is never a purely personal act of love, nor is there ever a sense of coherent selfhood. The plots and counterplots in the novel all share the paranoid suspicion of origin. The self is protean: moving, changing and shifting. This is the fate of the half breeds, like Vanilla and Gutte, but it is also shared by the white colonizers, the former rulers of an empire that is no longer there but that seeks to preserve its privilege and power by clandestine means. Thus, for example, the man heading the New Empire, Rudyard Wayland Smith, was an Anglo Indian officer who had undergone plastic surgery to make him look like the Egyptian king Ramesses. He has also changed his name, paying homage to Rudyard Kipling, the very symbol of empire. In a similar way, the head of Index, the rival organization, is a mysterious man with a number of aliases. Secret identities abound in the novel, suggesting that the very concept of identity is fraught and dangerous. The characters in the novel are forever changing their names, looks and loyalties to different causes. What emerges is a confused and confusing world, or rather worlds, in which secrets, plots and delusions are the order of the day.

Rushdie begins the novel on the set of a documentary film, which is supposed to reflect immigrant life in Bliss Grove. But the idea of the cinema as a medium that offers us illusions of the real is played out in the novel, as in *MC*. Cinema and its role as a maker of illusions is at the center of Rushdie's re-imagining of historical events in the novel. Thus, his narrator, Saleem Sinai, reflects on his role as the teller of his nation's story employing a cinematic metaphor:

> Reality is a question of perspective; the further you get from the past, the more concrete and plausible it seems—but as you approach the present, it inevitably seems more and more incredible. Suppose yourself in a large cinema, sitting at first in the back row, and gradually moving up, row by row, until your nose is almost pressed against the screen. Gradually the stars' faces dissolve into dancing grain; tiny details assume grotesque proportions; the illusion dissolves—or rather, it becomes clear that illusion itself *is* reality [197].

This telling passage contains one of the central metaphors in the novel—the movie and the movie screen—and expounds the novel's engagement with the idea of (virtual) reality and truth value. The inversion at the heart of the film metaphor (the past is clearer than the present) demonstrates how stories of the past that are already couched in historical terms may be easier to tell than the more present (in both senses of the word) events that may be too close for comfort. Saleem uses this metaphor to reiterate his "unbelievable claim" to supernatural powers of perception.

The film metaphor becomes real as Rushdie recasts the foundational historical event of Gandhi's assassination as an event that can only be narrated as the backdrop to a fictional film. He shifts the focus from the assassination to the announcement of Gandhi's death and Saleem's family's reaction to the historical event—a reaction that, from a Muslim family, is necessarily at odds with the Hindu view. Significantly, this scene takes place at a movie theatre. Saleem's uncle Hanif, a well known filmmaker, married to "one of the brightest stars of that celluloid heaven, the divine Pia" (167), comes to Bombay to seek his fortune in the film industry. Hanif's unique cinematic style involves a way of presenting erotic scenes on screen while circumventing the strict rules of Bollywood cinema that do not permit "lover boys and their leading ladies to touch each other on screen" (168). Hanif's ingenious solution involves the pair of on-screen lovers, Pia and Nayyar, "[kissing]—not one another—but *things*" (168):

> Pia kissed an apple, sensuously, with all the rich fullness of her painted lips; then passed it to Nayyar; who planted, upon its opposite face, a virilely passionate mouth. This was the birth of what came to be known as the indirect kiss—and how much more sophisticated a notion it was than anything in our current cinema; how pregnant with longing and eroticism! [168].

This scene takes place in the magical Kashmiri landscape ("by the foundations of Shalimar they pressed their lips to a sword"), only to be interrupted: "Against the larger-than-life figures of Pia and Nayyar, kissing mangoes as they mouthed to play-back music, the figure of a timorous, inadequately bearded man was seen, marching on the stage beneath the screen, microphone in hand" (168–169).

The idyllic on-screen moment, with its fake playback music and its exaggerated moves, is interrupted by an all too mundane, slightly ridiculous figure who nevertheless offers the ominous counter-story to Bollywood-style erotic play: "The Serpent can take most unexpected forms; now, in the guise of this ineffectual house-manager, it unleashed its venom" (169). The venom in this case is the announcement of Mahatma

Gandhi's assassination: "'This afternoon, at Birla House in Delhi, our beloved Mahatma was killed. Some madman shot him in the stomach, ladies and gentlemen — our Bapu is gone!'" (169). For the Muslims in the crowd, like Saleem's mother Amina, this announcement spells danger. Her brother Hanif warns her to leave the theatre: "'If a Muslim did this thing there will be hell to pay'" (169). Saleem's family remains in their house for the next forty-eight hours until the "radio gave us a name. Nathuram Godse" (169). Saleem's grandfather Aadam reacts: "This Godse is nothing to be grateful for." But Amina is overjoyed: "By being Godse he has saved our lives!" (169).

The major historical event is restaged as a cause of terror for one Muslim family. The linguistic pun, the killer is a "God sent" relief to the Muslim population by *not* being Muslim, provides a parodic insight of the effect of religious differences in India as a cause of national and personal strife. The loss of the nation's Bapu may be relevant to the Hindu population. For Muslims, it can mean something entirely different. Furthermore, Rushdie stages the dramatic moment as a literal and figurative interruption into the illusory world of *The Lovers of Kashmir* or the imagined land where things are done by indirection. The announcement becomes a rude foray of the mundane and real into the magical land of make-believe. And the snake in this Garden of Eden is not Gandhi's killer but the man who delivers the potentially lethal announcement. Moreover, he chooses this particular foundational moment in India's history and retells it as "[melodrama] piling upon melodrama, life acquiring the coloring of a Bombay talkie" (174).

Saleem's telepathic abilities, then, serve Rushdie as a way of reintroducing another key moment in India's history, perhaps *the* moment, as alternative reality. The adult Saleem is about to introduce the Midnight Children to Padma (who returns after an absence where she seeks a magical herb to cure Saleem's impotence). This cure makes him "delirious for a week" (232), and he ponders the ways this magic had "connected [him] briefly with that world of ancient learning and sorcerers' lore." In the later novel, Gandhi's assassination is revealed in the cinema, a place where the film shown to the audience provides both a sense of longing for love and for the idyllic Kashmir and also a mode of indirection, cut violently by the intrusion of the outside world in the form of political assassination that means one thing for part of the audience and quite another for Saleem Sinai's Muslim family. Thus, the cinema provides an indirect mode of

4. The Year of the Reverse

expressing collective and personal desires. And the intrusion of the real world into the film, dramatized by the announcer's presence as a disruption of the filmic attempt to circumvent reality, shows that there can be no escape from the real. It will always intrude on the imaginary world and violently upset it.

In *The Antagonist*, in an even clearer way, it is another film set that becomes an outright deception with explosive consequences. In one of the novel's most amusing, yet most horrifying, scenes, the Ahorgan, or human "sex-bomb," arrives at a border point between India and Pakistan on a motorcycle with the bomb strapped to his organ. He does not know that he has in fact arrived at a movie set, an elaborate ploy set up to deflect him from his purpose. The bomb, however, goes off in the wrong place, and the actors, spectators and director are blown up alongside the Ahorgan and his beautiful mate. War games become real war, causing very real and horrible deaths. This is one of the many instances in the novel in which the real and the imaginary collide, with destructive results. The film set is not what it seems. It is in fact an elaborately set up deception. Rushdie entitles the chapter "Doctormentally Fillum" giving us the Anglo-Indian version of "documentary film." The stage for this fake documentary is "the desert west of Jaisalmar" (211), and the man walking the desert is "Khan Abu Bakar Khan, Muslim and Northwest Frontiersman" and "an Indian spy" (211). He is "in control of one of Indian Intelligence's most daring, important missions; the capture of a nuclear device" (211). This mission is to be carried out on May 18, 1974, the day on which India conducted the nuclear experiment, authorized by Indira Gandhi, with the ironic codename "Smiling Buddha." This historical event is given a science fictional twist in Rushdie's re-imagining of the scene of the explosion as a documentary film set that turns real as the explosion occurs, killing and wounding numerous people. The figure of the warrior-spy in the desert that opens the chapter is a counter-figure to Saleem Sinai, the man whose name connotes deserts and destiny but who thinks of himself as a deserter — a man on the run from the weight of history. I shall elaborate further on the ways in which the desert figures both here and in *MC* as a symbolic locale.

The director of the film, shot by the Government of India Documentary Film Unit, is "Balsubramaniam Venkataraghaven, who is proud of his claim to be the film director with the longest name in India" (212). Balsubramaniam is also proud "of his command of the English language and of his hatred of art," which he combines in his saying "Art is an Ineffable Fart only, a flatulence without a beginning" (212). Rushdie is parodying this approach, providing a stereotyped representation of the filmmaker as a man who is more than willing to offer his services to Indian Intelligence: this "goldentooth glisterslipped suavepolished" (213) man is the epitome of a brand of "Indianness" Rushdie parodies here. The film director who had worked with the great Satayajit Ray as a "screenwriter and source" (212) is now a willing tool in the service of Indian Intelligence, willing to create an illusion that ends up blowing up in his and his crew's faces. Thus, the hatred of art comes to signal the mercenary quality of this new breed of Indian filmmakers. Interestingly, the two films in *The Antagonist* are documentaries, and both films present a version of "reality" that is manipulated and false. Gutte's film is commissioned by the BBC to show the alien nature of Bliss Grove, and the "doctomramentally fillum" in this chapter is meant to alter political realities by "capturing a nuclear device" (212).

Thus, the mounting political tensions between India and Pakistan are manipulated by the Indian government. Rushdie explains this manipulation as a result of a plot hatched by a pair of siblings, the Shahs, a brother and sister who take on the names of Egyptian royalty, Ptolmey and Cleopatra. Like the other plotters in Rushdie's novel, they take on a secret identity and weave their influence behind the scenes. After being banished from Pakistan, they plan "to reduce the political situation in Pakistan to such confusion that their advent, in the guise of injured innocents, would be hailed with relief" (214). The Shahs, part of the clandestine organization Rushdie imagines as the New Empire, are in possession of a "nuclear device so compact it can be carried by a single man." Their plan is to let the agent take the device through India, via the Rajasthan desert, across the border into Pakistan: "It will be detonated near Pakistan's border with India, and it will be construed as a horrendous act of war" (216). This devious plan, which will create havoc in both India and Pakistan, is discovered by the spy Khan Abu Bakar Khan. As he finds out that both Indian and Pakistani border-post guards would have been given bribes to let the agent through, he "was going to build a fake border, within Indian territory, let the carrier pass through and plant his bomb, then capture both agent and bomb. It would be a great coup" (216). Hence, the film set. That is, film acts as a medium of indirection here too, as it did in the episode of *MC* I discussed above. The Bollywood film imagines a fantasy land

(Kashmir) in which the realm of desire is acted out by indirection, signaling cinema's ability to create other worlds and remove us, if only for a while, from reality or at least offer a version of reality, an imaginative possibility, a dream that can perhaps never be realized but is there for us to long for; in this instance, in contrast, we have a more direct and more devious act of mimicry. The links between nation and cinema are shown to be fraught with danger, in both cases: in *MC*, it is the intrusion of Gandhi's assassination into the movie theatre that signals the enormous divide between the Muslims and Hindis. In *The Antagonist*, it is the India-Pakistan conflict, again hinging on Muslim and Hindi warfare, which is at the center. If cinema is in some sense a diversion from the real, here it only replicates it, with disastrous results.

As Sumita S. Chakravarty points out in "Fragmenting the Nation," the fiction film as a medium "can only present fragments of the nation and project them as evidence of the whole" (226). Film can only re-present a story of a couple, family or group to present the whole of which they are a part: "Thus, the 'nation' as an entity is always eclipsed in cinema and has to be reconstituted by viewers through its screen absence. It is the absence which marks the fullness of the nation. The fragment is therefore both the nation's source of fear and its object of desire, its threat and its promise" (226). Chakravarty concludes that "the paradox of cinema may well be that while its form of address is collective, its narrative organization and visual dynamics privilege the concrete and specific, the face in the crowd, the personal and singular" (226). It is this singular nature of the cinematic image that Rushdie represents in *MC*'s imaginary film, discussed above. But the elusive nature of the Indian nation as a object of filmic and literary representation is at the center of Rushdie's work from *The Antagonist* to this day. The choice of film as a medium that attempts to represent what cannot be represented — the nation as an entity — may also be a statement on the conflicted role of art, both visual and literary, in its attempts to construct a national narrative. The documentary film set in the novel enacts this idea of the fake doing battle with the real.

This vexed relationship between the very real bomb and the attempts to take it by Khan Abu Bakar Khan, the spy and instigator of the plot to both capture the agent carrying the bomb and keep the bomb itself from exploding, is presented in the short and hilarious exchange between spy and director. Khan tells BV, as he calls the director with the longest name in Indian cinema, that he is going to "film the most historical doctormentally fillum [he has] ever fillumed" in which they will "take an atom bomb" (217). Khan promises that although this is an actual bomb, it will not explode, a promise he cannot keep. The film director, who previously prided himself on his hatred of art, now muses: "I could have been an artist. Then at least I could stay alive, and make farts. Dead men break no wind" (217). Art, then, is a life force whereas what this particular "fillum" will create is history: The historical film will end up, like the history it seeks to imitate, a cause of death rather than life. And BV will die while the bomb explodes, making very accurate his prophetic remarks and the realization that he is "in the hands of a madman" (217), namely Khan, but on a larger scale, the kind of man Khan represents. The film set is not only a fake of the real; it also participates in creating deadly images in the service of Indian Intelligence — seen here as yet another clandestine and deadly instrument of the state.

The other player in this deadly game is the Ahorgan, the agent carrying the atomic bomb whose job is to "obscure the sunlight, blinding it in its own, brighter blast. Jude the Obscurer. Ahorgan Jude, marching as to war" (218). Rushdie, of course, plays here with the title of Hardy's novel *Jude the Obscure*, perhaps hinting at the lonely nature of the mission undertaken by the suicide bomber, the solitary life in preparation for one "Moment of Supreme Pleasure" (218) that is the explosion. The suicide bomber in this case is Jude, a "Wessexfathered and Hokkaidmothered" Englishman whose willingness to lay down his life for this moment of pleasure aligns him with the Kamikaze pilots which he feels a kinship for. This agreement is also a pact with Eros and with Thanatos. Jude stays at a hotel bearing the name of the Russian nuclear testing ground Novaya Zamlia.

The shared history of corruption is an ironic comment on the ways in which former alliances (Russia and India) bear traces in the most unlikely of places. Jude speaks fluent Hindi and asks for the most beautiful whore in the area from the hotel owner. The whore is "Shanta, the wonder of Jaislamar whose breasts curve as sharply as swords and whose energy can exhaust all comers" (218). The erotic is both lethal (swords) but also, ironically, a way to overcome war. *Shanta* means "peace." Jude "liked that idea too" (219). Rushdie is hinting here at the "peaceful" nature of the actual historical event: India's first nuclear test on May 18, 1974, under the Atoms for Peace program. This "peaceful nuclear explosion" is parodied in Rushdie's version of events. The oxymoronic nature of the "peaceful

4. The Year of the Reverse

explosion" is dramatized in Jude, the Ahorgan/suicide bomber who is literally a "sex-bomb," a human detonator of an atomic device. Rushdie's interest in the erotic as a destructive and redemptive site where the self is constantly renewed or destroyed is a major theme in many of his novels. It is interesting to note how he makes it the core of most of the intricate and intersecting plots in his earliest novel. Sexual energy, be it life affirming or death enhancing, or in some curious way, both, is at the center of the novel.

Eroticism and death are conjoined both literally and figuratively. In the Ahorgan's case, he is literally a "sex-bomb": Jude and Shanta make love on the night before his final day on earth. He feels grateful to the hotel owner for his "choice of a whore called Peace. There was a light that went on in her eyes when they wrestled that was the most erotic thing he's found in a woman in years. It was a soft light, but distant, an emanation from some unseen mother lode of desire, an outpouring of open, total, unashamed lust, a gentle, fierce, irresistible imperative" (220). The series of oppositions (gentle/fierce/peace/war) establishes the scene as the culmination of the kind of sublime moment that Jude seeks. He therefore asks Shanta: "How would you like to die?" to which she answers: "Like this, making love with you" (220). The moment of orgasm (this "little death") is literalized. Jude "finds his loins longing for the brief node of pain which will tell him he has been activated, and for the orgasmic fulfillment of the blast" (220). The bomb is strapped to his "organ," and it goes off after he has intercourse with Shanta.

Rushdie thus sets the scene for an explosion in more ways than one. The movie set, the fake border on which this suicide attack will take place, becomes a simulacra of the real event, in Baudrillard's term. The movie set functions as a mirror of very real tensions between India and Pakistan, two nations, formerly as much a "oneness of two" as Jude and his lover Shanta. Like them, Pakistan and India are now deadly mates, conjoining only as they blow each other up in numerous regional wars, culminating in the nuclear war games played by both nations.

The cinema also serves Rushdie, as in *MC*, as a space where reality and fantasy meet, sometimes with disastrous results. Rushdie thus describes the movie extras hired for the mock historical documentary as people in grip of a particular fantasy: the fantasy of being "in movies": "[The] presence of the paraphernalia of film-making gives them the illusion of fantasy-made-flesh. Which is, of course, the essence of the cinema. The extra is the most cinematic person on a lot; he is the one who believes most desperately in the medium, in the magic of the process" (221). So, it seems, does Rushdie: His fascination with the cinema as "fantasy-made-flesh," a vehicle of magic, is evident in fictional and nonfictional work, the most famous example being, of course, his book *The Wizard of Oz*, a meditation on the film's influence on his life and writing.

This fascination with the cinematic is also apparent in *The Antagonist*, in which film, as I have shown, figures very prominently. In the scene on the fake frontier the extras hired to play border guards perform their roles more vehemently than actors. Realism, then, is achieved when the fake couldn't be more convincing. The reality of the scene also comes from the true nature of the India-Pakistan bloody conflict. It will end up being very real when Jude and his mate arrive on the scene and the bomb goes off. Rushdie sets the scene for the explosion only to leave the readers hanging, as his narrator shifts the scene to Stoke Summerfield, Wiltshire: "[We] dolly slowly into the basement" of the Wayland-Smiths, the pair at the head of the New Empire, who operate Jude. The filmic metaphor ("we dolly") is a repeated narrative strategy in the novel, beginning with Trevor Gutte's film set. The Wayland-Smiths and the New Empire are the clandestine shadowy figures of brute (post-)imperial power. Thus, it is their command that sets the explosive event in motion. Jude, on his fast motorcycle with Shanta, feels "the point of pain and no return" (224). The narrator comments: "Behind him, Shanta holds on for what she takes to be dear life, and is in fact the Reverse" (224). As I have shown, the "year of the Reverse," 1974, is the year of undoing: death rather than birth. The ironies of the fake frontier are compounded when Shanta thinks they have arrived in Pakistan and begs Jude not to take her across the border: "I cannot go there. They will kill me over there. I'm Hindu" (224). Jude does not recognize the falseness of the border post. He assumes he was given the right location. As Jude and Shanta arrive on the scene, Jude says he "must have her now" (224) and proceeds to do so to the utter amazement of the film crew. When the climax arrives, so does the explosion: "There may have been an instant when Khan Abu Bakar Khan saw the thing happen, saw the man turn into *something*, a wave of unimaginable power. Perhaps he even appreciated the quality of the wave. But then the light came, and the fire, and the force of the blast, and the telltale mushroom, and there was no Khan left to think anything" (225). The film director finds something running down his face, "his eyes" (226). The final "shot," then, is real. The Big Bang, as Jude thinks of the bomb, has happened, and it has annihilated everything around it.

At the time Rushdie wrote *The Antagonist*, India and Pakistan had already been involved in three wars (1947–8, 1965 and 1971). India's nuclear capabilities, beginning with the "peaceful" experiment on May 18, 1974, have ushered in what would later be the nuclear age of the India-Pakistan conflict, a conflict that has not been resolved to this day. Thus, Rushdie's re-imagining his country's nuclear experiment as a post-imperial ploy with explosive results is a prescient observation of the ways in which the British Empire, responsible for the bloody Partition of India and Pakistan, has continued to wield its power in covert and overt ways, prolonging the conflict between the two sister nations, India and Pakistan.

Rushdie's retelling of Indian, Pakistani and British history also takes the form of a personal tale of one man, Saleem Sinai, and his alter ego, Black Saleem. *The Antagonist*, as I have suggested, is the blueprint for *Midnight's Children*, in which the personal and national fates are inextricably and pathologically linked in the figure of Saleem Sinai. The earlier novel first creates this character in a different form and makes the links between India and the British Empire even more personal: Saleem is married to the daughter of the leaders of the New Empire, a very unhappy union that he is eager to escape.

In the second part of this chapter, I turn to a more detailed reading of the Saleem Sinai character in both novels: How does the character evolve as the older author rewrites it? Is there a way of reading Saleem in both novels as Rushdie's alter ego at different stages in his writing career and life?

Deserts and Deserters: Saleem Sinai's Journeys

We first see Saleem Sinai in *The Antagonist* through Trevor Gutte's eyes. Gutte, captivated by the charms of Vanilla Icequeen, is led by her to a pub where he becomes the unlikely winner of a violent brawl, the pub's usual form of entertainment. Rushdie describes a rivalry between two pubs on Bliss Grove where Gutte is at work on his documentary film. Here too, antagonism is the ruling principle.

This antagonism, then, as Rushdie imagines it, is of east and west or rather east (the Turk's Head) facing west (the Hippo and Dromedary); the fighting side is the western one, and it "stands on the site of what was, in the mid–nineteenth century, the Great Turnstile of the Bliss Hippodrome, the gigantic racetrack which covered the entire area where Bliss Grove and environs now stand" (7). The legacy of the failed race track is now the legacy of the neighborhood where the "stink of failure" (7) is the prevailing aroma. As I already suggested, the ironically named Bliss Grove is the site of the post-empire immigrant nation, with its rich diversity of life but also the lack of hope. Gutte is led by Vanilla: "[His] ears, partially blue with cold, are filled with the siren's song" (9). Vanilla is the "siren" who will lead him away from his filmmaking career.

The third party to what Rushdie names "the first triangle" is Saleem Sinai, who appears in the pub after Gutte's triumph. He is "[a] bloodshot, dark-glassed mist of euphoria" (9). Sinai's first appearance on the scene is explosive and violent: "Now, says the bloodshot mist, bumping into Gutte, who has leapt to his feet in consternation. Who? It adds" (9). Saleem then is an entity, not an "I" but an "it": a presence that is both erotic and menacing. Gutte's response to this threat on his manhood hinges on the effect of naming: "Sinai, eh? That's an unusual name. Are you Jewish?" Adding: "I was in the peninsula, the Sinai peninsula. Your namesake, old chappie. I was there in the six-day war!" (9). As the bomb episode previously discussed demonstrates, deserts play a key role in the novel. Sinai, named after the desert, will prove to be the ultimate "deserter" figure in the text. His first appearance in the text, erroneously connected to Jewishness and the desert, is nevertheless symbolically true. Sinai is not Jewish, but he certainly is a wanderer and an unlikely prophet figure whose fate is linked to the fates of the British and Indian nations in the aftermath of empire. As he wryly answers Gutte: "Have a rest. This is the seventh day" (9). What happens in *The Antagonist* is the result of the "six days" or Creation. It's a world facing the aftereffects of national birth. In such a world, the desert as a place of becoming, a place from where the prophets emerge to lead a nation, becomes a space of violence and confusion. But Sinai's name retains its redemptive potential. He will not be able to stop his murderous alter ego, but he will return to India to die and be reborn at the enigmatic ending of the novel. Sinai's nature as a deserter is demonstrated in this first episode at the pub.

The next section, entitled "Sinai the deserter," follows the appearance of Sinai's British wife Susan, carrying a knife. The narrative shifts from the third person to Saleem Sinai's voice:

4. The Year of the Reverse

> Happy is the country that has no history. If history is his story, Man's, the poor dear, than a life, my life, is a my-story. Leading us by a false etymology into the unknown. Mystery: a religious truth or doctrine. From the same root as myopia. Ibn Sina, my putative ancestor, philosopher-mathematician, would have appreciated that. Sinai's the name. Seenaaaee not Sighnigh, though he's been reconciled to the second from the moment of his birth. Though, too, the Mosaic-Kissengerian allusions are correctly present within the name. The name: an old Persian mosaic [13].

Sinai's history, then, is linked to the history of his country and to the biblical story of Moses in the Sinai Desert. Rushdie's punning on the idea of "history," "story" and "mystery" locates Sinai's personal tale, much like the tale of his nation, in the realm of mystery and shortsightedness. If we add another pun to Rushdie's list, we may then say that it is also a story of misery. Sinai's name is his destiny. He is a deserter, a man running away from his destiny but to no avail. His physical body also corresponds to that state:

> Gaunt's the word that fits. Lean also and spare and always hungry. Incurable worms eat my lunch for me, which I do not grudge since it permits me to gourmandize with equanimity. Gaunt because of the enclosing desert. I have, you see, deserted my history and thus became happy. I wash regularly. Deserts are dusty [13–14].

Sinai's attempt to reinvent himself, to be born again at age thirteen — "I am now thirteen again, a second adolescence following gleefully upon the first" (14) — signifies the need for constant reinvention of self, a theme that Rushdie revisits in his later novels. The self as a protean entity is the state of a migrant, forever on the move, attempting to forget a painful past and construct a new one in its stead. Sinai's "comfortable, middle-class Indian childhood" ends at thirteen when he is sent to London, to a boarding school at "the heartland of empire" (14). This is, of course, an autobiographical detail: Rushdie, too, was sent to Rugby and received a British education. Sinai's "painful Birth" occurs, then, when his drunk father abandons him: "His father died at the instance of it; and he is Sinai sapiens, sui generis, innocence corrupted, worldly-wise baby off to school. No going back. Deserts are the desserts of the deserter" (14). The "new born" Sinai reflects, thirteen years later:

> It is February 1974 in my desert. Tell me: it is a desert of my own making. I'll agree. Desertion gets to be a habit, no, a way of life. The alternative is

folly, a leap from one edge into another. Hierarchies, archies of all kinds, shapes, duties, structures of confinement ... they're all back there in the womb I left. All shapes are cages; which means (to take the least important example) that all works of art, all philosophies, all of men's pitiful artifacts, are no more than monuments to repression. A book is a trap for its characters [14].

Sinai's monologue echoes Rushdie's belief in open-ended possibilities. The prison of selfhood, of history and nation is one his characters, trapped in books, continually try to desert. But the return to the womb, or Mother India, is the counter-force that shapes Sinai's life. In the later novel, *Midnight's Children*, we find a Saleem Sinai who has never left the mother country, a man shackled to its bloody history and who firmly believes that his fate affects his nation's history in meaningful ways. So how does this older, but not wiser, Saleem emerge in Rushdie's later novel? Does the "desert" in his name influence his destiny in the same way as it does his younger avatar?

It seems that Rushdie retains the name and its symbolic implications but creates a very different character in the later text. However, as I have suggested, Rushdie retains the melodramatic plot element (baby swapping) and the rivalry between two aspects of India in both novels. I shall therefore now turn to this aspect of the text to gauge how the later novel engages with this notion of duality in the national character of India. How does Saleem's doppelganger, Black Saleem in *The Antagonist*, turn into Shiva in *Midnight's Children*? I shall then turn to the final scenes in both novels to show how the idea of the atomic bomb, central to the first novel, re-emerges in the later one. Both novels end in a space of possibility for a different future. In both texts the protagonist ends up, like the desert and the prophets his name symbolizes, on a journey to a promised land. In both cases, however, this promise is just that — a promise for an unforeseeable future.

Deserts and Veils: Midnight's Children

Saleem Sinai, the deluded narrator, reflects on the role of the desert and the prophets that emerged from the (Sinai) desert. As in *The Antagonist*, where Sinai reflects on the Mosaic resonances of his name, in the later reworking of this theme, Rushdie returns to subject of prophecy and the role of the visionary individual, a false or true prophet of his nation's future. Saleem Sinai has telepathic powers: he can commune with the other Midnight Children born on the momentous night of India's birth in 1947. Rushdie presents the revelatory and visionary aspect of this gift. Saleem reflects on his role as one more prophet whose message is derided and ignored by his audience.

Saleem begins telling his tale with his impending doom in mind, voicing his ultimate fear of absurdity: "But I have no hope of saving my life, nor can I count on having even a thousand nights and a night. I must work fast, faster than Scheherazade, if I am to end up meaning — yes, meaning — something. I admit it: above all things, I fear absurdity" (*MC*, 4). Rushdie comments on his narrator's quest: "Saleem's greatest desire is for what he calls meaning, and near the end of his broken life he sets out to *write himself*, in the hope that by so doing he may achieve the significance that the events of his adulthood have drained from him" ("Errata," 24). In other words, Saleem's project is in effect a (vexed) attempt to write himself into a central role in his nation's history. The search for what Saleem calls "meaning," then, is qualified by his own position in the tale, or, as Rushdie puts it: "He is an interested party in the events he narrates" (24).

This never-ending quest for meaning seems to be at odds with the authorial presence in the novel: Rushdie's endorsement of alternative versions of history (rather than one coherent and meaningful tale) places him in the position of an eternal doubter. This position would appear to be the obverse of his narrator's place as an all-too-sure (however deluded) visionary figure. Saleem may believe he is indeed a prophet, but the author and readers are left in doubt as to legitimacy of his claim. Saleem's prophetic abilities are cast in largely comic terms in the novel. Rushdie constantly plays with the idea of prophecy and shifts its terms from the religious to the secular and back to the religious. As he observes in "Errata": "Saleem Sinai is not an oracle; he's only adopting a kind of oracular language" (25). The same can be said for Rushdie's manipulation of the figure of Saleem as prophet: Rushdie is only adopting the language of prophecy to deflate it and parody it, while pointing to its immense power at the very same time.

Saleem discovers his telepathic and visionary abilities as a result of a freak accident in a washing chest, where he likes to find refuge. Upon seeing his mother Amina's "black Alfonso mango" (191), he becomes unhinged and emits a tremendous sneeze. The effect is immediate. Saleem hears "noise, many tongued terrifying, *inside his head!*" (191). This incident heralds his telepathic powers of communication with his fellow Midnight Children. Saleem reflects on his prophetic role:

> On Mount Sinai, the prophet Musa or Moses heard disembodied commandments; on Mount Hira, the prophet Muhammad ... spoke to the Archangel. And on the stage of the Cathedral and John Connon Boys' High School, my friend Cyrus-the-great, playing a female part as usual, heard the voices of St. Joan speaking the sentences of Bernard Shaw. But Cyrus is the odd one out: unlike Joan whose voices were heard in a field, but like Musa or Moses, like Muhammad the Penultimate, I heard voices on the hill [192].

Saleem casts himself in the role of a Moses or Muhammad though he later comes to question his efficacy as prophet and imagines himself as the prophets surrounding Muhammad who were not heard. The introduction of Cyrus, his school friend, at this point is also significant, as Cyrus later becomes a "false prophet"— preaching sectarianism and racial hatred. At this stage (Saleem is only "barely nine" years old), he still imagines himself in the role of Muhammad; but, unlike the prophet, he gets no encouragement from his surroundings:

> Muhammad ... heard a voice saying, "Recite"! and thought he was going mad; I heard, at first, a heedful of garbling tongues, like an untuned radio; and with lips sealed by maternal command, I was unable to ask for comfort ... I struggled, alone, to understand what had happened to me; until at last I saw the shawl of genius fluttering down, like an embroidered butterfly, the mantle of greatness settling upon my shoulder [192].

Saleem is a solitary figure; he has to come to terms with his "greatness" on his own. Although Rushdie casts his ordeal in comic, not to say grotesque, terms, he nevertheless gives his protagonist a measure of greatness as well. Saleem, like all prophets, may be considered either a madman or a seer. Both options remain valid in the text.

Saleem's belief in his own prophetic mission, however, receives a literal and symbolic blow as he announces his new powers to his family. In a family meeting some time after the washing chest incident ("Family and ayah assembled in the sitting room"), Saleem prepares for his revelation: "'You should be the first to know,' I said, trying to give my speech the cadence of adulthood. And then I told them. 'I heard voices yesterday. Voices are speaking to me inside my head. I think — Amni, Aboo, I really think — that Archangels have started to talk to me'" (194). Instead of the expected "sweetmeats, public announcements, maybe more photographs," Saleem's revelation is "set upon from all sides" (194), culminating in his father's "hand which stretched out suddenly ... to fetch me a mighty blow on the side of my head, so that I could never hear properly in my left ear after that day" (194). Saleem understands that he has to hide his "superpowers" from his family. He tells his mother: "It was just fooling, Amma. A stupid joke, like you said" (194). But the older Saleem comments: "She died, nine years later, without discovering the truth" (194); his own faith in his prophetic abilities is not shaken. It is, however, qualified. Saleem realizes that "Archangels no longer speak to mortals ... the last prophet will come only to announce the End" (200).

This notion of the Apocalypse or the End is later played out in the novel's conclusion. Saleem returns to the notion of himself as prophet, albeit a failed one, not a Moses or Muhammad but the prophets preaching in Muhammad's time in the Arabian Desert:

> In Arabia ... at the time of the prophet Muhammad, other prophets also preached: Maslama of the tribe of the Banu Hanifa ... and Hanzala ibn Safwan ... and Khalid ibn Sinan. Khalid ibn Sinan was sent to the tribe of "Abs"; for a time, he was followed, but then he was lost. Prophets are not always false simply because they are overtaken, and swallowed up, by history. Men of worth have always roamed the desert [365].

In *The Antagonist* we find the early expression of this link between the name (Sinai) and the role (prophet or seer). The later novel recasts Saleem in the role of a "prophet" of sorts, but in a typical Rushdie move, this elevated status is popularized and parodied: Saleem is a telepath who hears the voices of India in his head in a multitude of languages he cannot understand. Saleem discovers, then, that "the voices ... far outnumbered the ranks of the angels" and "[decides], not without relief, that [he] had not been chosen to preside over the end of the world": "My voices, far from being sacred, turned out to be as profane, and as multitudinous, as dust" (200). This makes him decide that what he possesses are telepathic abilities: "Telepathy, then; the inner monologues of all the so-called teeming millions, of masses and classes alike, jostled for space within my head" (200). In a classic Rushdean move, the sublime becomes the ridiculous: "The kind of thing you're always reading about in the sensational magazines," only to be reread as something more: "It was telepathy; but also more than telepathy" (200). This way Saleem becomes "a sort of radio" or "All-India Radio" (197), the voice of the "multitudinous" India. Ironically enough, he cannot understand the many languages or the "polyglot frenzy" (200) in his head. Saleem's telepathic abilities then become a source of confusion rather than enlightenment or a true vision. The novel imagines an India inside Saleem's head, which is, like the real India, comprised of "teeming millions" who "jostle for space" (200). This vision of India as a confused and confusing entity that cannot be grasped and comprehended is at the heart of the novel. Saleem's confusion mirrors the confusion at the heart of the concept of "nation": If we return to Jacqueline Rose's term, it is a "state of fantasy" that is also a state of mind.

Midnight's Children is, as Rushdie comments in an essay from *Step Across This Line* entitled "A Dream of Glorious Return," "[his] first attempt at literary land reclamation" (180). Some critical readings of the novel thus see it as Rushdie's reconfiguration of India's national narrative.[1] In his "Notes on Writing and the Nation" (which also appears in *Step Across This Line*), Rushdie warns writers of becoming "the voice of the nation." He warns against what he terms the New Behalfism, which "[sees] literature as inescapably political" and ends up "[substituting] political values for literary ones" (60). This warning can be applied to his most famous narrative of nation, *Midnight's Children*. Thus Rushdie's choice to elide certain historical moments and highlight others in his tale of nation making is a literary choice but also a political one. Rushdie does not ignore his own subjective position as an expatriate (Muslim) Indian or the ways it influences his view of political and historical events. It is very present in the novel's treatment of the Gandhi assassination described above.

In his retelling of the Indian story in *Midnight's Children*, Rushdie recasts historical and personal memories as science fictional tales. As he observes in yet another essay from *Step Across This Line* entitled "Influence," what he tried to do in the novel is "to set against ... the canvas of a 'real' India, [his] 'unrealist' notion of children born at the midnight moment of India's Independence ... children who were in some way the embodiment of both the hopes and the flaws of that revolution" (65). Rushdie's very engagement with the (science) fictional and the fantastic as modes of telling a historical tale becomes a political and ideological gesture of a different kind. Rushdie employs this trope not merely as a means of dramatizing the inextricable links between the personal and the historical but also as a way of commenting on his authorial position. In the figure of Saleem, Rushdie then both parodies and reflects upon his own commitment to his role as a storyteller and questions to what extent he shares in the construction of national memory and in what ways he may become as implicated in this project as his narrator. In *The Antagonist* we can see how Rushdie first engages with the idea of narrating the self and the nation as two facets of a conflicted identity. As in *MC,* in the earlier novel too, Rushdie creates a narrator who is in some ways a skewed mirror of his own life. In both cases, it is an exaggerated and parodied version of selfhood but one that also resonates with the author's life in more meaningful ways. Rushdie chooses to locate the heart of the tale in the fantastic story of the Midnight Children. Saleem claims this tale is "the fantastic heart of [his] own story" (234).

Saleem's foray into the "fantastic heart" of his own story and his nation's are given mythical and archetypal proportions. Saleem promises he will "write in plain unveiled fashion, about the midnight children" (234). The notion of veiling and unveiling is linked to the story of national becoming or birth. The veiled woman is embodied in the novel in the figures of Saleem's grandmother, who is forced to give up the veil by his modern grandfather, but most notably in the figure of Saleem's sister Jamila, who becomes the national and veiled voice of the new Islamic nation, Pakistan. Jamila's betrayal in the novel and the dangers inherent in a totalitarian narrative of purity are symbolized by the veil metaphor. As Saleem draws nearer to the heart of his tale, he continually evokes the notion of unveiling as a counter-motif to the veil's repressive presence as an emblem of the totalizing narrative of the (Islamic) nation. Although Rushdie seems to resist this narrative, some critics claim that Rushdie rewrites the story of the nation (or *umma*) by recasting the (un)veiled woman as a figure of new nationhood.[2]

The language of unveiling is closely attached to the notion of revelation. As Teresa Heffernan reminds us, "[apocalypse] continues to be understood in a secular context as a revelation or unveiling ... and this paradigm underlines the ... teleological narrative of modern nationalism" (2). The nationalist narrative comes to "both replace and echo Revelation" (2). In this function, replacing the religious or traditional mode, it still manages to "satisfy the desire for origins, continuity and eternity" (2). This desire forms a significant part of Saleem's story of the emergent nation. The unveiling metaphor serves to underline the dark and apocalyptic potential of Saleem's tale — the Midnight Children's story is "unveiled"—

but its revelation also contains the seeds of its undoing. As Heffernan shows, however, apocalyptic narratives also express the wishes of the downtrodden: "Like the biblical story, secular apocalyptic writing about the nation also expresses the dreams of the ostracized and the oppressed about the renewal or rebirth of a community" (2). In Saleem's tale of nation, the secular and the religious are reconfigured. Saleem's prophetic stand is secularized. He is a telepath instead of the more exalted religious visionary.

The apocalyptic narrative is also a revolutionary vehicle: "[Apocalyptic] writing challenges the established order, confuses accepted rules, and ignores the prevalent code of reason" (Heffernan, 2). Saleem's narrative of nation is also a revolutionary vehicle. His confused tale will end up not only in an apocalyptic move but also in an affirmation of the power of narrative to challenge reason in favor of an alternate mode — which is a hallucinatory re-envisioning of both past and future narratives of nation.

As Saleem approaches the heart of his tale and proceeds to unveil the truth about the Midnight Children, he once again makes a plea for credulity: "Don't make the mistake of dismissing what I've unveiled as mere delirium.... I have stated before that I'm not speaking metaphorically; what I have just written ... is nothing less than the literal, by-the-hairs-of-my-mother's-head-truth" (240). But Saleem's next statement shows us that the metaphorical and the real cannot be so easily demarcated: "Reality can have metaphorical content; that does not make it less real. A thousand and one children were born; there were a thousand and one possibilities which had never been present in one place at the same time before; and there were a thousand and one dead ends" (240). The literal birth of (magical) children also becomes a marker of the destiny of the newborn nation. Saleem offers possible readings:

> Midnight's children can be made to represent many things, according to your point of view; they can be seen as the last throw of everything antiquated and retrogressive in our myth-ridden nation, whose defeat was entirely desirable in the context of a modernizing, twentieth-century economy; or as the true hope of freedom, which is now forever extinguished [240].

The Midnight Children are then made to embody possible past and future scenarios for the newborn nation.

Saleem appeals to the reader to "[understand] what [he's] saying" (234), a call for credulity in the face of a very fantastic narrative but also

4. The Year of the Reverse

expressing a wish to be understood and maybe also expressing his own attempt to make sense of the fantastic nature of his nation's coming into being. The narrative of the magical arrival of "no less than one thousand and one children ... born within the frontiers of the infant sovereign state of India" (234) links the infant state with the thousand and one magical infants in a bond that "handcuffs them to history." Like Saleem, these children symbolize the potential of the young nation. Saleem comments on the nature of this event:

> It itself, that is not an unusual fact (although the resonances of the number are strangely literary).... What made the event noteworthy (noteworthy! There's a dispassionate word, if you like!) was the nature of these children, every one of whom was, through some freak of biology, or perhaps owing to some preternatural power of the moment, or just conceivably by sheer coincidence (although synchronicity on such a scale would stagger even C.G. Jung), endowed with features, talents or faculties which can only be described as miraculous [234].

Saleem here again alludes to his role as Scheherazade and to the fantastic nature of his story. The "strangely literary" resonances of the mythical number are presented here at the very same time Saleem insists on the veracity of his tale. The magical number (and tale) interacts with the claim for truth value, as they do throughout.

In other words, the miraculous nature of the children's coming into being — or the "thousand and one nights" aspect — is given possible explanations by Saleem. He claims that he is talking in "plain, unveiled fashion" but asks the reader to "permit [him] one moment of fancy" in what will be "the most sober account [he] can manage" (234). The tension between the wish to tell a "plain" story and the pressures of the miraculous nature of his tale continually plagues Saleem; his attempt to recount a chronological, historical tale must perforce be vexed since this founding moment, as he tells us, is also one which steps out of history: "[As] though history, arriving at a point of the highest significance and promise, had chosen to sow, in that instant, the seeds of a future which would genuinely differ from anything the world had seen up to that time" (234–235).

Saleem relocates the moment when he became acquainted with his "brothers" at a historical moment in Indian history that he describes as "hallucinatory": "Certainly it was a hallucinatory time in the days leading up to my tenth birthday" (240). But Saleem locates this hallucinatory nature not in his "rambling mind" but rather in his nation's "state of mind," which is closely linked to his father Ahmed's altered state. Ahmed's disillusionment with his country is expressed in his withdrawal from society and his inability to tell his children imaginative bedtime stories. Saleem observes his "fading father" and his reaction on the "day on which taxes were raised and tax thresholds simultaneously lowered": "My father flung down the *Times of India* with a violent gesture.... 'It's like going to the bathroom!,' he exploded, cryptically; 'You raise your shirt and lower your trousers! Wife, this government is going to the bathroom all over us!'" (241). Saleem comments: "[He] had stomped off, leaving me with a clear understanding of what people meant when they said the country was going to pot" (241). Ahmed's critique of economic policies deflates the notion of "hallucinatory time," which his son attributes to the same events. As Saleem later comments, this is testimony to his father's loss of the imaginative faculties he had once possessed.

The tenth anniversary of the new nation coincides, then, with Ahmed Sinai's sense of failure and with what his son diagnoses as the "creaks and groans of a rusting, decayed, imagination" (241). Saleem describes his father's altered state: Ahmed Sinai "has succumbed to abstraction" and "entered a deep solitude, a condition so unusual in our overcrowded country as to border on abnormality" (241). Acting as an obverse mirror of his country's mythic and overly imaginative nature, Ahmed becomes a solitary figure. But he still engages in a different kind of fictionality: As he "enters an almost permanent state of intoxication," he purchases a fake "Indian nightingale," which ends up being nothing but "a talking budgie" with painted feathers (243). This bizarre act seems to indicate Ahmed's need to cling on to an idea of Indian/Persian mythology—a fairytale land of singing bulbuls and all powerful Chalifas. Like the new Indian nation, Ahmed becomes disillusioned. No longer able to recruit his imaginative faculties—a state reflected in his inability to tell his children convincing bedtime stories—Ahmed's abstraction (in both senses of the word) indicates that both he and his nation are not sure exactly where they stand.

This state of abstraction is also present in the earlier novel. Rushdie begins to explore the notion that the personal and the national tales will forever be inextricably linked. As previously shown, Saleem Sinai in *The Antagonist* comments on the idea of history as both "my story" and "mystery": The quest for understanding who and what you really are is at the center of both the earlier work and the later. In both texts, Rushdie chooses to dramatize this vexed relationship between self and nation, employing a trope characteristic of melodrama; Saleem's tale in *MC*, is, as noted before, described in terms of the "Bombay talkie," which involves "melodrama piling upon melodrama" (174). One of the staples of melodrama both on screen and in its literary form is the baby swapping plot: one baby is swapped for another, thus influencing their fates and disturbing the hierarchical structure of the society in which they were born and offering a comment on the ways in which one's birth affects destiny in both a personal and collective sense.

In the final part of this chapter, I turn to the ways in which this plot device serves Rushdie in his earlier work and is repeated in the later. In both novels, Rushdie employs this device to create mirroring characters who represent, as I have suggested, different aspects of the Indian nation. However, as I shall show, in the first novel, the two characters share the same name, indicating even more clearly that they are in fact doppelgangers—mirroring images of each other, representing different aspects of the same person. In the later novel, this is not the case. Rushdie chooses to name Saleem's antagonist Shiva, thus giving his character a mythical role, representing the destructive aspect of Indian nationhood.

The Shiva Principle

It is Shiva, Saleem's alter ego and nemesis, who becomes an emblem of all the aspects of India that Saleem cannot contain. Shiva is the god of destruction, and he then comes to symbolize the destructive principle, replacing Saleem's dream of brotherly love. Saleem reflects on his ambivalent feelings towards Shiva: "[He] became for me, first a stabbing twinge of guilt; then an obsession; and finally, as the memory of his actuality grew dull, he became a sort of principle; he came to represent, in my mind, all the vengefulness and violence and simultaneous-love-and-hate-of Things in the world" (358). Saleem comments on the way the "Shiva principle" operates in India:

> When I hear of drowned bodies floating like balloons on the Hooghly and exploding when nudged by passing boats; or trains set on fire, or politicians killed, or riots in Orissa or Punjab, it seems to me that the hand of Shiva lies heavily over all these things, dooming us to flounder endlessly amid murder rape greed war—that Shiva, in short, has made us who we are [358].

Shiva, then, is the dark side of the Midnight Children's (and India's) historical promise: "He, too, was born on the stroke of midnight; he, like me, was connected to history" (358), comments Saleem, implying that the course of history is affected as much by the dark forces—operating at the most optimistic moment of national birth. The Shiva principle, then, becomes a metaphor for the ways the new Indian nation, from its very inception, contains the dark seeds of its own undoing. This destructive force is given the form of an army man: Shiva is a general and a murderer. His dark deeds symbolize the murderous potential of nationhood. The fate of the new nation could not be more bleak: The "murder rape greed war" that characterize it from its inception continues; Aadam, who is Shiva's biological son but is raised by Saleem, is an emblem of the new India, where greed is the order of the day. The promise of a new generation is not fulfilled.

Saleem returns to his beloved Bombay only to find it drastically altered. He discovers that the Midnite Confidential Club is an underground club, run by an Indian playboy. The "new Indian" is a "businessman-playboy," a strange entity in Saleem's old India, but seemingly the marker of the new India in which he no longer fits. Saleem is bothered by the club's name, ominously calling to mind his own club:

> [And] we entered that place whose name had already unnerved me somewhat, because it contained the word *midnight*, and because its initials has once concealed my own, secret world: M.C.C., which stands for Metro Cub Club, once also stood for the Midnight Children's Conference, and had now been usurped by the other secret night-spot [541].

This club, then, comes to stand for the "usurpation" of the new generation over the old. Saleem sees it as a hellish location and comments (parodying Sartre): "Hell is other people's fantasies; every saga requires at least one descent into Jahannum" (541).

He descends into this underground world with his infant son, thereby marking Aadam's inauguration into the future of the nation. They are led by a blind hostess who explains the true nature of the club: "[Nobody] who comes here wants to be seen. Here you are in a world without faces or names; here people have no families or past; here is for *now*, for nothing except right now" (541). This new M.C.C. becomes the obverse version or the flipside of the original. This (postmodern) version of hell, then, is a "place outside time" or a "negation of history." It marks the wish to escape

4. The Year of the Reverse

ties of family and past. Or as Saleem discovers: "[This] was a new world in which I had no place." His son, Aadam, however, "sat ... with ears burning with fascination; his eyes shone in the darkness as he listened, and memorized, and learned" (542). Aadam clearly belongs in this new world: He reappears as a character in Rushdie's *The Moor's Last Sigh* as a "businessman-playboy," an avatar of the Mammon-led India that Saleem envisions and dreads.

In *The Antagonist*, the rivalry between Saleem Sinai and Black Saleem is expressed in a series of letters. Black Saleem sends these letters to his alter ego, the man who stole his destiny unwittingly when they were swapped in the cradle by an Ayah influenced by the communist ideology of her lover. Thus, the baby swapping act is an act of social rebellion: the poor baby will take the rich one's place as a comment on the ills of an unjust society. The letters gradually reveal this secret to Saleem. They end in a threat: Saleem is to return to India at a certain date to stop the murder of the Ayah by Black Saleem. He receives the letter too late and upon his arrival discovers that the dark deed has already been done. This leads to his complete breakdown. The letters thus are a way of unfolding the melodramatic story, which is later repeated in *MC*. However, the difference lies in the ways Rushdie presents this doppelganger figure in the earlier novel, suggesting at one point that the two Saleems are really one and the same person, a kind of Jekyll and Hyde duo that represent different aspects of the same persona. Although this explanation, resulting from the fact that Black Saleem's handwriting and Saleem Sinai's handwriting are identical, is later discredited — we know that there is a Black Saleem in India and that he had committed the murder when Sinai was still in England — the symbolic significance remains. The two Saleems are aspects of one persona; when one dies, the other breaks down. No longer able to maintain the fiction of a coherent selfhood, Saleem Sinai recedes into a catatonic state and is institutionalized by his parents. This breaking down of self begins when Saleem returns to India: the idea of return to the motherland unhinges him even before the shock of the murder is revealed. The plane ride, in which the fact of India already imposes itself on Saleem and Vanilla Icequeen, who travels with him, becomes a liminal space: a limbo-like state before the descent into hell.

The final scene in *The Antagonist* dramatizes the novel's engagement with the idea of selfhood as a precarious state, one that can break down at any moment but also one that can be revived: Saleem experiences another "new birth" when he is whisked away from the mental hospital by a nurse who finds him appealing. The nurse smuggles Saleem out of the hospital, attempting to take him home with her. But the novel ends with yet another escape: The seemingly catatonic Saleem wakes up and runs away from what would appear to be another form of enslavement by the lustful nurse. In the later novel, *Midnight's Children*, we find a similarly ambiguous ending. Saleem is on a wedding pilgrimage to Kashmir, the place signifying the potential for redemption and peace in India's bloody history, a symbolic Eden and a space of longing. But the final scene enacts the total breakdown of self and the feeling of potential at one and the same time. The image of the nuclear bomb appears here as a symbolic marker of the way India's move into the nuclear age further embroils it in a seemingly never-ending conflict with Pakistan and pushes it further away from the imagined realm of peaceful coexistence symbolized by the Edenic Kashmir.

The Bomb in Bombay: Saleem's Last Stand

The novel's final scene finds Saleem still struggling with his conflicting positions: Is he still "handcuffed to history"? Does he still play an active role in his country's history and story? Or does his impending marriage to Padma inaugurate a different phase in his life—can it be a new beginning or rather the end? The novel does not fully resolve these questions. It ends in a series of questions that ponder the future of the Indian nation at what seem to be the final moments in the life of one of her first-generation children. Saleem envisions his wedding day to Padma and their consequent honeymoon trip to the Edenic Kashmir as an apocalyptic scenario. He declares his mission as a true prophet: "I shall have to write the future as I have written the past, to set it down with the absolute certainty of a prophet" (550). He immediately qualifies this over-certain statement, however, claiming that "the future cannot be preserved in a jar" (550). Saleem is uncertain whether he will indeed have a future, reach his thirty-first birthday or marry Padma. He tries to envision the scene of his birthday/wedding, taking place on Independence Day, and the final paragraphs of the novel are couched in the linguistic and prophetic mode of the future tense.

4. The Year of the Reverse

Saleem envisions the crowds and celebrations of Independence Day and pictures, with a growing sense of terror, the "many-headed multitudes" (551) that threaten to engulf him. He pictures the scene of separation from Padma in the throng as a nightmarish scene, where he is ultimately left "alone in the vastness of the numbers, the numbers marching one two three" (551). In this hallucinatory state, Saleem encounters the "familiar faces in the crowd"—his long-dead family members who "throng around [him] pushing shoving crushing" (551). He is suffocated not only by the anonymous multitudes but also by his own history. He feels that "the cracks are widening" and comes to the final prophetic revelation: "I see that I shall never reach Kashmir, like Jehangir the Mughal Emperor I shall die with Kashmir on my lips, unable to see the valley of delights to which men go to enjoy life, or to end it, or both" (551). Like Moses, Saleem will never then see the Promised Land. In this last hallucinatory moment, Saleem feels that he, like the great prophets and rulers before him, will never reach the land of his dreams.

In his final moments, Saleem does not relinquish his idea of himself as a seer. He still believes he has the power to envision his own death and at the same time glimpse the future of his country, to which he still feels inextricably bound. Therefore, when his sees the "mythological apparition ... the Black Angel," he discovers that "its face is green its eyes are black, a centre-parting in its hair ... its eyes the eyes of Widows" (551–2): even Death takes on the form of Saleem's nemesis and prime rival for centrality in his nation's history. Saleem cannot escape history. It follows him to the grave and even beyond.

The final passages in the novel dramatize the breakdown of syntax: both as an ordered system of meaning and (in its alternative dictionary meaning) as an organism. The breathless series of broken sentences seem to reflect the breakdown of both narrative and body. Arriving at the moment of ultimate narrative aporia, the moment of the narrator's death, instead of a narrative closure and a return to origins (symbolized by Kashmir, the ultimate unreached goal of Saleem's journey), marks the ways in which Rushdie's novel refuses closure and finality. Saleem's final words reflect this disintegrative moment:

> Shiva and the Angel are closing, closing, I hear the lies spoken in the night, anything you want to be you kin [sic] be, the greatest lie of all, cracking now, fission of Saleem, I am the bomb in Bombay, watch me explode, bones splitting breaking beneath the awful pressure of the crowd [552].

Saleem's wholeness is finally compromised: He is now India's Bomb —
marking the fission at the heart of the country's foray into the nuclear age
and possibly its ultimate undoing. We can see how Rushdie reworks the
idea of the human bomb that he began exploring in *The Antagonist*. As I
have shown, in the earlier novel the "sex-bomb" is both a literal entity
and a figurative embodiment of the destructive potential of India's entry
into the nuclear age. In the later novel, Saleem's undoing is metaphorically
linked with the nuclear age, suggesting that this entry into a seemingly
unending and potentially destructive nuclear standoff with Pakistan is the
work of the deathly elements in India, symbolized by Saleem's alter ego,
Shiva. In the earlier novel, Rushdie begins to explore this idea of the fission
of selfhood. Saleem in *The Antagonist* will finally break down but will also
envision a new birth. The ambiguous ending of *The Antagonist*, which I
shall describe in more detail below, imagines a possibly happier future for
Saleem. The novel ends in a space of an imagined possibility, one of many
options to end the tale. As I have shown, this open ended option is one
Rushdie returns to in his later novels, signaling his belief in the imagined
option as the only space where hope may be found.

Saleem envisions himself literally breaking down. He is no longer
able to delude himself that his many selves can be integrated into a (fictive)
whole. Saleem attributes this final breakdown to his multiple selfhood:
"[Because] I have been so-many too-many persons, life unlike syntax
allows one more than three, and at last somewhere the striking of a clock,
twelve chimes, release" (552). The moment of death, then, is again, like
the moment of birth, marked by the ever-ominous number twelve. The
novel ends with the individual voice crushed down beneath the power of
the multitudes. But as Saleem "contains multitudes," this trampling also
marks the ways the individual voice, like the "voice of the people," is a
reflection of both national and personal hope and despair.

The novel closes with the ultimate act of re-membering: Saleem's
narrative of memory breaks down. The text ends on a prophetic note, but
this prophecy, unlike Saleem's claim for "absolute certainty," is anything
but certain; rather, it dramatizes the inability to prophecy the future.[3]
Saleem prophecies the final trampling down of all future generations by
the multi-headed crowd — which is, for better or worse, an embodiment
of India:

> [They] will trample my son who is not my son ... until the thousand and
> one generation ... because it is the privilege and the curse of midnight's chil-

dren to be both masters and victims of their times, to forsake privacy and be sucked into the annihilating whirlpool of the multitudes, and to be unable to live or die in peace [552].

The inextricable link between personal and historical fates cannot be undone, it seems. Rushdie presents the impossibility of escaping this bond(age). In the figure of Saleem, Rushdie offers us a secular prophet, a deluded narrator, a teller of tales who constantly battles with the impossibility of telling his nation's tale. Rushdie claims that it may ultimately be the fate of historical tales and tellers to be forever bonded to history and committed to the task of telling it. Despite at times longing to escape this bond in favor of the personal, Saleem finds he cannot do so. I believe that Rushdie intimates that this may be our fate as well. As readers and tellers of our own national and personal tales, we cannot escape this bond with our national stories.

Rushdie does not offer us a clear teleology or a neat ending. He does not construct new myths of nation to replace the old founding ones. This end, in both senses of the word, cannot be reached. What remains is the role of the teller of tales, the reminiscer, erecting a monument of words to his beloved and lamented India of dreams. It may be the only way, Rushdie tells us, one can ever come to terms with a conflicted idea of both nation and self. Even so, this gargantuan effort may prove to be the unmaking of this teller of tales. For, if one is committed too deeply to the notion of himself as a "national body," this may lead to very dire consequences. Finally, then, the novel leaves us pondering the nature of this tenuous bond between our role as historical beings and our attempts to forge our own tale. The novel poses the unanswerable question: Can we ever truly come to terms with our existence as national beings? Are we, like Saleem, doomed to fall apart when the pressures of history prove too much? Are we as yet unwilling, or unable, to detach ourselves from the handcuffs that bind us to our own conflicted national tales?

This Is the End: The Antagonist

The ending of Rushdie's first novel finds Saleem returning to India, where he faces his inability to change the course of history. He arrives in India to find that Black Shiva has murdered Mary Pereira, the ayah responsible for the baby swapping.

The effect of her death on Saleem is profound. Her death "dropped Saleem into the Black Hole" (315). His breakdown is reflected in speech or in the inability to speak. He feels that Mary Pereira's last scream remains lodged in his throat. When he does speak, he "enters the third person" (318). The narrator reflects on this choice of pronoun: "There is the latent possibility of a pun. He has been a deserter, and an antagonist and is now entering a third person" (318). This "third person" or third state is a reflection of Saleem's attempt to be objective about his life: "He has adopted it because he has become aware of the corrosive effect of his present environment upon his language — of the corrosive effects of all his environments" (318). Saleem reflects on his current state: "The murder of Mary Pereira means he can no longer duck the central issue, the question of responsibility. To what extent has he been responsible for causing to happen the things that have happened?" (318). As in *MC*, the question of personal responsibility for the "things that have happened" is the main dilemma.

In both novels, this question undermines the protagonist. It would seem that its burden proves too heavy to bear. Saleem feels that "by getting here too late ... [he] had played a part in his abdication" (319). The use of the word plays on the idea of responsibility. If Saleem abdicates his responsibility for Mary's death, then he may become free. But the word abdicate, of course, is also related to a king abdicating his throne. Saleem chooses to abdicate the throne of self in favor of a different state of being.

This description seems to reflect Rushdie's own sense of not belonging in either India or England. Saleem's solution to the problem therefore is to "remain in this room ... in this neutral, controlled environment and continue the process of reshaping himself. Given the disappearance of the possibility of redemption, this seems the only option" (319–320). Saleem's turning inward is read by Vanilla Icequeen as the "birth of a butterfly" (320); Vanilla thinks Saleem will "perform the miracle of transformation" (320). This optimistic view is brought up only to be questioned by the narrative voice: "At least, that is what she thinks" (320). We are left to see whether this new birth will in fact occur.

Vanilla becomes the catalyst for Saleem's final descent into a selfless state. She offers Saleem her love. It is the act of love, or rather love making, that will "set something off inside Sinai" (326). This "something" is Mary's scream that is finally released. Saleem descends into the "Black Hole." Before descending into this state, Saleem tells Vanilla that his act "is not to be constructed as a failure. Or surrender. It will be a choice, an act of optimism" (329). The place of optimism, the "contagious disease," as Saleem Sinai calls it in *MC*, appears in *The Antagonist* at the very moment when it seems the least likely of options. Vanilla's view of Sinai's transformation is hinted at as a possible ending. But the doctor at the hospital to which Saleem is taken has a less optimistic view: "It is some form of cataleptic illness" (328). The doctor offers an explanation for Saleem's autistic behavior: "An inability to cope with society. One withdraws into oneself, to hide" (329). Is Saleem indeed hiding from society or is there a different reason for his withdrawal?

Imitation of Life: Saleem's Escape?

Saleem's withdrawal into an autistic state may be Rushdie's comment on the impossibility of reconciling conflicting selves into a coherent whole. As in *MC*, here too, the protagonist can no longer maintain the fiction of selfhood. He chooses, instead, to renounce his links to the world and retire inwards. This form of escape, however, is not a defeatist option. Saleem's withdrawal is a comment on our inability to ever form a meaningful narrative of our chaotic lives. Rushdie provides us with a different perspective on this choice through Vanilla's encounter with another possible version of Saleem. Vanilla receives a gift while in India, a book by the Bengali reformer Ram Mohan Roy.[4]

This inability to achieve a peaceful fusion between cultures is symbolized by Saleem's breakdown. His inability to bridge the cultures is a collective failure of peaceful assimilation. Rushdie laments an imagined option of peaceful coexistence of East and West, as in the other novels I discuss. The merging of cultures is an impossible dream, turned into the nightmare of history.

Saleem here, like his namesake in *MC*, is a "disaster area." His withdrawal into his personal "Black Hole" reflects the Indian nation's "Black Hole": its final breakdown with England and the continued history of violence after the enforced Partition. The historical nightmare is also a personal one and vice versa; collective identity is reflected in personal trauma. Rushdie does not resolve the trauma, but he does offer a way out of the bind. The "Black Hole" is also the place of a potential rebirth:

> The astronomer's black holes, like Saleem Sinai's psychological version, are usually presented as collapses.... Within the black hole, the collapsing star

could, in theory, continue to collapse to infinity. So that, at the hypothetical point at which the collapsing star can no longer collapse, the event horizon has stretched outwards to swallow up the entire universe. The collapse of one star has created a new world [331–332].

Saleem's new condition, then, has the potential to create a "new world." His retreat into the "Black Hole" may end up being, as in Vanilla's metaphor, merely the cocoon out of which a butterfly will emerge. Saleem reflects on liberty and fantasy: "Fantasy is ... a means of explaining the world to yourself, it is at the same time a flight and a widening of perceptions. Liberty is only possible in fantasy. The rest is a cage" (334). This sentiment reflects Rushdie's credo, as I have explored in his later works. The imagined, fantastic or science fictional option is the only locus where liberty and possible redemption can be attained. Saleem's only option of freedom from the cage is an imagined one. It is the option to which Rushdie returns time and again in his writing: The notion of possible lives and alternate worlds are the only way to achieve a measure of freedom and hope. Saleem rearranges the events in his life and remakes them:

> He can rearrange his life into a dozen different shapes. Thus destroying the rightness-idea. None of the shapes are right or wrong. They are all possibilities. There is a political shape, a metaphysical shape, a pyramid and a Great Circle. There is a seamless garment and a spiral. The Black Hole is a super-Sinai, in which he exists as part of a many-headed monster, stretching over years and continents; he is a crowd. Everything's that's happened is a part of him [335].

Some of the images here (like the crowd) reappear in the *MC* version. The Walt Whitman echo from *Leaves of Grass* ("I contain multitudes") appears in both novels. But in this early version, the cosmological metaphor dominates. Saleem is a collapsing "star," a "Super Nova," or rather "Super-Saleem," imploding into himself only to be born again: "The further you go into yourself, the wider your event horizon spreads. Eventually, you'll swallow the universe" (334).

Saleem's story will end, in one version, as a reincarnation of the baby swapping event. The idea of swapping is replayed in Saleem's mind as he encounters a nurse in the nursing home to which he had been admitted by his reluctant parents. He reflects that "[nurse] Sharmila might easily be a richer incarnation of Mary Perreira" (336). She is the one who "gives Saleem Sinai the possibility of yet another Independence Day" (336). As

4. The Year of the Reverse

in *MC*, personal independence is couched in national terms. Saleem is offered another birth, and Nurse Sharmila performs another act of swapping, one that will enable his escape from the nursing home and from the electric shock treatment that the doctors plan to perform.

Saleem's "twin" is the patient in the next room who is kept under sedation. Whenever his drugs wear off, he screams; "His screams are loud and feminine, like the last visceral yells of Mary Pereira" (336). This man is another mirror image of Saleem. Saleem has not seen him but knows that "[the] man in the next room is screaming because he knows he's trapped in a cage, because he knows he can't get out, and because he doesn't know that the way out is to get in" (336). Saleem's double, then, is the man who, unlike Saleem, doesn't withdraw into his own world and is therefore "going to die" (336). Saleem's knowledge of the man's impending death and the presence of the rich and kind Nurse Sharmila give Saleem "an idea, a fantasy" (336). The novel ends with the detailed working out of this fantasy in Saleem's mind: "This fantasy is one of the possible ways out of his cage. Either it will come true, or it won't. He has no control over what happens" (336). The ending, then, is merely one option, one possibility among many. The final section in the novel thus begins after this disclaimer: "So it will either happen, or ... Either" (336). The "either-or" option — or as I have called it in the Introduction, following Iser's model of fictionality, the "what if" construction — is played out in the novel's possible ending.

The final section is entitled "A Fantasy: or, Towards Mahalia Jackson Cinema." The cinema appears both as a metaphor and a literal stage where explosive events may take place, makes an appearance in the novel's final, imagined episode. Rushdie is alluding to Douglass Sirk's 1959 film *Imitation of Life*, where Mahalia Jackson appears in the final funeral scene. In Sirk's film, Jackson sings "Trouble of the World." In Rushdie's version, Saleem imagines her singing the famous spiritual "He's Got the Whole World in His Hands." I shall relate in more detail to this choice in my discussion of the final scene. At this point, it is interesting to note that Rushdie chooses to locate the allusion to the film as a signpost for the reader: The film is a melodrama with a tragic ending, but it is one that also offers a chance of redemption. In a similar vein, Rushdie's novel imagines a redemptive option, symbolized by Mahalia Jackson's uplifting voice and her presence as a figure of spiritual redemptive potential.

Imitation of Life, Sirk's remake of the 1934 John M. Stahl film, tells the story of two widows, one white and one black, who both have daughters of the same age. The two women become friends, and the film follows their relationship with their daughters. The film's main concern is the question of racial passing. The black widow's daughter is light skinned and passes as white. The film ends with the tragic death of the black mother and the daughter's final acknowledgment of her mother at the scene of death. The film deals with survival and identity in the context of American race relations. Why then has Rushdie chosen to end his first novel with a direct allusion to this classic film?

The most obvious answer would relate to genre. The melodrama and its Bollywood version are prominent features in Rushdie's oeuvre. As I have shown, Rushdie places great importance on cinema's role as an imitation of life. The title of the film suggests that it is as much about fictionality and the (un)making of self as it is about the conflicts of race and culture. If cinema is the vehicle by which we attempt to create versions of the world, then Sirk's film becomes the epitome of such an endeavor, if only by virtue of its evocative title.[5]

Saleem's fantasy then takes the form of another melodrama. Nurse Sharmila is attracted to Saleem and decides to get him out of the nursing home and "look after him herself, like a mother, like a lover, like a nurse" (337). The death of Saleem's "twin" comes "conveniently enough the night before Sinai is due for his first toasting" (337–338). Saleem's fantasy scenario hinges on the kind of convenient consequences that are the staple of melodrama. Nurse Sharmila switches the bodies and puts the corpse of the dead man in Saleem's place. By the time the doctors discover the switch, it is too late. Saleem's parents do not insist on identifying the body, and the plan succeeds. Again, in true melodramatic form, coincidences determine fate. Nurse Sharmila smuggles Saleem out of the nursing home in her car, unaware that "as he told Vanilla Icequeen, whatever he's doing is from choice. There is no physical reason why he can't get up and make a run for it" (339). Saleem indeed "makes a run for it": "He rises from the floor at the back of the car like a waking Kraken, Ouroboros rising from the Sundering Seas" (339).

Saleem's rebirth is cast in mythological terms. His escape from underneath a pile of Nurse Sharmila's laundry bag full of "bony bras and ample knickers" (339) is described in comic terms. But the mythological allusions remain to give the scene a different edge. The mythical allusions cast the story of Saleem's escape as a resurrection tale. He had died to one world

4. The Year of the Reverse

only to emerge in another. The image of the serpent, or as it appears in the novel in the form of Saleem's worms, is another symbol of the cyclical and self-contained nature of both character and text. The Ouroboros, a symbol in Egyptian, Greek and Roman mythologies, becomes, in Rushdie's ironic recasting, also a symbol of the autistic nature of the self-enclosed, feeding-on-its-own-"tail" character, Saleem Sinai. Plato describes the Ouroboros as a creature created as a self-sufficient being: "Of design he was created thus, his own waste providing his own food, and all that he did or suffered taking place in and by himself. For the Creator conceived that a being which was self-sufficient would be far more excellent than one which lacked anything" (Timaeus, 33). Saleem's autistic, self-sufficient state is a distorted image of this immortal, mythological being.

The narrative of Saleem's life is cyclical, ending where it began with an act of swapping, which creates a new life. The Ouroboros also symbolizes a self-sufficient organism, able to survive on its own without any outside source of nourishment: a being that feeds upon itself. Rushdie gives the myth an ironic twist when he gives his hero intestinal worms that feed on him from the inside. That Saleem arises from a pile of woman's underwear is, albeit ironically, also a symbol of sexual potency. Nurse Sharmila, after all, rescues Saleem because she finds him sexually alluring.

Thus, the novel's final scene rewrites the mythological tale of rebirth in the guise of a comic melodrama. Saleem emerges out of the womb (Nurse Sharmila's laundry bag) to be reborn. In *MC*, Saleem finds his prophetic powers in a laundry bag as well. And the later novel also links the maternal and the sexual: the description of Saleem's mother's ample derriere provides the background for the scene, as I have shown. We can clearly see here, as in the other instances discussed, how the mature Rushdie reworks the themes of the early unpublished piece and incorporates them into his later novel. In both novels, the melodramatic and the comic are inseparable. If in *MC*, we have "melodrama piling upon melodrama" (157), here we have *Imitation of Life*.

Saleem runs into the streets of Bombay that had previously unhinged him. Now, he finds that the "street-plan of Bombay leaps unbidden into his mind. He knows where he is and dives into the twisting alleys" (339). No longer afraid, Saleem leaps into his new life. He emerges from a "passage of darkness" (339) and "re-emerges into the light" (340). He finds himself near the Regal Cinema: "The Regal is showing an old American movie, starring Lana Turner, John Saxon and Sandra Dee. The old movie features a guest appearance by the great woman-mountain of a hot-gospeller, Mahalia Jackson. One day, Begum Sharmila will probably look like Mahalia Jackson. The old movie is called *Imitation of Life*" (340). The novel ends then with another encounter with the cinema. Rushdie's novel begins and ends "in the movies." The novel begins with Trevor Gutte's film set on Bliss Grove, moves to the fake movie set where the real atomic bomb explodes, and ends with a movie that, unlike the two documentary films before it, offers a different "imitation of life." Unlike the documentary film, Sirk's movie offers a fantasy version of life. This is in keeping with the nature of Saleem's escape: it is, after all, a fantasy, which may or may not occur.

The "Mammy" figure, Mahalia Jackson, is compared to the other "Mother": Nurse Sharmila. Both women are symbolic saviors. Sharmila saves Saleem from the nursing home. Mahalia Jackson's song becomes the appropriate soundtrack for Saleem's redemption: "There is a song Saleem Sinai has always associated with Mahalia Jackson. The song is in his head as he walks away, even though, as far as he can remember, she didn't sing it in *Imitation of Life*" (340). As mentioned, the song does not appear in the movie. But Rushdie chooses the song most associated with Mahalia Jackson, a spiritual that offers an uplifting message of hope. Mahalia Jackson's "huge, pure voice" (340) is a symbol of the ways in which the human spirit triumphs over adversity.

The novel ends with the song's lyrics together with the director's stage instructions: "Bring in the backing around here, low in the background, a piano, a drum, maybe a tenor sax or two. The backing swells up like tears, a great wail of victorious noise, a definition of life. And take it away: 'He got the whole world, in his hand, He got the whole wide world, in his hand'" (340). This staging of a "victorious" song offers one version of a happy ending. Whereas *Imitation of Life* ends with a funeral and a different song called "Trouble of the World," Rushdie's novel ends with a vision of having the "whole world in your hand." The spiritual imagines a world in the safe care of a benevolent, father-like God who takes care of his children. Choosing this imagined option chimes in with Saleem's promise to Vanilla of an optimistic ending. This version, at least, ends on a soaring note: a definition of life as an uplifting spiritual, a celebration of life over the forces of death. Although this is, as in the other Rushdie novels I discuss, only an imagined option, it nevertheless remains the last written and aural image we are left with. The novel officially ends with the word: "Or:" followed by "******." This is only one version of many possible ones. But it would seem that optimism, that "contagious disease," remains the organizing feature of Rushdie's oeuvre. This optimistic belief in the power of regeneration of hope informs his work, even as it charts the darkest moments in his nation's history. If we return to Jacqueline Rose's "states of fantasy," we may say that in *The Antagonist* Saleem imagines a different homecoming. In Bombay, near the Regal Cinema, he finds a fantastic space, an imagined option for redemption. This is not the "Bomb in Bombay," the more dire version of *MC*. Here we have an explosion of song, a swelling up of tears and joy. Rushdie's first, unpublished piece may thus prove to be one of his more optimistic works. It is certainly one of his finest and most moving creations. However, this optimistic moment remains, as I have shown, an imaginary one. The novel ends in a space of possibility, one of many.

As I have shown, Rushdie's novels often locate hope and possible redemption within a fictional space, whether a song, a film or a re-imagined land. It is interesting to note that the novel that best exemplifies this optimistic Rushdean spirit emerges in the darkest moments of the author's life, following the announcement of the *fatwa* in 1989. It was then when Rushdie decided to fulfill his promise to his son Zafar and write a book for him. In *Joseph Anton*, Rushdie recounts the moment at which his son becomes the agent of his redemption and brings him back to writing: "It was Zafar who finally brought him back to himself" (166). Rushdie recalls, "[It] was the only time in his working life that he knew almost the whole plot from the beginning. The story dropped into his head like a gift" (167).

Rushdie locates the origin of the tale that will become *Haroun and the Sea of Stories*, the topic of the following chapter, in "the title of an old Sanksrit book ... usually rendered in English as The Ocean of the Streams of Story" (167). Although the original book has no actual sea, Rushdie decided to invent such an "ocean" of stories. What changes in Rusdie's vision of the tale—first conceived as a modern book "in which the broken family stayed broken, and the boy became used to it, dealt with it, as his own son was doing" (167)—is the ending: "A happy ending had to be found and he agreed with himself that he was ready to find one. He had of late become extremely interested in happy endings" (167). Rushdie's most personal answer to the *fatwa*, the refusal to remain silent and the continued need to tell stories with (qualified) happy endings, reflecting the author's wish for such an ending in his own life, is couched in a science fictional form. The writer as an "antagonist of the State," who began his writing career in a demonstration of the power of the literary text to create alternate and subversive versions of known reality, here embarks on a tale that would examine the very nature of storytelling as a life giving force.

5
Haroun and *Shalimar*: Kashmir and Koshmar

> *He knew what he knew: that the real world was full of magic, so magical worlds could easily be real.* —Haroun and the Sea of Stories
>
> *What is the use of stories that aren't even true?*
> —Haroun and the Sea of Stories

Although my focus is on Rushdie's later novels, I locate *Haroun and the Sea of Stories* (1990) as a template for the unique science fictional spaces created by Rushdie in later novels. The novel tells the story of Rashid Khalifa, a storyteller who lives in the country of Alifbay, in a sad city, "so ruinously sad that it had forgotten its name" (*Haroun*, 15). Rashid lives in this city with his wife Soraya and his son Haroun. He loses his storytelling abilities when his wife leaves him for Mr. Sengupta, a town clerk who hates fictional stories. In an attempt to recover the father's lost storytelling abilities, Haroun accompanies Rashid on his journey to the beautiful Dull lake in the Valley of K. The father and son are hosted on a boat called *Arabian Nights Plus One*. Following a change of beds with his father, Haroun encounters the Water Genie, a creature from one of his father's tales, who takes him to the Earth's second moon, Kahani, to the land of Gup and shows him the Ocean of the Streams of Story. The Ocean has been polluted by a tyrannical "Cultmaster" (148), or "Khattam-Shud," the leader of the Chup nation at war with the Gup nation. This ominous figure certainly echoes the Ayatollah Khomeini, but he becomes a much broader allegorical signifier of the will for domination and the wish to police language. Haroun is the hero of the tale as he manages to stop the poisoning of the Ocean. As a reward, the Walrus—the Grand Comptroller of the Processes Too Complicated to Explain, the head of the Eggheads in the land of Gup—awards him and his sad city with a synthesized "happy ending": Haroun and Rashid return to the sad city that has now found its name — Kahani ("story"). Soraya returns to her husband and son. Haroun wakes up on his birthday to find that all is well in his family. Time, which had stopped when Soraya left Rashid and Haroun, is now "definitely on the move again" (210). Haroun's adventure, which takes place out of ordinary time, in a dream, ends up affecting a return to the ordinary course of time in the real world. A similar narrative device is at work in *Luka* where the son's adventures in the world of magic save his dying father's life in the real world.

One of the characters in the novel, the Walrus, a figure of a benevolent scientist, or an Egghead, synthesizes a happy ending for the novel in potion form. Thus the magical science of creating fictions and finding fictional resolutions to life's travails becomes a trope both for Rushdie's endeavor as a writer as well as for the fictive attempt to provide magical solutions to real problems. The Walrus's happy ending only cheers things up for a little while. It is not meant to be a solution or a recipe for solving personal and national problems. However, this happy ending marks Rushdie's belief in the power of fiction to create alternate spaces in which the problems of real life are reworked and sometimes resolved within the fictional space. In *Haroun*, an allegorical fairy-tale-like narrative, written for Rushdie's son Zafar, following the infamous *fatwa* in 1989 — the event that shook Rushdie's life and the life of his family and caused an enforced separation from his beloved son — Rushdie nevertheless provides an optimistic tale in which the powers of the child, Haroun, help the father, Rashid, to regain his storytelling powers.

This allegory of the writer's plight at the time when dark forces try to silence his artistic voice is transformed into a magical quest for the lost artistic voice. Rushdie's title alludes to two Eastern collections of stories: The epic of ancient Sanskrit literature by the poet Somedava (c. A.D. 1000) known as the *Katha Sarit Sagara,* which translates as "the sea of stories," and the *Arabian Nights,* which features the famous caliph Haroun Al Rashid. The father-son duo in Rushdie's novel are named Rashid and Haroun. The explicit allusion to the ancient Sanskrit text, itself a collection of tales, appears in *Haroun* when Rashid is shown "the entire collection of tales known as *The Ocean of the Streams of Story*" (*Haroun*, 51). Rashid is told that if he ever "runs out of material," he "will find plenty in here" (51). Rashid, who had lost his storytelling powers, is alarmed at the suggestion: "Run out? What are you saying?" (51).

5. Haroun *and* Shalimar

Thus Rushdie both plays with the allusion to the canonical text and with the idea of a source of stories that may dry out or become polluted as it does in the course of the novel. *The Arabian Nights'* influence on Rushdie's oeuvre is evident, for example, in the ending of the final chapter of *The Satanic Verses* entitled "A Wonderful Lamp," where the *Arabian Nights* are invoked, as Catherine Cundy reminds us, to represent "the magic of love regained" (85). Cundy locates the role of the *Arabian Nights* in *The Satanic Verses* and in *Haroun* as texts that bring back the magic of childhood, what Saladin sees in *The Satanic Verses* as the place where "the true djinns of old had the powers to open the gates of the Infinite, to make all things possible, to render all wonders capable of being attained" (*SV*, 546). This relationship between *The Arabian Nights* and the ability to return to a sense of childlike wonder is also at work in *Haroun* in its allusions to the tales' significance as a source as well as in the choice of the protagonists' names and metaphorical roles. I shall relate in more detail to this relationship in my reading of the novel below.

At this point, however, one can note Rushdie's manipulation of names and naming as he chooses a title that evokes two famous story-collections that become a metaphoric reference for the novel's engagement with the notion of a sea of stories that can be dipped into to create new strands and streams in a never-ending succession.

In typical Rushdean mode, these Eastern allusions are accompanied by foundational Western texts. Rushdie's most obvious Western influence is the 1930 movie *The Wizard of Oz*. In his 1992 monograph on the film subtitled "A Short Text About Magic," Rushdie locates the magic not only in the film's special effects but also, and more widely, in the role of cinema as a creator of magical locales, a theme to which he returns in his novels time and again. Rushdie comments on the relationship between *Haroun* and *The Wizard of Oz*: "When I first saw *The Wizard of Oz*, it made a writer of me. Many years later, I began to devise the yarn that eventually became *Haroun and the Sea of Stories*, and felt strongly that if I could strike the right note it should be possible to write the tale in such a way as to make it of interest to adults as well as children" (*The Wizard of Oz*, 18). Rushdie indeed writes a tale that is, like the film, a work that can be enjoyed by both children and adults. His densely allusive text is nevertheless a fast paced and entertaining adventure for "children of all ages."

Haroun also serves as a marker of Rushdie's different brand of fantasy. This is not Magical Realism, where fantastic events and miraculous occurrences interpose into the realism of the novel's surface. In *Haroun*, there is no such distinction. The world of Rashid and Haroun is always-already a fictionalized version of India, or at least of certain aspects of Indian life. The magical world of the Walrus and the other fantastic beings in the novel is just another version of this fantastic world, another alternative universe, one of many, all existing at the same time. Rushdie's alternative histories and science fictional sites do not avoid the inherently violent nature of his nation's coming into being and the never-ending bloodshed that is not mitigated even in the imagined versions of true historical events. In *Haroun*, Kashmir appears as the "Valley of K.," an Edenic locale that Rashid hopes will help restore his lost storytelling abilities. I shall relate this imagined version of Kashmir and its relationship to the history of Kashmir below. The second part of this chapter will address the reappearance of Kashmir as a place of bloody conflict in Rushdie's 2005 novel, *Shalimar the Clown*, where the bloody history of Kashmir, although imagined employing science fictional tropes, is no less violent and painful than a more realistic rendering of the same tale.

Haroun and the Sea of Stories is one of Rushdie's most impassioned hymns to the power of storytelling to create worlds. The novel appeared shortly following the infamous *fatwa* in 1989 and has been read as Rushdie's response in fictional form to the real threat on his life. Some critical readings of the novel accused Rushdie of writing a simplistic allegorical response to the *fatwa* in the guise of a children's book. Thus, Srinivas Aravamuden claims that in the conflict between the lands of Gup and Chup, or silence and free speech, Rushdie created a "banal didactic fiction," which presents an essentialist view of "censorship and literature as Manichean opposites" (Aravamuden, 327). This reductive reading ignores the novel's complex intertextual collage of different literary, filmic and cultural influences and its nuanced representation of the war between speech and silence. In my reading of the text, I shall show how Rushdie masterfully creates a fable without a didactic purpose or tone.

It is interesting to note Rushdie's own evaluation of the role of his novel as a modern day fable without a clear moral. In "Influence," a lecture delivered in 1999 at the University of Toronto, Rushdie relates to the nature of his text: "Although the form of this novel is that of a children's fantastic adventure, I wanted the work somehow to erase the division between children's literature and adult books. It was in the end a question of the right tone of voice. The secret was to use the language of the fable while eschewing the easy moral purpose of, for example, Aesop" (*Step Across this Line*, 67). In the same lecture, Rushdie relates to the issue of literary influence. *Haroun* becomes a marker of Rushdie's art: He describes the writer's work employing a sea metaphor that closely resembles the description of the "Sea of Stories" in the novel:

> I have always envisaged the world of the imagination not so much as a continent, but as an ocean. Afloat and terrifyingly free upon those boundless seas, the writer attempts, with his bare hands, the magical task of metamorphosis. Like the figure in the fairy tale who must spin straw into gold, the writer must find the trick of weaving the waters together until they become land: until, all of a sudden, there is solidity where once there was only flow, shape where there was formlessness; there is ground beneath his feet [*Step Across this Line*, 62–63].

Rushdie here gestures both at the inherent dangers of writing and its status as a magical feat. The writer must weave the different streams into a story, but the many streams influence his writing and without them, Rushdie seems to say, no worthy piece of literature will ever be written. We also hear an echo here of Rushdie's *The Ground Beneath Her Feet*, which is, as I have already shown, another fictional response to the *fatwa*.

In the same lecture, Rushdie presents *Haroun and the Sea of Stories* as an example of the ways in which literature is created: "In my novel *Haroun and the Sea of Stories*, a young boy actually travels to the ocean of imagination. By using what is old, and adding it to some new thing of our own, we make what is new" (*Step Across this Line*, 66). The description of that "sea of stories" in the novel suggests, indeed, that the work of literature is made up of many story streams. It also alludes to the thousand and one tales in *The Arabian Nights* as a metaphor for that multiplicity of voices and tales:

> He looked into the water and saw that it was made up of a thousand, thousand thousand and one different currents, each one a different colour, weaving in and out of one another like a liquid tapestry of breathtaking complexity. Different parts of the Ocean contained different sorts of stories. And because the stories were held here in fluid form, they retained the ability to change, to become new versions of themselves; so that unlike a library of books, the Ocean of the Streams of Story was much more than a storeroom of yarns. It was not dead but alive [*Haroun*, 71–72].

This telling passage encompasses Rushdie's artistic credo, which can be located throughout his oeuvre. The importance of the continuing life of stories in different versions and forms, the ability to create new tales out of old ones, and the idea of the fluid nature of the literary work — its metamorphic quality — are all present in what would seem to be a fantastic, fairy-tale-like description of an imaginative locale.

Furthermore, Rushdie again mentions his source of influence by name — "The Ocean of the Streams of Story" — thus acknowledging the importance of the Indian source as a defining metaphor for his unique brand of storytelling. The "Ocean" is also the writer, however. Rashid is known "to his admirers" as the "Ocean of Notions" (*Haroun*, 15). The writer, like the stories, contains multitudes. *Haroun* enacts both the perils and the joys of the writer's endeavor to create new tales. Rashid's loss of creative powers reflects Rushdie's own fear, expressed in the interview with James Fenton: "I spent an awful lot of time thinking I would never write again" (31). This fear is dramatized in the quest at the center of the novel. If Rashid is to regain his storytelling abilities, he must do so with the help of his son, accessing the father's magical world of multiple tales as a source of inspiration. A similar theme resurfaces in *Luka and the Fire of Life*, which I address in my final chapter.

If *Haroun* is, at least to some extent, Rushdie's response to the *fatwa*, then his depiction of the war between the worlds of speech and silence is more nuanced than his detractors have given him credit for. Rushdie constructs contesting textual worlds that fight for domination as the novel stages a battle between two warring nations, the Gups and the Chups, or speech versus silence. This battle, however, is not a simplistic showdown between the powers of light and powers of darkness. Rushdie creates a more complex tale, and his fictional resolution of the conflict is indeed reconciliation between the two worldviews rather than a triumph of one over the other. In a 1991 interview with the poet James Fenton, Rushdie spoke of writing *Haroun and the Sea of Stories* partly in fulfillment of a promise to his son, Zafar, "that the next book I wrote would be one he might enjoy reading" (31). Thus, *Haroun* is indeed a story that is Rushdie's personal gift to his son, a book that he would enjoy reading. However, the book also paradoxically deals with doubt. The question that invades the world of fantasy created by Rashid and that permeates the tale is "What is the use of stories that aren't even true?" (*Haroun*, 22). This question is one that both Rashid and Haroun will set out to explore in the course of their journey to restore Rashid's storytelling powers. *Haroun* explores the concept of the fictional narrative as it connects with the problems of the real world. In his reading of the novel, Daniel Roberts points out that the novel "deconstructs normative distinctions between fantasy and reality, posing 'real' issues of politics and governance in fairy-tale form" ("Rushdie and the Romantics"). In my reading of the "Valley of K." episode in the novel, I shall relate to the ways in which real political issues are played out in fairy-tale form in Rushdie's re-imagining of Kashmir as an Eden on earth.

Rushdie further comments on the relationship between the *fatwa* and his decision to write a book for his son in the James Fenton interview: "Children blame themselves for the misfortunes that befall the adults in their lives. It is a place to write from. A terrible thing happens to a father, the child blames himself and wishes to rescue the father. And in the novel not just the father, but the whole world, while doing it, and why not?" (32). Rushdie grants the child the ability to effect change in his world and in the world at large through the power of imagination. This is a repeated theme in his work and one that receives the most poignant expression in *Haroun*, written at a time when Rushdie's life was in very real danger. However, *Haroun* remains an optimistic text, celebrating the power of storytelling to affect change in the real world. Thus, when Rashid delivers what is supposed to be an election speech for a corrupt politician, Mr. Buttoo, at the end of the novel, he ends up telling *Haroun and the Sea of Stories* instead. The audience responds to the allegorical meanings of the tale and acts upon them: "Whenever Rashid was talking about Khuttum-Shud and his henchmen from the Union of the Zipped Lips, the whole audience stared hard at Snotty Buttoo and *his* henchmen" (*Haroun*, 206). The audience turns against Mr. Buttoo, and he "went slinking with his henchmen off the stage" (206). The fictional story ends up transforming the real world: "Mr. Buttoo was never seen again in the Valley of K., which left the people of the Valley free to choose leaders they actually liked" (207). Rushdie here demonstrates the power of the tale to effect political change. In this case, it is a change for the better. But Rushdie is well aware of the potentially lethal effect of fictions, as *Fury*, for one, demonstrates. *Haroun* engages with the transformative power of fiction while also presenting the ways in which fictional rhetoric can be abused. Rushdie does not present a simplistic dichotomy between the two opposing forces of speech and silence or Gup and Chup. Rather, he offers a nuanced meditation on the roles of the fictive and the real in our construction of our worldviews.

Haroun offers us two worlds that are in dialogue with each other: The fictive land of Alifbay (Alphabet), which is the textual equivalent of an imagined India, as I shall later show, and the imaginative land of Rashid's tales, a science-fictional or fantastic domain where flying mechanical birds, Water Genies, Eggheads in charge of Processes Too Complicated to Explain headed by a Walrus in the land of Gup are confronted by the Cultmaster, Khuttam-Shud, and his army of shadows in the dark land of Chup. Rushdie delights in manipulating the science fictional elements of his tale with the allusions to multiple Eastern and Western canonical texts. In the figure of the flying mechanical bird, Butt the Hoopoe, for one, Rushdie creates a lovable and humorous machine that wryly comments on his own nature to the bewildered Haroun: "You maybe have some objection to machines? But but but you have entrusted your life to me. Then am I not worthy of a little of your respect? Machines also have their sense of self-esteem.—No need to gawp like that, young sir, I can't help it if I remind you of someone" (*Haroun*, 66). The machine that reads Haroun's mind and communicates with him telepathically (66) is a magical world incarnation of the driver who takes Haroun and Rashid on their journey to the Valley of K. His wry comments echo the many science fictional tales dealing with the sometimes blurry divide between the machine and the human. Rushdie explores this theme in a less humorous vein in *Fury*. In *Haroun,* the "science" in "science fiction" is addressed in a parodic manner. When Haroun seeks to understand how the mechanical bird works, he gets the answer, repeated many times in the course of the novel, becoming its ironic refrain: "By a P2C2E, a Process Too Complicated to Explain" (*Haroun*, 66). The P2C2E is Rushdie's bemused answer to hard core SF's engagement with "factual" scientific explanations. Rushdie's use of the generic tropes of SF is, as I have shown, a more bemused one, as Haroun finds out, but the Hoopoe is a bird with a "deadpan" sense of humor: "Butt the Hoopoe's eyes were twinkling. Really, there were major difficulties involved in talking to machines, Haroun thought. With their deadpan expressions, it was impossible to know when they were pulling your leg" (*Haroun*, 80). Rushdie, it seems, delights in pulling our leg with his "scientific" descriptions.

As in Rushdie's favorite film, *The Wizard of Oz,* here too, characters from Haroun's real life are transformed into characters in the fantasy world. Mr. Sengupta, the clerk who runs away with Soraya, Haoun's mother, is like Khuttam-Shud, the evil ruler of Chup, and the friendly driver who takes Rashid and Haroun to the Valley of K., Mr. Butt, is transformed into the friendly mechanical bird, Butt the Hoopoe. Haroun's wish to meet the Walrus echoes Dorothy's quest to meet the Wizard who will grant her wish to go back home, and the revelation that the dreaded Khattam-Shud is just a "skinny, scrawny, sniveling, driveling, mingy, stingy, measly, weaselly, clerkish sort of fellow" (190) echoes the unveiling of the Wizard of Oz as a small man with no magical qualities who relies on technology to effect his "magic." *Haroun* ends, as does *The Wizard of Oz*, with a return to a happier domesticity.

Rushdie also alludes to the *Alice* books in his evocation of a quest that takes place in a dream. Like Alice, Haroun finds out that he has been asleep while engaged in his adventures. When he wakes up, he realizes that in the real world only one night had passed. But he finds a "golden envelope lying by his pillow," a note from his friends from the magical land he has visited. The note reads: "Come whenever you want. Stay as long as you like. Remember: when you fly with Butt the Hoopoe, time is on your side" (204). This relationship with time, cast not as a linear trajectory with a definite end point but as a fluid, flowing presence that is "on our side" rather than our mortal enemy, appears again in *Luka and the Fire of Life*, in which the threat of the father's death is a central theme. In *Haroun*, Rushdie plays with the notion of parallel times and parallel story lines to indicate the ways in which our views of time and narrative, which must occur in time, are affected by the imaginative possibility to travel "out of time" and live in multiple worlds that may be the only ones in which we can find solutions for our real life problems. Although *Haroun* is a children's book, expressly written for one child and meant to amuse "children of all ages," Rushdie nevertheless addresses in this seemingly playful way some of the most pertinent issues in his oeuvre. If the idea of fiction as a life-saving force is a constant refrain in Rushdie's work, then *Haroun* dramatizes the idea of storytelling in the most concrete way by imagining a "sea of stories," its pollution and final rehabilitation as the main image in the novel. This device allows him to expound on the roles of stories, at times in a parodic, playful way but more often in an urgent way, showcasing how, in the aftermath of the *fatwa*, the allegorical becomes too close to the real to be merely a metaphor.

The Valley of K.: Rushdie's Imagined Kashmir

The novel explores storytelling and examines the act of reading. It dramatizes the process of reading as a navigational act, thus alerting the reader to the process of signification or of generating meaning from multiple linguistic signs. My focus will be on one instance of literal and figurative navigation. I examine the role of Kashmir, the Eden-like locale and place of longing in Rushdie's oeuvre, in a text that does not mention it by name but only alludes to it. In *Haroun*, Kashmir appears only as a partially erased road sign. I claim that by using this literary device, Rushdie reinvents both Kashmir and India as textual and fantastic sites. In this fairy-tale universe, Rushdie explores his personal and national dilemmas and offers magical solutions to difficult, seemingly impossible, political situations. In *Haroun*, he offers a provisional happy ending, thus reflecting perhaps his own wishful projection for the future of the troubled nations of India and Pakistan. He celebrates the powers of language over the attempts to silence it while also being acutely aware of the powers of language and rhetoric, especially political rhetoric, to do harm in the world. Although this tale is more optimistic than some of his other novels, it is by no means a naïve celebration of cultural hybridity and multiplicity as some critics have insisted. Even the novel's happy ending[1] is qualified; Rushdie winks at his readers' wish for happy endings by reminding them that in art, as well as in life, all they do is "cheer up things for a while" (*Haroun*, 202). After examining the erased figure of Kashmir in the text, I turn to Rushdie's novel *Shalimar the Clown* where Kashmir takes center stage and question whether Rushdie still envisions a "happy ending" in the bloody war zone that has transformed idyllic Kashmir into a "Koshmar" or nightmare.

Kashmir appears time and again in Rushdie's fiction as the ultimate Eden-like site, a land of origins and a place of longing. It is the promised land that Rushdie's characters long for and imagine as an alternate space in the midst of civil strife and the rivers of blood that seem to wash over Indian history. It is the land Saleem will never reach at the end of *Midnight's Children*, but he is forever on his way there. In his later novels, *The Ground Beneath Her Feet* and *Fury*, other, more urban sites may replace Kashmir as imagined, possibly redemptive locales, but the idea of Kashmir as an earthly Eden still hovers above. It is only in *Shalimar the Clown* that Kashmir, the land and the ideal, becomes the central character, if you will.

5. Haroun *and* Shalimar

In his reading of the novel, Daniel Roberts points out that *Haroun* "deconstructs normative distinctions between fantasy and reality, posing 'real' issues of politics and governance in fairy-tale form" ("Rushdie and the Romantics"). Roberts relates to another major literary influence in the novel: Samuel Taylor Coleridge's "Kubla Khan," which appears in the acrostic reference to Zafar that appears as a dedication:

> Zembla, Zenda, Xanadu,
> All our dream-worlds may come true,
> Fairy lands are fearsome too,
> As I wander far from view
> Read, and bring me home to you.

The reference to Xanadu provides the connection between Rushdie's novel and Coleridge's poem, which, as Roberts points out, "has been connected with Kashmir." The Coleridge poem is subtitled: "A Vision in a Dream," thus also linking it to *Haroun*'s engagement with dreamscapes and alternate realities. The poem's first stanza describes a landscape that is echoed in Rushdie's novel in the description of the Valley of K.:

> In Xanadu did Kubla Khan
> A Stately pleasure dome decree
> Where Alph, the sacred river, ran
> Through caverns measureless to man
> Down to a sunless sea.
> So twice five miles of fertile ground
> With walls and towers were girdled round;
> And here were gardens bright with sinuous rills
> Where blossom'd many an incense-bearing tree;
> And here were forests ancient as the hills,
> Enfolding sunny spots of greenery

Roberts locates the role of the Romantic imagination in constructing an "Orientalist stereotype of an earthly paradise" ("Rushdie and the Romantics"). This earthly paradise is, as Roberts points out, an evocation of Kashmir, a central locale in Rushdie's oeuvre. Coleridge's landscape is echoed in the description of the "pleasure gardens built by the ancient Emperors" (*Haroun*, 25) in Rashid's description of the Valley of K. As Roberts rightly points out, *Haroun* sets out a number of parallels between its different magical locales, which are all connected in some way to Kashmir:

With the Oz-shaped logic of the story, the Valley of K is paralleled quite evidently by that of Kahani, the earth's second moon: while Mr. Butt, the mail-coach driver takes Haroun into the Valley of K, his counterpart Butt the hoopoe bird carries him on an equally manic journey to Gup City on the moon Kahani. In Gup City we again encounter the same garden, carried over from the Romantic Orient, from Coleridge, from the Valley of K, and now transformed to the Guppee landscape" ["Rushdie and the Romantics"].

There is, however, a significant difference between the despotic Orientalist vision of Coleridge's poem and the democratic land of Gup. As Roberts shows, the novel departs from the despotic vision to offer a version of a democratic, though chaotic, India: "Whereas Kublai's palace is the sole architectural feature within the wild and expansive garden, Rushdie introduces three important buildings, the Palace of King Chattergy, the Parliament of Gup and the towering edifice of P2C2E House, the technological heart of Gup city" ("Rushdie and the Romantics"). This inversion indicates that "the despotic Orient of the Romantic period is now displaced by the bungling bureaucracy of modern and democratic India, represented by the technologically complex but administratively chaotic emblem of the P2C2E House. The Orient is represented as irrepressibly democratic, and perhaps glancing too at the chaotic resilience of modern Indian democracy" ("Rushdie and the Romantics"). Indeed, Rushdie's loving depiction of the Gup nation, which, despite their fondness for chatter, as the name of their king suggests, and their love of endless debates, prove to be better warriors than the shadowy, secretive Chup nation. Rushdie clearly favors this brand of democracy, chaotic as it may be, over the totalitarian order represented by Khattam-Shud's silent and silenced people, who end up turning against one another in the final battle against the Gup nation. Rashid marvels at the Gup army's abilities in the face of what he perceives as the Guppees' weakness: "Meanwhile the Guppees were still busily arguing over every little detail. Every order sent down from the command hill had to be debated fully, with all its pro's and con's, even if it came from General Kitab himself. 'How is it possible to fight a battle with all this chatter and natter?,' Rashid wondered, perplexed" (*Haroun*, 184). The final outcome, however, proves him wrong:

> Rashid saw, to his great surprise, that the Chupwalas were quite unable to resist the Guppees. The Pages of Gup, now that they had talked through everything so fully, fought hard, remained united, supported each other when required to do so, and in general looked like a force with a common

5. Haroun *and* Shalimar

purpose. All those arguments and debates, all that openness, had created powerful bonds of friendship between them [*Haroun*, 184–185].

"Openness" wins over close-minded suspicion. This is definitely the Rushdean credo, expressed here in very passionate terms, at odds with the more light-hearted tone of some of the novel's episodes. Although Rushdie is careful not to create too facile a dichotomy between the forces of light and the powers of darkness, he nevertheless reiterates his belief in the merits of democratic debate and chaotic chatter over the totalitarian will to dominate and silence its opponents.

The reference to Coleridge's "Kubla Khan" also contributes to the meta-fictional quality of the novel. If one looks at Coleridge's poem as a comment on the creative process in which the "pleasure dome" built by Kubla Khan can be read as a representative of the poem itself, then Rushdie's novel engages in similar ways with the role of fiction in real life and with the ways in which imaginative spaces are constructed in literature to reflect real-life problems. Rushdie alludes to another Coleridge poem, *The Rime of the Ancient Mariner*, in his description of the dark side of his allegory: the "shadow ship" where the ominous Khattam Shud and his minions imprison Haroun. The allusion to the poem, however, first appears in the description of the "Ocean of the Streams of Story." Upon arriving at the land of Gup, the confused Haroun exclaims: "Water, water, everywhere; nor any trace of land" (*Haroun*, 66), evoking the famous lines from Coleridge's poem: "Water, water, everywhere, And all the boards did shrink; Water, water, everywhere, Nor any drop to drink" (*The Rime of the Ancient Mariner*, part 2, lines 119–122). This evocation of a watery surface that is polluted evokes the pollution of the "Ocean of the Streams of Story" that we learn of shortly after this scene. The following allusion to Coleridge's poem occurs, as I have mentioned, on Khuttam Shud's "shadow ship," evoking Coleridge's deathly ship in the poem: "The Sun's rim dips; the stars rush out, At one stride comes the dark, With far-heard whisper, o'er the sea, Off shot the spectre-bark" (*The Rime of the Ancient Mariner*, part 3, lines 199–202). In Rushdie's novel, Haroun realizes that the "Dark Ship" he is on is a ship of shadows: "So they are all shadows here. The boat, the Zipped Lips gang, and Khattam-Shud himself. Everything and everyone here is a Shadow made Solid, except for Iff, Mali, Butt the Hoopoe and me" (*Haroun*, 166).

The allusion to Coleridge reinforces the death-like quality of Khuttam-Shud's reign of shadows, which is opposed to the life force represented by the Gup nation and by Haroun, their ally. Furthermore, the two Coleridge poems are concerned in some way with the work of the poet as world maker. In *The Rime of the Ancient Mariner*, the mariner, like the poet and the visionary, has "strange powers of speech" (*The Rime of the Ancient Mariner*, part 7, line 587). He is compelled to tell his tale to the worthy listener. In Rushdie's novel, storytelling equals continued life. The attempt to stop the wellspring of tales is a death wish, practiced by "shadows." Thus, both "Kubla Khan" and *The Rime of the Ancient Mariner* resonate in *Haroun*, a novel that dramatizes the power of telling to construct alternate worlds.

Haroun provides an interesting instance of the way Kashmir figures in a text that never once alludes to it by name. Rashid Khalifa and his son Haroun embark on a journey to the Valley of K.,[2] where Rashid is engaged by a corrupt politician named Buttoo[3] to aid in his election campaign. In an interview following the theatrical production of the novel, Rushdie talks about the genesis of the tale:

> *Haroun* came in the first place from fragments of stories that I used to tell my son — Zafar, who was at that time 10 or 11— in the bath.... Haroun is my son's middle name. Another germ was a short story I wrote years before and never published.... Then, when I was coming up with Haroun's adventure — by that time, I guess I had become involved myself in a sort of war between language and silence — I suddenly understood the meaning of the story that I haven't previously understood [26–27].

In this way, the novel becomes both a story of Rushdie's own war with the silencing impetus of the *fatwa* and a father-son story. Rushdie tells of his years in hiding following the *fatwa* that have also had an impact on Zafar's life: "So for me, the father-son relationship is at the heart of *Haroun*. As it was for him" (48).

In his reading of the novel, Aron Aji comments on the fictional characters of father and son and on the ways they become aspects of the same person: Aji reads the father and son's names, Rashid and Haroun, as two manifestations of the same person — namely Haroun al-Rashid, the famous caliph from Bagdad: "Between the father and son, then, Rushdie's fairy tale offers us two caliphs rather than one: Haroun Khalifa and Rashid Khalifa. In his own manner, each is the custodian of the Sea of Stories, and, as importantly, each is incomplete without the other. Haroun is after the essence of stories, while Rashid gives them shape and form" (Aji, 5). This importance of naming and names is one of the central aspects in Rushdie's fairy-tale universe. The father and son live in a country called Alifbay (or alphabet) and reside in a "city so ruinously sad that it had forgotten its name" (*Haroun*, 15). This city is later re-named Kahani, or "story," thus indicating the power of naming and names to create and recreate reality.

Rashid describes the destination of the journey, the Valley of K., in magical terms: "But the Valley of K! Now that is different. There are fields of gold and mountains of silver and in the middle of the Valley there is a beautiful Lake whose name, by the way, is Dull" (*Haroun*, 25). This is, of course, an allusion to Kashmir's Dal Lake, which here, by a change in spelling, becomes "Dull Lake." Thus Rushdie alludes to an imagined version of a magical Kashmir in his alternate version of India. The Khalifa family dwelling is described thus in the novel: "The Khalifas lived in the downstairs part of a small concrete house with pink walls, lime-green windows, and blue painted balconies with squiggly metal railings, all of which made it look (in Haroun's view) more like a cake than a building" (*Haroun*, 18). As Suchismita Sen points out, "Haroun provides us with a child's eye view of a world that urban Indians will have little difficulty in recognizing as their own childhood environment.... The house in which the Khalifas live, for example ... can be found in the less fashionable middle-class quarters of any Indian city" (Sen, 6–7). This imagined, but all too familiar, version of India as Alifbay, then, also encompasses the magical land of Kashmir as a dream of earthly Paradise. Rushdie only alludes to Kashmir, choosing not to name it explicitly in the text. His renaming of Kashmir's "Dal Lake" as "Dull Lake" constitutes another renaming gesture that points to the actual place yet leaves it in the realm of fable.

The same playful manipulation of place names as signifying real places occurs often in the course of the novel. Place names become ways of signifying meaning or of pointing out the problematic relationship between a place *name* and an actual location. In one such instance, the narrator explains the reason for naming towns by their first initial: "I should explain that in the country of Alifbay many places were named after letters of the Alphabet. This led to much confusion, because there were only a limited number of letters and an almost unlimited number of places in need of names" (*Haroun*, 24). Rushdie here offers a parodic twist to the realist convention of nineteenth century novels in which this naming device (naming places only by their initial letter) was used to protect the "real identity" of fictitious characters and places thereby maintaining the realist illusion. By placing this convention in an Indian locale where place names get confused and misplaced or even forgotten, Rushdie pays a parodic homage to realist novels, while also pointing out the different nature of his novel and of India in his fairy-tale version of it.

Rushdie's fable continually draws attention to its (linguistic and actual) links to the real world. The novel presents two mirroring textual worlds: The country of Alifbay or, if you will, a fictive India, and the lands of Gup and Chup, or speech and silence, which can be read as versions of India and Pakistan, or India and Iran, respectively. Both sets of textual worlds in the novel are imaginatively constructed as being in and of language. The war between silence and language is complicated when a defector from the Chup camp — the Shadow Warrior Mudra and his shadow — offer to help Rashid, Haroun, Prince Bolo and General Kitab (literally "book") of the Gup camp in their fight against the Cultmaster Khattam-Shud (literally "completely finished, over and done with").

As Daniel Roberts points out, Mudra's presence is crucial as he "teaches Haroun that Gups and Chups might after all learn from each other." After seeing Mudra's performance, Haroun reflects on the meaning of silence and speech: "The Shadow Warrior showed him that silence had its own grace and beauty (just as speech could be graceless and ugly); and that Action could be as noble as Words; and that creatures of darkness could be as lovely as the children of the light" (*Haroun*, 125). The two opposing sides come together: "At the sight of Mudra, many Chupwalas threw in their lot with the Guppees" (*Haroun*, 185). As Roberts claims: "The Guppee 'victory' is thus acceptable to the Chupwalas because it implies not a foreign rule, but rather the installation of a suitable leader from among their own people" ("Rushdie and the Romantics").

In an elaborate set of reversals, Rushdie hints at the traditional Indian theatre's language of hand gestures or *mudras*. The Shadow Warrior cannot speak but performs an elaborate routine of hand and face gestures, interpreted by Rashid. This language of face and hand gestures is a description of an ancient theater art form of Kathakali (native to the state of Kerala), which literally means "story-play." This by now almost extinct art form contains remnants of the ancient ritual plays of Hindu temples and various dance forms, but these were crystallized as an art form in the seventeenth century when the Rajah of Kottarakkara wrote plays based on the Hindu epic Ramayana. The Kathakali actor undergoes a long period of physical training and instruction in *abhinaya* (acting) and uses *mudras*, the descriptive and symbolic movements of the hands and fingers to signify an object or action. The Kathakali actor uses *mudras* instead of the spoken word.

Thus, the idea that silence can also be a form of more elaborate speech is introduced, and the binary opposition between light and darkness and self and shadow is deconstructed. Mudra describes the change in the land of Chup:

> Khattam-Shud's black magic has had fearsome results. He has plunged so deeply into the Dark Art of sorcery that he has become Shadowy himself—changeable, dark, more like a Shadow than a Person. And as he has become more Shadowy, so his Shadow has come to be more like a Person. And the point has come at which it's no longer possible to tell which is Khattam Shud's Shadow and which is his substantial Self—because he had done what no other Chupwalla has ever dreamt of—that is, he has separated himself from his Shadow! [129].

The idea of the shadow self taking over the real man may hint at the darkness and shadow selves that take over totalitarian regimes, such as Khomeini's Iran and others, where shadows follow you wherever you go and where you find yourself no longer sure of your own identity, as an elaborate game of masking becomes a survival technique; but it may also relate to the ways in which the self is as fluid as it is substantial—a theme Rushdie revisits in his more adult novels and which he links to the notion of the migrant as a fluid or what he calls protean being—a shape-shifter who is never a whole and complete self. Rushdie is also playing an elaborate game of multiple allusions here; he mixes the Eastern or Indian tale of theatres, shadows, masks and mirror selves (one of the props in the Kathakali theatre is a mirror), and he also hints at Hans Christian Andersen's famous 1847 tale "The Shadow," which takes place in a "warm climate" where the people "are negroes" as a result of the constant sunlight and where a learned man travels from the north and finds that his shadow has detached itself from him and created an identity of its own. By the end of this story, the "shadow/slave" becomes the master and enslaves the man; they switch roles and the man is executed by his own shadow. As in the allusion to the realist nineteenth century European novel mentioned earlier, Rushdie here gestures at the fairy-tale or fantastic genre and offers another twist on this motif, which can, of course, be read, even in Andersen's version, as a critique of social hierarchy and maybe also racial hierarchy as the story's setting in a "dark" country suggests.

The novel offers its imagined version of the Valley of K. as a sign—

both literally and figuratively. It alerts the readers to the very process of reading and interpretation as a form of navigation between various and confusing road signs. This process invariably leads to multiple meanings and resists an easy "happy ending" or clear resolution. Haroun and Rashid travel to the Valley of K. and pass by a "a sign that had originally read WELCOME TO K; but somebody had daubed it with crude, irregular letters, so that now it said WELCOME TO KOSH-MAR" (*Haroun*, 39–40). This sign arouses Haroun's curiosity. He is interested in finding out what "kosh-mar" is. The reluctant driver does not offer an answer other than stating that "[not] every person in the Valley is happy, as you may find" (40). But Rashid offers the linguistic answer to his son's question: "It's a word from the ancient tongue of Franj.... In those long-gone days the Valley, which is now simply K., had other names. One, if I remember correctly, was 'Kache-Mar.' Another one was this 'Kosh-Mar'" (40). This possible reading of the K. as Kache-Mer or "under the sea" hints that there may be hidden meanings beneath the surface of the text. As the Sea of Stories in the novel generates endless versions of stories, it also hides the very sources of these stories or their true origins. Rushdie may be hinting here at the limits of linguistic signs and more broadly the limits of literary representations to uncover meanings. As Aji rightly points out, "'Kache-Mer ... may be take to refer to each of Rashid's fairy tales which come from and contain the Ocean of the Stream of Story; 'Kosh-Mar' is a 'nightmare,' which suggests the 'fearful' potential of fairy tales already mentioned in the dedication to the book" (Aji, 4). The dedication is a five-line poem to "Zafar: Zembla, Zenda, Xanadu: All our dream worlds may come true. Fairy lands are fearsome too. As I wander far from view. Read and bring me home to you." The first letters of every line spell Zafar, and Rushdie's longing for his son is expressed in this form. The act of reading becomes a way of crossing the gap between father and son: "Bring me home to you." As Rushdie describes: "We got ripped apart, you know. I couldn't live with him.... I could see him but only under conditions of ridiculous secrecy" (Fenton, 48).

Haroun, however, insists on the true meaning of the name. Rashid explains: "All names mean something.... 'Kache-Mar' can be translated as 'the place that hides a sea.' But 'Kosh-Mar' is a ruder name" (*Haroun*, 40). The name is linked to the nature of the place it represents. In other words, the sign may indicate what the inhabitants of the Valley of K. think of it or how they "place" it. Rashid seems reluctant to reveal the "rude" meaning and insists on the more neutral interpretation (the Franj, or French meaning, although both meanings come from the French). However, Haroun urges him and he finally replies: "In the old tongue ... it was the word for 'nightmare'" (40). The "old" or original meaning then locates the Valley of K., or Kashmir, as a nightmarish locale. As Aji points out, however, the

> qualitative difference resulting from a slight phonetic variation (Kache-Mar/Kosh-Mar) signals the negative potential of a positive name, and vice versa — hence the kind bus driver Butt, the corrupt politician Bhutto, and Haroun's benevolent companion Butt the Hoopoe. These early instructions by Rashid are as much for readers as for Haroun, and they guide our interpretation of the names of the fairy tale's main characters and setting [Aji, 4].

In the novel's fairy tale universe then we find a "Kashmir" that is a "Kosh-mar"— not the Edenic Valley but rather a place of lost hope and despair. The significance of names and the power of naming to change the nature of a place or its inhabitants is a repeated motif in the novel. This belief in the power of stories as either life affirming or death enhancing is, of course, never far from Rushdie's vision in any of his novels. But in *Haroun and the Sea of Stories*, he shifts his fictional universe and places it in fairy-tale setting. This device allows him to demonstrate his artistic credo in less ambiguous terms. If we have a sea of stories to dip into, we are also responsible for the kinds of stories we choose. We have to make sure not to pollute this invaluable source of life as do the powers of darkness in the novel. When this source of all stories, hidden under the sea of stories, is polluted, we get the nightmare or "Koshmar." The novel's resolution, however, reaffirms the belief in the power of (re)naming to create a new reality, if only for a little while.

The novel ends with a truce between the warring nations of Gup and Chup, achieved with the help of Haroun and Rashid and with the recovery of Rashid's storytelling abilities. Haroun's defeat of Khattam-Shud's diabolical plans is effected by his conjuring the sun to shine on the land of darkness, an action that causes the darkness and shadows to melt away and disappear. But Haroun does not merely reverse the order of things. He restores the natural balance of day and night to fall on both lands. As Roberts rightly points out, "Rushdie is careful to suggest that the peace achieved by this victory is not one-sided, but bilaterally acceptable" ("Rushdie and the Romantics"). The peaceful situation is described as a "peace in which Night and Day, Speech and Silence, would no longer be separated into Zones by Twilight Strips and Walls of Force" (*Haroun*, 191). The peaceful solution is, as Roberts claims, "at one level a fantasy solution" because "part of the decisive action takes place on the lunar Kahani ('Kahani' meaning 'story' in Hindi)" ("Rushdie and the Romantics"). The solution takes place in a fictional or "story" locale. If we return to Rushdie's evocation of the Valley of K., then, as Roberts reminds us, "Kahani is a displacement of 'K.,' as well as (twice-removed) of Kashmir, but it is also a fantasy version of both." Thus, the novel's end in the "sad city" that finds its name (Kahani/story) becomes yet another displaced locale where another "happy ending" can take place.

The sad city re-finds its name as "Kahani," or "story." The power of storytelling wins over the attempts to silence it. Haroun, who longs for his estranged mother and father to reunite, asks the Walrus, the Grand Comptroller of the Process Too Complicated to Explain who resides in Gup City and is in charge of the Eggheads,[4] to grant him his wish for a happy ending: "I come from a sad city, a city so sad that it has forgotten its name. I want you to provide a happy ending, not just for my adventure, but for the whole sad city as well" (*Haroun*, 202). The Walrus explains that "[happy] endings are much rarer in stories, and also in life, than most people think. You could almost say they're the exception, not the rule" (*Haroun*, 202). This statement may be Rushdie's comment on the call to provide a happy ending that may be directed at the (not always willing) author. But the Walrus has a scientific solution to the problem: "'It is precisely because happy endings are so rare ... that we ... have learnt how to synthesize them artificially. In plain language: *we can make them up*'" (202). Making up a happy end, then, is the narrative solution offered by the Walrus, or the author, if you will. Furthermore, the Walrus offers another problematic aspect of too-neat closures or endings: "Happy endings must come at the end of something.... If they happen in the middle of the story, or an adventure, or the like, all they do is cheer up things for a while" (202). Haroun's response may be Rusdie's too: "That'll do."

The provisional happy ending is the only one that can work in Rushdie's fictional world. When Rashid and Haroun return home and find their sad city transformed into a happy (story) city, Haroun is skeptical at first: "It isn't real. It's just something the Eggheads got out of a bottle. It's all fake. People should be happy when there's something to be happy about, not just when they get bottled happiness poured over them from the sky." Rashid does not share his son's skepticism: "If it is the Walrus ... then the city owes you a great vote of thanks" (208), he tells his son. The magic of storytelling, then, is still very powerful in the real world. When, however, Rushdie turns to an examination of the "real" situation in Kashmir, the optimistic worldview that characterizes *Haroun* is no longer that evident. Encountering the transformation of the beloved, Edenic Kashmir to a hellish war-zone, Rushdie's text is bleaker and seems to have lost its belief in the power of regenerative fictions. However, as I shall show in the last section of this chapter, the redemptive option still surfaces at the end of the novel in the form of an imagined future for the Kashmiri option.

Returning to Kashmir: Shalimar the Clown

In *Shalimar the Clown* Kashmir takes center stage. Rushdie tells the tale of the gradual transformation of this Eden into a nightmarish zone of civil war, slaughter and bloodshed. The novel becomes his lament for the loss of Kashmir as a locale that had once practiced peaceful coexistence between Hindis and Muslims. It can therefore be read as a dirge, bemoaning the quality that Rushdie calls "Kashmiriness, the belief that at the heart of Kashmiri culture there was a common bond that transcended all other differences" (*STC*, 110).

Thus, when he encounters the grim realities of Kashmir in *Shalimar the Clown*, Rushdie's narrator laments them with an almost uncharacteristic vehemence. The novel is indeed a lament for a lost paradise on earth, which has been transformed into a bloody and murderous zone or, to borrow the language of Rushdie's fairy-tale, a "Koshmar" or nightmare. Is the Kashmiri option, then, finally vanquished by the bloody realities of civil war? Does Rushdie abandon his belief in the potentially healing power of redemptive spaces when facing the loss of this ultimate dream of transcendence? In her review of the novel, entitled "Salman Rushdie Loses His Cheerfulness," Annabella Pitkin claims that Rushdie's novel — though still possessing the "sprawling scale, the cinematic aspects ... and the fabulistic characters that readers have come to expect from Rushdie" (Pitkin, 257) — soon changes: "The writing begins to feel ... like a reportage, like bulletins from the front" (257). Pitkin contends that this is "exactly what Rushdie intended" (257). She concludes her mixed review of the novel by claiming that it offers "no solution or specific form of hope." The novel does not promise a "redemptive ending," according to Pitkin: "Despite the clown of the title, one is left with the sense that in writing this novel ... Rushdie is no longer laughing" (262).

In what follows, I attempt to address these questions and assess whether Rushdie is indeed "not laughing" as he faces the Kashmiri tale. I claim that Rushdie's vision, although much bleaker in this novel, nevertheless still retains the belief in the power of dreams and remains committed to the idea of redemptive textuality. I shall show how Rushdie creates a different option of "Kashmiriness" in the figure of India/Kashmira, another bastard/hybrid child, who offers a different vision of transcendence. I claim that Rushdie still remains committed to the idea of dreams (even if they turn out to be "koshmars" at times) and still maintains his belief in the possibility of "happy endings" even if they only "cheer up things for a while" (*Haroun*, 202).

Shalimar the Clown tells the story of the European-born, Jewish-American ambassador to Kashmir, Maximilian Ophuls. Ophuls had a glorious past as a fighter in the Resistance but later becomes a secret negotiator for shady American interests around the globe. In Kashmir, he meets Boonyi, a beautiful Kashmiri dancer, whom he seduces, corrupts, impregnates and finally abandons. His daughter, India, born out of this illicit affair, is taken from her mother by Ophuls' wife and is raised in America. Boonyi's husband, Shalimar, embittered by the loss of his wife, becomes involved in guerrilla conflict. Having trained in Afghanistan using weapons that Ophuls has himself provided when the U.S. was covertly arming Islamic terrorists after the Russian invasion in 1979, Shalimar becomes an assassin in Europe and the U.S. He finally takes his revenge on Ophuls: He becomes Ophuls' driver, and manages to get close enough to slay him, using Ophuls' own kitchen knife, on the doorstep of his daughter's apartment building.

In his reading of the novel, Andrew Teverson states, "[As] is the case in all Rushdie's fictions, the political conflicts with which he is primarily concerned are played out micro-cosmically in the lives of his central characters" (Teverson, 2). Rushdie again shows how personal stories both mirror and are mirrored by national and political ones. In some sense, then, Boonyi becomes a stand-in for Kashmir: she is seduced and abandoned by America. As Teverson points out: "America's power seduces, its affections imprison, its commodities corrupt, and it abandons once it has taken what it wants" (2). In a similar vein, Shalimar represents the brutal resistance to American global influence that takes the form of fanatic Islamic

5. Haroun *and* Shalimar

doctrine and murderous practice. Shalimar, however, is another stand-in for Kashmir. As Ophuls' daughter, India, comments when she first sees him: "A driver from paradise. His hair was a mountain spring. There were narcissi from the banks of rushing rivers and peonies from the high meadows growing on his chest, poking out through his open collar" (*STC*, 11). Shalimar, like Boonyi, becomes Kashmir: India sees him as the living embodiment of this earthly paradise. It is his *body* that becomes the trope for the land's beauty but also signals the site of ruin and future disaster. The next time India sees Shalimar, her vision is transformed: "Flowers grew out of the concrete sidewalk at his feet and his hands and clothes were red with blood" (*STC*, 23). This vision, then, is both a foreshadowing of Ophuls' death at the hands of his driver but also a marking of the Kashmiri body/landscape with blood.

This bleak vision of Kashmir as a former Paradise on earth now covered in blood informs Rushdie's novel. In the words of his character, Max Ophuls, lamenting Kashmir's fate in a television interview shortly before his assassination: "In Kashmir, it is paradise itself that is falling; heaven on earth is being transformed into a living hell" (*STC*, 28). This vision of a living hell makes this novel one of Rushdie's bleakest, most pessimistic novels. Although there are still many instances of Rushdie's sense of humor and delight in the more bizarre aspects of human existence, his optimistic spirit is less in evidence.

The novel does feature the science-fictional or fantastic elements that characterize Rushdie's writing. To name but a few: there is a character who can hear colors; the leader of the warrior troop that Shalimar joins is the "Iron mullah," who is literally made of iron; and India Ophuls, Max's daughter, possesses visionary and telepathic powers. In the description of the fierce "Iron mullah," Rushdie hints at the supernatural powers of the fanatic leader:

> The Iron mullah Maulana Bulbul Fakh was their appointed superior. He still spoke in the old, harsh way as if human speech were painful to him. Was it possible that he had grown bigger and more attractive over the years? As for his being made of iron, there could no longer be any argument about that. There were places on his shins and shoulders where the knocks of a hard life had rubbed away the covering of skin and the dull metal beneath had become visible, battle hardened, indestructible [*STC*, 264].

This description, however, can be read metaphorically rather than literally. Rushdie plays with the idea of a comic-like "Iron Man," but he does so more as a metaphoric device, suggesting the man's ultimate "hardness" and lack of flexibility, than as a more direct science fictional device as in his other novels. Similarly, India/Kashmira's visions are employed more as a way of enhancing the metaphorical dimension of Kashmir in the text, as when she first sees Shalimar and envisions Kashmir etched on his body. India's "strangeness of seeing," her "otherness of vision" (*STC*, 6), is invoked as a way of explaining her complex and disturbed personality, the effect of a troubled childhood. Therefore, as in the "Iron mullah" example, here too, the science fictional element is less prominent.

It seems, then, that in *Shalimar the Clown*, the pressures of reality prove too much for characters and author alike. The magical quality of Kashmir can no longer withstand the brutal realities of the civil war that tears it apart. This becomes most painfully clear when Rushdie expresses his outrage at the systematic slaughter carried out in Pachigam by both Islamic insurgents and the Indian army. This expression of helpless and hopeless rage reaches its climax on two occasions in the novel. On both occasions, all the narrator can do is repeat two related questions: "why?" and "who?"

The first instance occurs after a week-long orgy of violence against Kashmiri Hindus during which the Indian army stood by:

> There were six hundred Indian troops in Kashmir but the pogrom of the pandits was not prevented, why was that? Three and a half lakhs of human beings arrived in Jammu as displaced persons and for many months the government did not provide shelters of relief or even register their names, why was that? When the government finally built camps it only allowed for six thousand families to remain in the state, dispersing other around the country where they would be invisible and impotent, why was that? ... There was one bathroom per three hundred persons in many camps why was that ... and the pandits of Kashmir were left to rot in their slum camps, to rot while the army and the insurgency fought over the bloodied and broken valley, to dream of return, to die while dreaming in return, to die after the dream of return died so that they could not even die dreaming of it, why was that why was that why was that why was that why was that [296–7].

The second occasion occurs after the Indian army takes revenge on the village of Pachigam for managing to hold out against them for so long. Rushdie's narrator asks the unanswerable question: "Who killed the children? Who whipped the parents? Who raped that gray-haired lazy-eyed woman...? Who raped that woman again? Who raped that woman again?

Who raped that woman again? Who raped that dead woman? Who raped that dead woman again?" (308). This rhetorical device is more than just a way of highlighting the desperate nature of Kashmiri reality. As Teverson points out, "the very act of posing the question, of bearing witness to atrocity, constitutes a potent political gesture: a demand for attention and a demand for redress" (5). In Rushdie's fiction, he constructs imaginary locales that may end up as the only way of offering hope in what seems to be an unsolvable political situation, like that in Kashmir. This is also the case in a novel that seems to offer the most hopeless Rushdean vision to date.

In his assessment of the novel's message, Teverson claims, "Rushdie sees nothing that allows for hope in contemporary Kashmir" (3). Teverson contends that in *Midnight's Children*, a novel that also shares the bleak and bitter subject matter of *Shalimar the Clown*, "there was an *outside* to the fictional world into which a more utopian hopefulness could be projected, even if it was never shown" (3). This is not the case in *Shalimar*: "In *Shalimar*, there is no hope for the continuity of the idea of Kashmir outside the fiction. Kashmiriness is annihilated without redemption" (3). The novel laments the idea of Kashmiriness, but Rushdie does offer us hope in constructing another *version* of Kashmiriness *within* the fictional space of the novel. The "utopian hopefulness" that Teverson seeks *outside* the fictional text is to be found *within* Rushdie's fictional and potentially redemptive spaces.

It is, however, in the spirit of provisional "happy endings" that Rushdie offers us even in the midst of one of his more optimistic texts, *Haroun*, that I want to read *Shalimar*'s ambiguous ending and show how Rushdie still manages to offer us a chance of a "happy ending," depending, as in *Haroun*, on the magical power of naming and renaming to influence reality.

In *Shalimar*, it is again the act of renaming and reinvention of self as place and place as self that may offer a redemptive potential. India Ophuls, Max Ophuls' and Boonyi Noman's daughter, re-invents herself as Kahmira Noman. After finding out from her stepmother, Max's ex-wife, who had taken her from her birth mother, that her given name is Kashmira, she decides to adopt the name as well as its implications. She returns home to Kashmir in order to recover her mother's fate. It is in Kashmir that she finds out that Shalimar is responsible not only for her father's death but is also her mother's murderer. Kashmira returns to America and begins to hone herself for the final encounter with her parents' killer. After Shalimar is caught and arrested in America, Kashmira comments: "Kashmir lingered in her.... She no longer saw this as an American story. It was a Kashmiri story. It was hers" (*STC*, 372).

Kashmira devotes herself to this Kashmiri story: She sends Shalimar letters in which she defines her intentions: "Now you are my target and I am your marksman however my arrows are not dipped in love but hatred" (274). In this inverse Cupid image, Kashmira becomes an avenging goddess. This Kashmiri story, it seems, is one in which love has no place. Kashmira now inhabits a "combat zone": "She no longer lived in America. She lived in a combat zone" (382).

In her final encounter with Shalimar, after he has managed a daring, almost magical prison-break, Kashmira literally becomes the embodiment of an avenging goddess. Armed with bow and arrow, she faces her assailant:

> She was ready for him. She was not fire but ice. The golden bow was drawn back as far as it could go. She felt the taut bowstring pressing against her gritted teeth, allowed the last seconds to tick away, exhaled and let fly. There was no possibility that she would miss. There was no second chance. There was no India. There was only Kashmira, and Shalimar the clown [398].

This annihilation of Shalimar as an embodiment of the bloody Kashmiri option ends the novel. Its final words pit "Kashmira" against "Shalimar the clown" as two warring entities. We are meant to understand that Kashmira will not miss her mark.

Even if she does, we are also informed of police sirens in the background and can assume Shalimar's final moment has arrived. Is this vengeful ending, then, what Rushdie leaves us with? Even though Shalimar does embody Kashmir as a bloody option, it would still seem a rather bleak ending. Is the new Kashmir embodied in Kashmira as another bloody avenger?

Rushdie provides us with another Kashmir, however, in the form of Kashmira's lover, Yuvraj. On her trip to Kashmir, Kashmira meets and falls in love with Yuvraj, a Kashmiri merchant who buys and sells Kashmiri handicrafts. Yuvraj, whose name literally means "prince," waxes poetic as he describes his work to Kashmira: "'So many artists together make every piece, the final work is not one man's alone, it is the product of our whole culture, it is not only made in but in fact made by Kashmir" (359). Yuvraj,[5] who still lives in a magical garden that he describes as a "heaven inside a heaven" (361), now laments the loss of the Kashmir outside the garden: "But now Kashmir is no longer heavenly" (361). Yuvraj's magical garden, however, may still replace the bloodied Shalimar Gardens that India/Kashmira envisions on Shalimar's body and that represent Kashmir as a former garden, now covered in blood. Yuvraj represents the dream of maintaining this possible heaven on earth, even in the aftermath of ruin and destruction. He embodies another kind of "Kashmiriness" that may still prevail. His love for Kashmira and the possible union between them may project a happier future for the next generation, even if the old Kashmir will never be a heaven on earth again.

Finally, then, it is in the next generation that we may find hope for a different future.[6] As in *Midnight's Children,* the next generation projects a different future vision. Whether it will be a happy ending or another "koshmar" remains to be seen. In the figure of Kashmira, the daughter of a Jewish father and a Kashmiri mother, we may find a path for a different, less nightmarish, future and a re-instatement of Kashmir as Paradise on earth. India Ophuls, who chooses to rename herself Kashmira in memory of her dead mother whom she had never met, may still provide a more optimistic ending. Although the novel ends with India/Kashmira poised to kill her father's assassin, the eponymous Shalimar the Clown, there is another possible "happy ending" in which Kashmira may be united with Yurjav, the Kashmiri "prince," who still believes in the Edenic qualities of his homeland.

As in *Haroun* and other novels, Rushdie chooses to leave the readers and the characters in a space of potential and possibility rather than offer a clear and unambiguous ending. The hope inherent in future generation can become a bitter joke — such as when Saleem Sinai's son appears again in *The Moor's Last Sigh* as a not very flattering embodiment of the new Mammon-led India — but there are instances, as in *Shalimar,* where there may still be a hope for a better future, coming as it does from the hybrid daughter of East and West.

Rushdie does not offer a direct *political* solution to the national and personal dilemmas of his characters. What he does offer in his fictional, unresolved endings is a different kind of solution within the fictional space. In the world outside the fiction, war rages, but the fictional space still remains open to the possibility of change and reinvention. There we may find the "happy endings" that "cheer up things for a while." This "happy ending," sought after by the writer and readers alike, again appears in what may be termed the sequel to *Haroun*. This time, it is Rushdie's younger son, Milan, who is given a book by his father. Rushdie revisits the idea of the textual as a potentially life saving force in even clearer terms. In *Luka and the Fire of Life*, examined in the next chapter, Luka embarks on a quest to save his dying father. The novel ends in a scene of happy domesticity, but death is ever present as the novel imagines and dismisses the idea of (techno-)immortality.

6

Immortality Now:
Luka and the Fire of Life

> *Luka had just been wondering how it would be if he, his brother, his mother and father could all live for ever. The idea struck him as more frightening than exciting.*
>
> *Our dreams are the real truths — our fancies, the knowledge of our hearts. We know that Time is a River, not a clock, and that it can flow the wrong way, so that the world becomes more backward instead of less, and that it can jump sideways, so that everything changes in an instant.*
> — Luka and the Fire of Life
>
> *Why art thou silent & invisible*
> *Father of jealousy*
> *Why dost thou hide thyself in clouds*
> *From every searching Eye* — William Blake, *To Old Nobodady*

Rushdie's latest novel (2010) is about time, death, immortality and the power of storytelling to ward off death. These are familiar Rushdean themes, made ever more poignant by the no-longer-young writer's grasp of time as that river that "flows the wrong way," as it did when the *fatwa* of 1989 turned his world upside down. His oeuvre has since been occupied with notions of time and its twists and turns, its loopy spirals and unexpected endings. It is in this later novel, however, I would suggest that, as in its prequel *Haroun and the Sea of Stories,* Rushdie addresses the most urgent concerns in his fiction. I claim that Rushdie employs the computer game form not merely as a playful narrative device or, as some of the reviewers of the novel claim, as a cheap appeal to his teenage audience. Rather, Rushdie's choice of this form as the organizing feature of the novel fits with his ongoing attempt to explore storytelling as a life saving force.

In recent years, computer games are increasingly at the center of groundbreaking work on narratology as it is reconfigured in the space of the game and its online "reality." One may say then, with Steph Aupers, that the "fast-growing genre of computer games on the Internet called *Massively Multiplayer Online Role-Playing Games* (MMORPGs) ... largely based on the fantasy genre ... have evolved into full-fledged virtual worlds that defy the definition of fiction" (Aupers, 250). These games, which are "like real life, only better" (251), then, offer "imagined histories" (262) and magical worlds that defy what Aupers calls "ontological fundamentalism" (267) and offer in its stead "ontological pragmatism": "Not hindered by cognitive evaluations about 'what is real' and 'what is fake,' people increasingly choose realities that are experienced as real, meaningful and enchanting" (267), and thus this "contemporary era of hyperreality instigates a re-enchantment of the world" (268) rather than, as Max Weber and later Baudrillard would have it, a "disenchantment of the world" brought on by scientific and technological progress. This radical reevaluation of the ontological realm of the computer game as a reality generating mode and as a vehicle for "re-enchanting" the world is an apt description of the fictional project Rushdie began in charting the fantasy world of *Haroun*. This imagined world becomes the computer game world of *Luka*, thus providing Rushdie with a vehicle for re-enchanting the world by offering alternative versions of multiple worlds. Rushdie borrows the thematics and form of the computer game and ingeniously employs its narratological options to explore the main concerns of his work to date.

This later text grapples with the notion of mortality and storytelling in different ways than *Haroun* did. Whereas *Haroun* addressed the silencing impetus of the *fatwa*, *Luka* grapples with the twin roles of Death and Time as the defining contours of the storytelling animal, man, in his attempt to ward off death or perhaps to come to terms with mortality. Thus, in what can be read as the novel's motto, the character who embodies Rashid Khalifa's "Death" (and as such is Rashid/Rushdie's doppelganger) ruminates on the power of storytelling as the defining feature of man's humanity: "Man is the Story Telling Animal ... in his stories are his identity, his meaning and his lifeblood. Do rats tell tales? Do elephants elephantasize? You know as well as I do that they do not. Man alone burns with books" (Luka, 34).

These are the words of Nobodady, Rashid Khalifa's transparent double, delivered to Rashid's son, Luka, about to embark on a quest to save his real father from the "Big Sleep" he had mysteriously fallen into. Borrowing William Blake's neologism, Rushdie here gestures at the great Father figure in the sky, the figure of a cruel and invisible god who is associated with death rather than with life and the pursuit of knowledge. "Why darkness & obscurity / In all thy words & laws / That none dare eat the fruit but from / the wily serpent's jaw" are lines from William Blake's "To Nobodady," which resonate throughout Rushdie's novel. This deathly figure is, as Thomas Wharton puts it in his review of the novel, "the spectre of his (Luka's) father's death" ("A Return to the Land of Haroun"). As Wharton rightly points out:

> [Like] its predecessor, *Haroun*, Luka's story rushes along at breakneck pace from one wonder to the next, fuelled by the anti-gravitational magic of Rushdie's story-spinning and wordplay. The narrative catapults with dream-like illogic through numerous story-worlds — there are riddling demons, goddesses from plethora of pantheons and various Alice in Wonderland-style creatures, such as the prissy Elephant Birds ["A Return to the Land of Haroun"].

However, Wharton finds fault with what he and other critics have regarded as the novel's failing:

> But this isn't Haroun's adventure, this is the world of Magic 2.0, where the logic of video games holds sway. Luka must collect enough lives to survive the increasingly dangerous "levels" on the way to the Fire of Life. An obvious effort to appeal to kids' changed tastes, this is the one element of the story that doesn't quite fly. Luka spends a lot of time checking his life-count, wondering if he's collected enough to get through and, accordingly, the perils he encounters feel less urgent ["A Return to the Land of Haroun"].

In my reading of the novel, I contend that since this *is* a text about (im)mortality, it is this very ingenious use of the trope of the computer game as a venue offering techno-immortality that gives the novel its most persuasive edge. Rushdie uses the form of the computer game to enhance his grappling with the issue of storytelling as a potentially life saving force. As Wharton points out, "the World of Magic, as chaotic as it seems, is really the world of Rashid's tales, and this is Luka's edge when confronted with seemingly impossible odds. He already knows these stories and understands the rules they obey." What Wharton sees as the "lingering question raised by this recurring *deus ex poppa*" of "whether Luka truly grows beyond his father's own authority as storyteller" is an interesting one. I would suggest, however, that the impetus of the tale is the very idea that stories can and do save lives. It is Luka, the boy, who is endowed with the power to save the doomed father figure. As in other Rushdie texts, like

Fury, the father-son bond is seen as life enhancing, though not without its perils and tribulations. The son can be a "life saver," but he is also the figure that signifies the father's own fear of mortality. Luka does not fail to grow and mature. He finds his own powers throughout the game and is the one who figures out the solution to its many riddles. The point is then not Luka's failure but rather Rashid's realization that he is no longer the sole master of his own tales, a theme that Rushdie began exploring in *Haroun*.

Encapsulating Rushdie's belief in the vital role of storytelling in the world, conjuring up the image of fire and burning (books), reminding us that *Luka and the Fire of Life* is the sequel to *Haroun and the Sea of Stories* written in the aftermath of the *fatwa* when Rushdie's books were burned by angry Muslim mobs— the striking short passage that tells us that "[m]an burns with books"— alerts us to the ways in which Rushdie's latest work is in dialogue with his former texts and to how it comments on both his own status as the Shah of Blah, the ever talkative storyteller, and the role of fiction as a life saving force, one that would even contest death. If man "burns with books" rather than burns books, then, Rashid/Rushdie claims, he may still remain human.

However, in a text where elephants do play a major speaking role, as do rats, there may be more to this quip than is first apparent. In keeping with Rushdie's world making, this novel offers a mirror image of the real world, where talking animals are the norm and where the protagonist fights a battle as old as Prometheus': stealing the "Fire of Life" to ward off his father's impending death. As noted above, the novel employs the form of a computer game: Luka has to "save" his progress to advance to the next level of the game; he can collect lives and loses lives, and the ultimate prize is a return to the real world where his father awakes from his "Big Sleep" and returns to life. This narrative device allows Rushdie to address the grand notions of time, space, death and life, or even the meaning of life, in what would seem to be a playful, at times ominous but never really threatening, tale for children.[1]

I would claim, however, that the novel employs this device to query some of the most pressing and urgent issues in Rushdie's life as a no longer young man, his relationship with his readers, his reevaluation of his role as a writer of fiction and ultimately his ongoing engagement with death threats and the possibility of impending death, which have been at the center of his oeuvre since the infamous *fatwa*. It is interesting to note here that Rushdie himself relates to the novel as a text dealing with immortality and fatherhood. In an NPR interview, Rushdie comments on the life and death issues at the heart of his "fun" book for children: "I think the book is kind of fun, but the serious thing at the heart is this question of life and death. You know, the existential question, will you live to see your child grow up? And when Rashid falls into this coma-like sleep, it becomes the child's duty to try and save his life" (Evans). This serious subject matter at the heart of the "fun" tale is what gives *Luka* a more ominous edge. Although the novel has a happy ending, which seems less qualified than that of *Haroun*, the novel's darker moments still resonate. Rushdie's savage social critique, which I shall discuss later, is one instance where the playful nature of the novel, in both senses of the word, becomes, to borrow Rushdie's term, (dead) serious.

Writing Hieroglyphics: Luka *as Cybertext*

Rushdie's novel takes on the form of a computer game and employs some of the narrative elements of computer games that center on a quest: Luka is on a quest to find the "Fire of Life" that will save his father from the death-like sleep he had suddenly fallen into. The road is filled with many obstacles and foes, and it is only Luka's deep knowledge of his father's imagined "World" that finally allows him to "win" the game and rescue his father. In this mission, he is also aided by Soraya—the queen of—a nation of rude, betel-chewing and lovable "Otters"—who is, as Luka discovers, a younger version of his beloved mother. In this vein, Rushdie again conjures up his favorite film *The Wizard of Oz*, in which Dorothy encounters her real-life buddies in different forms in the magical land of Oz. The narrative remains, or so it seems, a linear one. Rushdie's use of the game format would seem, then, a way of appealing to his young readers who have grown up with this technological wizardry at their fingertips.

If we examine Rushdie's novel carefully, however, we shall see how he comments on his own (or rather Rashid's) ineptitude where computer games are concerned precisely as a way of highlighting the ways in which this new generation, embodied here by Luka, has the ability to "save" the "World"—if only by his mastery of the computer console. The novel opens, not in cyberland, but in the magical land readers know from *Haroun*, the land of Alifbay or, if you will, Rushdie's imagined India. Luka is the hero of the day as he challenges the evil ringmaster, Captain Aag, master of the GROF (Great Rings of Fire) circus. Luka is appalled at the ringmaster's cruelty to his animals and curses him: "May your animals stop obeying your commands and your rings of fire eat up your stupid tent" (*Luka*, 3). The curse works, and Luka finds himself with two new pets: "A dog with a tag on its collar reading 'Bear' and a bear with a tag on its collar reading 'Dog'" (5). In Rushdean mode, tags and signs may not always mean what they say or say what they mean. This frame story establishes the nature of the later quest: Luka will encounter his nemesis Captain Aag in a parallel computer game world and will vanquish him, thus restoring peace to the Khalifa household.

Thus, the main adventure or, if you will, Luka's quest, is a reflection of his adventures in the "real" world or, rather, in the imagined land of Alifbay. The tale will end where it began: in a scene of domestic bliss where mother, father, older brother (Haroun) and young brother (Luka) are happily dancing under the stars: "And we'll leave them there, the rescued father, the loving mother, the older brother, and the young boy home from his great adventure, along with the lucky dog and the his brotherly bear, up on the roof of their home on a cool night under the stationary, unchanging stars, singing and dancing" (*Luka*, 216). The characters in the novel become (or perhaps have always been) types: the "mother," "father," "son" and "brother" in a nigh–Dickensian moment of bliss.

The opening also establishes Luka's knowledge of computer games:

> Fortunately for Luka, he lived in an age in which an almost infinite number of parallel realities had begun to be sold as toys. Like everyone he knew, he had grown up destroying fleets of invading rocket ships, and been a little plumber on a journey through many bouncing, burning, twisting, bubbling levels to rescue a prissy princess ... and metamorphosed into a zooming hedgehog and a street fighter and a rock star [*Luka*, 11].

The phrase "like everyone he knew," which is repeated three times within the space of three paragraphs, establishes Luka as a product of his time:

> Like everyone he knew, Luka possessed a wide-assortment of pocket-sized alternate-reality boxes, and spent much of his spare time leaving his own world to enter the rich, colourful, musical, challenging universes inside these boxes, universes in which death was temporary (until you made too many mistakes and it became permanent) and a life was a thing you could win, or save up for, or just be miraculously granted because you happened to bump your head into the right brick, or eat the right mushroom, or pass

6. Immortality Now: Luka and the Fire of Life

through the right magic waterfall, and you could store as many lives as your skill and good fortune could get you [12].

This passage encapsulates the template for the later quest. Luka will "enter" a magical world where he has to store up "lives" and where his ability to store these "lives" will have "life and death" consequences in the "real" world: his skills will determine whether his father lives or dies. In that sense, the "alternate-reality" box, described here in slightly mocking yet affectionate tones, becomes a metaphor for real life, where death is, after all, inevitable, and for the game, where immortality and resurrection are both common and plausible options.

The move from "your world" to the "rich, colourful, musical, challenging" universes is what the book and the computer game do. In that sense, Rushdie's novel attempts to both describe and enact the gaming experience. Rushdie, however, is careful to insert the ironic note of the less than technologically apt parents into the novel to showcase both the fear of technology as dark magic and its enchanting possibilities:

> Once again it was his father Rashid Khalifa who encouraged Luka, and who tried, with comically little skill, to join him on his adventures. Soraya was unimpressed, and, being a commonsensical woman who distrusted technology, worried that the various magic boxes were emitting invisible beams and rays that would rot her beloved son's mind. Rashid made light of these worries, which made Soraya worry even more. "They are useless skills," Soraya retorted. "In the real world there are no levels, only difficulties. Life is tougher than video games. This is what he needs to know, and so, by the way, do you" [13].

This dialogue again stresses the affinity between the imagined worlds of video games and the imagined worlds created by Rashid Khalifa, the storyteller and maker of alternate worlds of his own. The father and son are presented as the counter-forces to the mother's "commonsensical" approach. Clearly, the readers are meant to take Rashid and Luka's side in this battle between the commonsensical and the magical. The computer game console, which Soraya says makes her "in-console-able" (114), becomes the source of "consolation" or redemption in the novel. Rashid is "useless on the Muu" (14) — Rushdie's punning name for the game console Wii. His strength lies in *words*. If we are to view this as a meta-fictional comment on *Luka*, Rushdie may be saying that his novel, albeit taking place in an imagined virtual world and attempting to replicate its rules, is still to be judged for its word power. After all, it is Rashid's magical world and its rules that are the template for the game. Without knowing them, Luka would never have been able to pass any of the game's nine levels.

What are we to make, then, of Rushdie's choice of the game console device? And how does this choice influence our reading of the narrative? If we take Stuart Moulthrop's account of the gamer's "misadventure" while playing an unfamiliar game as a creative process, we may use this process, akin to the process of reading a text that attempts to convey the game experience, as such a creative venture into what could be a new form of engagement with an otherwise seemingly conventional work of fiction. Moulthrop suggests the affinities between literature and computer/quest games: "Like print products, computer games address a range of audiences, so their quality and sophistication may be expected to vary. Like literary texts, games also have meaningful affiliations and genealogies" ("Misadventure: Future Fiction and the New Networks"). The similarities between the book and the computer game as forms of literature are also in the realm of response to the text. In his influential work on cybertexts, Espen Aarseth locates the differences between player or user and reader:

> The concept of cybertext focuses on the mechanical organization of the text, by positing the intricacies of the medium as an integral part of the literary exchange. However, it also centers attention on the consumer, or user of the text, as a more integrated figure than even reader-response theorists would claim. The performance of the reader takes place all in his head, while the user of cybertext also performs in an extranoematic sense. During the cybertextual process, the user will have effectuated a semiotic sequence, and this selective movement is a work of physical construction that the various concepts of 'reading' do not account for [Aarseth, 1].

Aarseth claims there is a crucial difference between the experience of reading a text and the engagement with cybertexts, whether computer games or texts like the Chinese *I Ching*, which "is not meant to be read from beginning to end but entails a very different and highly specialized ritual of perusal," or "the text in a multi-user dungeon [which] is without either beginning or end, an endless labyrinthine plateau of textual bliss for the community that builds it" (Aarseth, 2). Thus "[a] reader, however strongly engaged in the unfolding of a narrative is powerless. Like a spectator in a soccer game, he may speculate, conjecture, extrapolate, even shout abuse, but he is not a player. The reader's pleasure is the pleasure of the

6. Immortality Now: Luka and the Fire of Life

voyeur. Safe, but impotent" (4). In stark contrast to what he conceives as passive enjoyment, Aarseth posits the "cybertext reader" who

> is not safe, and therefore, it can be argued, she is not a reader. The cybertext puts its would-be reader at risk: the risk of rejection. The effort and energy demanded by the cybertext of its reader raise the stakes of interpretation to those of intervention. Trying to know a cybertext is an investment of personal improvisation that can result in either intimacy or failure. The tensions at work in a cybertext, while not incompatible with those of narrative desire, are also something more: a struggle not merely for interpretative insight but also for narrative control: "I want this text to tell my story; the story that could not be without me." In some cases, this is literally true. In other cases, perhaps most, the sense of individual outcome is illusory, but nevertheless the aspect of coercion and manipulation is real [4].

In this sense, then, *Luka and the Fire of Life* does not fulfill the required interaction that the word *cybertext* entails. It does not offer the readers an active role in the construction of Luka's story. The novel progresses in linear fashion from the crisis at the beginning to the happy ending on the rooftop. Rushdie could have used what Aarseth calls "manipulation" and "coercion." He chooses not to do so. Instead, he manipulates the narrative trajectory of the quest, common to adventure (or, if we follow Moulthrop's lead, misadventure) games, to create a text that enacts "narrative desire" in a broader sense. Moulthrop, unlike Aarseth, leaves room for a space between the active player and the passive reader in the figure of the "misadventurer" who stumbles into the game's world without knowing exactly how to traverse it. Moulthrop describes his experience with two quest games, Myst and Riven and his use of a "Hints and Solutions" book in order to traverse them.

> After many hours of dilatory play in which I solved occasional puzzles only in order to reach unseen portions of the world, I finally succumbed to temporal economy and took the book tour. Life is linear and short, but computer art, alas, tends to be fractal ["Misadventure"].

I suggest applying this model to a reading of *Luka*: Only by "taking the book tour," or by knowing the Rushdean universe, can we benefit from the ultimate experience the book offers. Rushdie makes this clear by indicating that the "book" to be followed is the World of Magic, created by Rashid Khalifa. This orally transmitted text, told to his son Luka, is also the "World" readers of *Haroun* know well. *Luka* is then a game for the dedicated Rushdie reader. Following Luka on his quest to save the "author" of the book we're reading takes on more ominous dimensions when we consider Rushdie's life in the shadow of the (never lifted) *fatwa* as being continually fraught with very real danger.

Over the Top: Rushdie's Attack on Political Correctness

I therefore turn to the novel's recasting of familiar Rushdean themes in a new narrative form. I shall examine some of the key scenes in the novel to establish how Rushdie revisits the concerns of his earlier novels. My focus will be on the twin themes of storytelling and immortality. However, I believe that a discussion of the novel should address some of its political and ideological aspects. As in *Haroun*, Rushdie offers a scathing critique of society. However, whereas *Haroun* imagined the nations of Gup and Chup as rivaling options of speech and silence, *Luka*'s imagined worlds offer us a different social critique. Rushdie seems to be getting back at the British nation, which offered him protection from the *fatwa* yet turned against him at his time of need. The two "nations" described in *Luka*, the Rats and the Otters, represent two opposing worldviews and behavioral codes. Whereas the Rats are obsessed with the notion of "respect" and "borders," the Otters are very disrespectful, delightfully irreverent and insulting. Their queen Soraya is thus named the "Insultana of Ott." Ott stands for Over the Top and that is the Otters' defining quality. The Otters chew betel and throw rotten eggs at their Rat opponents. It would not be too far-fetched to assume, as I shall show, that the Rats represent a dour and "respectable" nation, which takes offence very easily and takes great pains to avoid being offended and disrespected. Their grey uniformity and the description of their land reads at times like a very bitter representation of the unbecoming aspects of "Englishness." The Otters, on the other hand, led by the stand-in for Luka's mother (or at least her younger and irreverent version), represent the betel-chewing, insulting and yet compelling Indians, who delight in a good insult and care nothing for political correctness.

This is established in the frame story in which Luka's arch enemy, Adi Ratshit, is described as a part of the Imperial Army, whereas Luka belongs to the Intergalactic Penguins: "Luka's greatest adventure to date had taken place during the Great Playground Wars at school, in which he

6. *Immortality Now:* Luka and the Fire of Life

had led his gang, the Intergalactic Penguins Team, to a famous victory over the Imperial Highness Army led by his hated rival, Adi Ratshit, aka Red Bottom, winning the day with a daring aerial attack involving paper planes loaded with itching powder" (*Luka*, 6). This victory is re-enacted in the game world as Luka manages to vanquish the Rats using the very same method. The rivalry between the "Imperial Highness" and the "Penguins" hints at the opponents' ethnicity without stating it explicitly. We can see, however, that Luka and his Penguins (not quite white) are also "Intergalactic" (or not of one nation) whereas Ratshit belongs to the Imperial Highness Army, implicitly allied with the notion of empire.

In the game world, the allegorical underpinnings become clearer and more disturbing. Luka and his friends find that the Rats' territory, a part of the World of Magic, does not seem very magical. In fact, the description of the border station with its barbed wire and guards reflects the perils inherent in border crossings. The arrival at a "strange, sad land," barred by a "scary-looking border post, with its floodlights on high pylons and its tall reconnaissance towers containing lookout guards wearing mirrored sunglasses and carrying powerful military binoculars and automatic weapons" (*Luka*, 69), stresses the role of surveillance and force in policing borders. As in *Haroun*, where road signs are ways of both deciphering and obscuring meaning, here too we have a revealing sign (of the times). The sign reads: "YOU ARE AT THE FRONTIER OF THE RESPECTORATE OF I. MIND YOUR MANNERS" (69). The twin notions of "manners" and "respect" (Respect-orate) are the defining features of the Rats who rule this land. As Nobodady comments: "I'm sorry to say that the World of Magic is not immune to Infestations. And this part of it has been overrun, in recent times, by Rats" (69). Nobodady further explains the nature of the land to the bewildered and alarmed Luka: "This barbed-wire contraption, the O-Fence goes all around the Respectorate of I — it gives the place, you could say, its I-dentity — and as the sign warns you, many of its present occupants take Offence very sharply indeed" (70).

Clearly, Rushdie is allegorizing. But what is the allegory about? Readings vary. Christopher Rollason, who takes offence at what he sees as the novel's "obsessive intertexuality" claims that "[the] Rats and their Respectorate rather too obviously allegorize the political mindset of Rushdie's detractors over *The Satanic Verses* — in this case, not so much his Islamic opponents as the postmodernist anti–Rushdie faction on the Western left, the proponents of cultural relativism, identity politics and 'respect for religion'" ("An Unsurprising World of Magic"). The allegory may not have been as obvious as Rollason contends. Antonia Peacocke comments on the allegorical significance of the novel: "Luka encounters a dystopian society run by easily offended rats who demand an unsupportable degree of tact and respect from all those who enter. The "Respectorate of I" — ostensibly a stand-in for Iran — is a colorless prison of a nation" ("Rushdie Rekindles Old Myths"). Iran? Not quite.

As in every successful allegory, Rushdie's "Respectorate of I" can be read in different, though not mutually exclusive, ways. Although I believe that the "I" (as we are clearly told) does not stand for "Iran" but for "Identity" and "identity politics," as Rollason points out, this is not the whole story. Rushdie's ingenuity provides us with the counter-option — the Otters. If we examine the description of the Rats and Otters doing battle, to the detriment of the Rats, we may find that the allegorical significance may be a bit less obvious than Rollason would have us believe.

I would rather borrow Alex Clark's formulation in his review of the novel: "*Luka and the Fire of Life* zings along with a palpable sense of Otter-like excess: its exuberance is inextricably linked to its profligacy with puns, rhymes, one-liners and snippets of nonsense." The Otters are presented as irreverent creatures who, much like their creator, balk at the notion of censorship and political correctness. In a BBC interview, Rushdie comments on this episode:

> I think we live in a very timid age and a part of our timidity arises from our unwillingness to offend people. And, as a result, there are whole tribes of people now who define themselves by their offendedness. You know, I mean, who are you if you are not offended by anything? Nobody, or even worse, you are a liberal. And I just think that this whole business of defining yourself by anger is very problematic and the idea that we all sort of bend over backwards not to induce that anger also becomes a problem and a kind of cowardice, if you like [Buchan-Terrell].

In the first encounter between Luka and his friends and the Border Rats, this insistence on political correctness is presented as a blend of the comic and the menacing. The Border Rat demands "papers" and ends up confiscating Luka's pockets. Luka is forced to hand over his swap cards, paper airplanes and "orange sweets in their transparent wrapping" (71) in the manner of an unruly school boy at the mercy of a stern teacher. The Border Rat warns Luka: "Here in the Respectorate we expect visitors to behave. We're very thin-skinned. If you prick us, we bleed, and then we make you bleed double: it that clear?" (71). This speech echoes Rushdie's sarcastic dismissal of people who define themselves by their "offendeness." It also alludes, of course, to Shylock's famous speech in Shakespeare's *The Merchant of Venice*, making the Rats very vindictive Shylocks.

The scene's most comic stab at political correctness, however, centers on gender issues. The guard asks: "'Are any of you female? That dog, is she a bitch? That bear, is she a ... bearess? A bearina? A bearette?' 'Bearina indeed,' said Dog the bear. 'Now I'm the one that's offended.' 'And I,' said Bear the dog. 'Not that I have anything against bitches'" (71). Rushdie is playing the scene for all its comic potential here. The issue of defining and naming, deconstructed at the very beginning of the tale (the dog is named Bear and the bear is named Dog), is here given another twist. People (or rather Rats) who are so insistent on naming are both ludicrous and dangerous in the Rushdean universe. The repeated use of the word "bitch" signals how a word might be termed offensive even if it is not meant as such. The Border Rat's insistence on policing becomes absurd as he invents feminine endings to the word "Bear," culminating in the absurd "bearette." The notion of policing and controlling the boundaries of language also comes into play in the exchange between Nobodady and the guard. Nobodady promises the Border Rat, "We will most definitely mind our p's and q's, Sir." The Rat answers: "What about the other twenty-four letters of the alphabet? You can do a lot of damage with those, and never use a q or a p" (71). Doing damage with language, instead of treating it as sacred, is what the Rushdean credo is all about, after all.

The Rats are led by the self-appointed Over-Rat, who, as Luka finds out, bears an uncanny resemblance to his arch enemy, Ratshit. The Otters are also led by a youngster: a green-eyed girl with fiery red hair, riding a "famous flying carpet, *Resham*, which is to say, the Green Silk Flying Rug of King Solomon" (77), or "Salman"; this is, after all, Rashid Khalifa's World of Magic. And Salman Rushdie is also "Solomon," at least in translation. The Otters save Luka and his friends from the Rat attack, after Luka challenges the Rats' insistence that "two and two make five" and that "the world is flat" (75). Again, it is Nobodady, Rashid and Rushdie's stand-in, who explains the nature of Otter land:

> Over in that direction, Over the Top of these mountains, is the unusual land of Oh-Tee-Tee, a land ringed by bright waters, whose denizens, the Otters, are devoted to all forms of excess. They talk too much, eat too much, drink too much, sleep too much, swim too much, chew too much betel nut,

and they are without question the rudest creatures in the world. But it's an equal-opportunity impoliteness; the Otters lay into one another without discrimination, and as a result they have all grown so thick-skinned that nobody minds what anybody else says [77].

This land, unlike the "sad, strange" Respectorate, is "a funny place, everyone laughs all the time while they call one another the worst things in the world" (77). This is the reverse mirror image of the Respectorate. But although Rushdie seems to suggest here that the Otters may also be flawed, in much the same way as was the otherwise loveable nation of Chup in *Haroun*, it is clear where his sympathies lie. The Over the Top Otters, as I have claimed, are a stand-in for Rushdean linguistic exuberance and excess. They are also seen as possessing some "ethnic" markers; they chew betel nut, they use vegetables as weapons, and their queen is named the Sultana and appears astride a magic carpet that seems to have wandered in straight out of Arabian Nights.

These Eastern markers are posited in contrast to what seems to be the Western markers of the Respectorate. The dominant color in the Respectorate is grey: "the houses, the curtains at the windows, the clothing worn by Rats and people alike (yes, there were people there, Luka was relieved to see), all grey. The Rats were gray too and the people had acquired a grayish pallor. Overhead, grey clouds allowed a neutral sunlight to filter through" (72). Nobodady explains the reason: "They developed a Colour Problem here a little while ago. The Rats who hated the colour yellow because of its, well, cheesiness were confronted by the Rats who disliked the colour red because of its similarity to blood. In the end, all colours, being offensive to someone or other, were banned by the Rathouse" (72). The Otters, on the other hand, are very colorful. Their intrusion into this grey scene takes the form of "red rain" (78), consisting mostly of betel juice. In that sense, the "color problem" can be read as Rushdie's tongue-in-cheek comment on the nature of the immigrant "problem." The colorful Otters are an emblem of this rude Eastern affront on grey, Western respectability. The Otters are a loud and rude reminder of the Otherness of the "colored" people. Their disrespect, then, can be seen as a marker of rebellion against implicitly Western codes of proper behavior.

Luka is attacked by both camps. However, he clearly belongs to the Otter camp. Recognizing that the Insultana's voice is in fact his mother's leads him to this moment of revelation. Nobodady tells Luka: "What a sharp little tongue! You'd make a good Otter" (83). And indeed, it takes a measure of "chutzpa" of the Otter kind to be able to win the quest. Rushdie positions Luka, the left-handed boy, on the side of the Otters: not angelic but rather quick tongued and fiery, much like his "magic world" mother Soraya.

This revelatory moment also stops time. Luka's powers in the World of Magic hinge on the knowledge of his father's world. In that world, Soraya is the "most important female person" (85). Luka meets a young avatar of his mother, Soraya, and in *Back to the Future* mode seems smitten with her. The novel does not explicitly explore this option but toys with it as one of the many intertexts that Rushdie delights in exploring. Soraya's sharp tongue and "rough Otter way" belies a "kinder nature" (85): she acts as a surrogate mother, aiding her "son" to save his father. However, here, in the World of Magic, it is the young boy who calls the shots. Even the powerful queen needs his help to vanquish her foes.

Luka resorts to his schoolyard weapons: itching powder bombs. The Rats are "possessed of their last and lethal Frenzy" (89): "The thin-skinned masters of the Respectorate were literally scratching themselves to bits, actually ripping themselves apart, until there was nothing left of them but lumps of mangy fur, and grey, ugly meat" (90). A very disturbing description, especially for what is meant to be a "fun" book for children. And although Rushdie assures the readers that the "not–Rats" were not harmed, but rather rejoiced and tore down the fences of their "prison" (90), there seems to a fair deal of authorial rage here. It is, after all, clear, that the Rats are a stand-in for the kind of people Rushdie abhors.

"And that was the end of that" (90) is the conclusion following the scene of the Rats' demise. Rushdie seems to be getting his own back at the rats of the world who get their just deserts for being so "thin skinned," unable to take an insult or a joke. The violence of the final scene and the rest of the Respectorate episode indicate Rushdie's emotional and ideological investment in stopping what he considers the evils of the censoring, politically correct West. This episode stands out in the novel. Although we are meant to see the Rats' insistence on their (mistaken) beliefs as ridiculous, there is nothing really fun, or funny, about the scene. Later scenes of conflict are not couched in such violent terms. I shall look at the ways in which Rushdie engages with a recurring theme in his work — the power of mythologies to shape our world — to demonstrate how this conflict, between Luka and the angry gods, remains in a more playful mode and does not seem to carry the same emotional weight as the Respectorate episode. The mythological gods and goddesses re-emerge on a different, less grand stage. Rushdie delights in invoking the gods of Western and non–Western mythologies as a way of reiterating his never-shaken belief in the power of stories to shape lives and change worlds.

The Gods Reenter the Stage

Rushdie's fascination with all things mythological is most evident in *The Ground Beneath Her Feet*, Rushdie's rock 'n' roll novel, where he invents a counter-mythology of East and West. The protagonist and narrator, Rai, who is fascinated by the mythological duo Ormus and Vina, reflects after their demise about the end of the mythological age. After the gods leave the stage, it's time for ordinary men and women to go about their daily lives. But the power of mythology remains. It provides us with stories that we live by or try to undo. The myths provide blueprints for our experiences. Rai explains the central role of mythology in his life:

> The old religions' legacy of living stories—the Ash Yggdrasil, the Cow Audumla ... the vain Olympians, the fabulous monsters, the legion of ruined, sacrificed women, the metamorphoses—continues to hold my attention; whereas Judaism, Christianity, Islam, the Market, utterly fail to enthrall. These are faiths for the front pages, for CNN, not for me. Let them struggle over their old and new Jerusalems! It's Prometheus and the Nibelungs, Indra and Cadmus, who bring me my kind of news [*TGBHF*, 555].

This sentiment closely echoes Rushdie's worldview and is given a further twist in *Luka*. The mythological gods and goddesses, now out of favor, still have the power to enthrall. In *Luka*, the coming together of gods from every conceivable land and culture serves Rushdie as a means of highlighting, yet again, his call for multiplicity over oneness; he reaffirms his unshaken belief in the power of stories while presenting his own magic world as an ascendant mythological tale that joins the ranks of the mythologies of old and creates a new myth for our times.

In Claude Levi-Strauss's seminal work on myth, he locates the seeming discrepancy between the myth's apparent arbitrariness—"It would seem that in the course of a myth, anything is likely to happen. There is no logic, no continuity"—and the "astounding similarity between myths collected in wildly different regions" (Levi-Strauss, 429). Levi-Strauss pro-

6. Immortality Now: Luka and the Fire of Life

poses a model to explain the singularity of myth as a linguistic phenomenon whose "substance lies not in its style, its original music, or its syntax, but in the *story* which it tells" (430). That is why "[whatever] our ignorance of the language and the culture of the people where it originated, a myth is still felt as a myth by any reader throughout the world" (430). Levi-Strauss rejects the quest for the "true" version of the mythological tale. Rather, "we define the myth as consisting of all its versions" (435). In this sense, then, "not only Sophocles but Freud himself, should be included among the recorded versions of the Oedipus myth on a par with earlier or seemingly more 'authentic' versions" (435). In other words, it is the different, at times contradictory, versions of the myth that provide us with its fullest meaning. And the reworking of the mythological tale, from Sophocles to Freud and beyond, is as much a part of the study of myth as the earliest versions. This rejection of the idea of an authentic mythological text in favor of its many shifting versions and variations is in keeping with Rushdie's fictional project in *Luka and the Fire of Life*. For the book can be read as a retelling of the Promethean myth. Stealing the fire of life in order to bring a father back to life fits, after all, the kind of mythological structure outlined by Levi-Strauss that depends upon "the awareness of oppositions towards their progressive mediation" (440). The organizing framework of the mythological text, then, hinges upon "discovering a mediation between life and death" (437). It is this "mediation" that Rushdie's novel performs as he rewrites the Promethean myth.

This rewriting takes the form of a fantasy or science fictional tale, which is, as Margaret Atwood points out in *In Other Worlds: SF and the Human Imagination*, the most suitable form of the rewriting of the mythological tale to suit our (post-)modern era. As Atwood puts it: "[Every] question that myths address, SF has addressed also. Indeed, it's arguable that this form and its subforms have subsumed the mythic areas abandoned by literature after the meta-theological poetics of *Paradise Lost* and the meta-fabulations of *The Pilgrim's Progress*" (55–56). In this sense, the reworking of the mythological tale in SF terms is what Rushdie's novel achieves. His rewriting of the myth as a computer game narrative is, as I have suggested, a way of re-enchanting the world, but it is also a comment on the ways in which new myths are formed in a post-mythological age. If we take Paul Ricoeur's observation about myth's role as a "disclosure of unprecedented worlds, an opening to other *possible* worlds which transcend the established limits of our *actual* world" (Ricoeur, 490), we can see that it is as much a description of SF: a mode that engages with possible worlds that transcend the limits of our actual world as much as mythology does. Rushdie's novel creates such a possible world in the fictional computer game Luka traverses to save his dying father.

As Spiros Orfanos reminds us, "[myths] are stories not usually bound by time and place. Like many such stories, myths change in tone and meaning. It is often difficult to tell where a myth actually begins and where it ends. Yet we can pick our entry points, and find all kinds of interesting and phantasmagorical elements in them to spark our imagination and creativity" (Orfanos, 482–3). This fluid and changing nature of the mythological tale means that myths "can be at once radical and conservative. Myths can be uncomfortably ambiguous and they can often wind up affirming what they deny. Because there is usually no official text for myth, the storyteller's persona often becomes part of the myth-making process" (483). In *Luka*, the myth-making process is a shared one. Rashid's magical worlds and the mythologies of the ancient world, whether Greek, Roman, Native American, Japanese or a host of others, are remade in the process of storytelling and myth-making. Luka becomes part of this process, as he has to employ the power of his father's tales in order to save his father's life. This process is enacted by employing one of the foundational myths of Western culture: the Promethean myth that enacts both man's creation and the possibility of violent destruction of the world embodied in Pandora's entry into the scene. Although Pandora's box is absent from the Rushdie version of the tale, the "fire of life" that has to be stolen in order to revive the dying Rashid is evoked, as it was in the Greek myth, as a symbol of a creative force as well as an act of rebellion against old gods and of putting man at the center of his world.

The final confrontation in *Luka* is thus not, as the readers have come to expect, with the angry captain Aag, the cruel circus master defeated by Luka at the beginning of the novel. Aag's threatening "Rings of Fire" turn out to be illusions, easily recognized by Dog and Bear. This fake fire is also reflected in Captain Aag's red hair, a sign of his impotent rage and lack of real power. In a scene that echoes *The Wizard of Oz*, the villain is deflated—this time not by water, which is the cause of the wicked witch's undoing in the film, but by his own element, fire: "[when] the flame died away, there was no more Captain, just a small pile of angry-looking ash" (125). The final encounter, then, has to be between the representatives of the old mythologies that are now out of favor and the new mythology represented by Luka, who had internalized his father's mythological world and is therefore the most appropriate hero for such a showdown between old and new tales. The foundational myth — Prometheus steals the fire from the gods and is eternally punished — is reworked alongside other non–Western myths about stealing the scared fire in order to suggest that in this new age of re-enchantment by different means, the stealer of fire is not longer punished. Rather, he is rewarded. The "fire of life" will revive Luka's sleeping father. It is the power of life over death emblematized in the ability to continue telling new stories and creating new myths of creation and becoming.

The old gods are no longer relevant: They are portrayed as a pathetic and self-centered group of has-beens, more like aging Hollywood stars and starlets than the all-powerful entities they once were. As Otto Rank sees it, what he terms "the Prometheus complex" is a central stage in human development. According to Rank, this stage occurs in puberty and marks the "first revolt by the child against subjection of his ego by parents" (Rank, 201). Rank reads the Greek myth as a symbol of the need or desire to create. Prometheus creates men just as well as the gods, thereby symbolizing the dethroning of the gods created by man and the installation of himself with his fully developed personality and his need to create. Prometheus creates real men after his own image just as earlier men created the gods. The myth creates not only man but woman — the love object, Pandora. Pandora brings the element of death into the world, and Prometheus is unable to stop the intrusion of death and misery although he has the prophetic gifts that warn him of what Pandora's *pithos* ("jar") contains.

Rank reads Prometheus's punishment by Zeus as representing an inhibition of the tendencies of the personality to create. Interestingly, Rank links the Prometheus myth to the pedagogical situation, claiming that "the pupil should be brought *from* the Oedipus complex, *through* the Promethean complex, *to the creation of his own personality*" (203). He sees the Promethean stage in human development as one that few adults attain. It is the pinnacle of human maturity. Rushdie's choice to retell the myth chimes in with Rank's notions of creation and education. Luka becomes his own master, realizing in the process that though he has his father's Magic World of stories to rely on, he is the one who has to find his own creative solution to the problem of his father's waning powers, symbolized by his "Big Sleep." Luka, the adolescent boy, is, as Rank tells us, at the perfect stage for both rebelling against the totality of parental authority and for creating "his own personality" in the process. However, as Rank points out, the parent still has a crucial role in the pedagogical process. His interaction with his child must be one in which both parent and child learn how to form this new bond between them. No longer the infantile Oedipal connection, the Promethean stage leads the parent and the child to a better understanding of one another: "The pedagogic situation must be transformed and developed in to a mutual emotional relationship in which parents and children grow up with — and develop — one another" (210).

In *Luka*, Rushdie provides two sets of parents: Rashid and Soraya, Luka's parents in Aliphbay, and their doubles, Nobodady and the Insultana of Ott in the magical world of the game. In the world of the game, Luka cannot rely on his real parents. Their doubles offer him only limited help and, in the case of Nobodady, are not there to help him but to see that he fails in his mission to save the real father from death. In this sense, these parent doppelganger figures are there to educate Luka how to succeed on his own, without the presence of controlling parental authority. The first chapters show us that both Rashid and Soraya are very involved in their son's life. In the world of the game, Luka has to fend for himself. This is part of the process of growing up and, Rank points out, also a part of creating the self.

Rushdie's choice of the Promethean myth, then, signals his interest in the creative process as a life affirming but also potentially destructive force. Stealing the "fire of life" may have deadly consequences. They can only be averted by resorting to the creative force within — a force that is revealed at times of great crisis. The Promethean myth of course is also a story about the ways in which a symbolic father figure (Zeus) punishes his wayward son (Prometheus) for his independent deed: giving human beings fire and thus raising the humans above mere brutes but also providing them with what can be a destructive force. The Promethean myth can also be read as a tale of technological progress that carries disastrous implications. Mary Shelley's *Frankenstein* is subtitled "the modern Prometheus" since it is the story about what science and technology can do when pushed to their most dangerous ends. The father figures in Rushdie's novel (Rashid and Nobodady) function as aspects of this patriarchal power. However, in Rushdie's reworking of the Promethean tale, Luka becomes another version of Prometheus, but instead of being punished by the father, his transgression is what is needed to save the dying father. If we consider Rushdie's reinvention of the myth in a virtual realm, we may say that here it is the young son's knowledge of technology, his computer game know-how, which will enable him to become the hero of his own tale and his father's redeemer. The fear of technology voiced by the mother is not shared by the father or his son. Luka's mastery of computer games, is, as the first part of the book demonstrates, what will later aid him on the most important quest of his life.

The Promethean myth is not only one of the foundational Western myths; it is also a story that has different meanings in different times and different cultures. Rushdie seems to suggest that in our own day and age, the quest for immortality at the center of the Greek myth is to be found in the realm of the virtual: the computer game with its endless possibilities for "re-living" offers this option. Luka dies many times only to find that he had more lives not yet used up. In the world of the game, this option remains viable. In the world of the novel, Rushdie questions the dream of immortality. Luka realizes that immortality is not something to wish for. Thus, the novel's conclusion celebrates a moment in time: the reunited family on a rooftop epitomizes the joy of such moments in time while emphasizing that they are just moments. Nothing lasts forever. Rashid, though rescued from death at this point, is mortal. The "fire of life" only works to awaken him from his "Big Sleep" but does not promise endless life. Whereas the virtual realm imagines a world where multiple lives replace one, finite life, the world inhabited by Luka and his family still functions, despite incursions into the fantastic, as the real world where death is final and life is short and transient.

Playing with Fire: Rushdie's Reinvention of the Promethean Myth

Although the Promethean myth is at the center of *Luka and the Fire of Life*, Rushdie chooses to offer its many alternative, non–Western versions as a way of highlighting the multiplicity of mythological tales and their endless variations. Luka is faced with the ultimate challenge of stealing the "fire of life" from the Aalim, who are in charge of the Heart of Magic and guard the fire. The Aalim, or as Rushdie playfully calls them, the three Jos, are the embodiments of past, present and future: "Jo-Hua knows even the smallest details of the Past, Jo-Hai can even see the smallest incident in the Present, and Jo-Aiga can foretell the Future" (139). Thus Rushdie suggests that the powers of the gods are in fact the powers of narrative: the three Jos can see into past, present and future and thus are the authors at the heart of Rashid's Magic World. The power to know, see and foretell is the power of the author over his creation. The Aalim control that power, which is also the life-giving element: the fire of life. Choosing to name the guardians of the fire by resorting to both Old Testament gods (Aalim or Elim in Hebrew) and the Hindi mythology inherent in the names of the three Jos (Jo-Hai, for example, literally means "life as it is") demonstrates Rushdie's playful manipulation of language and myth.

In Rashid/Rushdie's Magic World, mythological creatures of different cultures, times and places gather together and try to stop Luka from stealing their fire. The Promethean myth, in Rushdie's retelling, becomes another story among many. Although Prometheus is acknowledged as the "First thief. Oldest and Greatest. King of the Hill. Inspiration to us all" (*Luka*, 150), in the words of another fire thief, the wily Coyote, he is still only an example of one of the many fire thieves in the history of the World of Magic. Soraya tells Luka about the fire thieves of Native American mythology: "The Algonquin Indians got Rabbit to steal Fire for them. Beaver and Nanabozho the Shape-Shifter did the same for other tribes. Possum tried and failed but then Grandfather Spider stole Fire for the Cherokee in a clay urn.... And so on" (149–150). The multiple mythologies then playfully evoke the double meaning of "Indian": Soraya, implicitly linked to "Indianness," as I have shown, is the bearer of the clay pot, the Ott Pot, which contains the Ott Potatoes that Luka will use to keep the fire of life burning. Instead of Pandora's jar in the Prometheus story that brings about death and destruction, here we have the Ott Pott that preserves (the fire of) life. Rushdie's revision of the Promethean myth also involves the inclusion of Captain Aag, Luka's mortal enemy and a fiery character of a different sort, as Prometheus's brother. Rushdie hints here at the original myth where Prometheus is the brother of Atlas, and the links between the grandmaster of the circus and the mythological figure who carries the world on his shoulders are also hinted at. Captain Aag is a ruler of a self-enclosed world that is the circus ring, and his despotic rule of this world is the cause of his undoing. Soraya tells Luka: "The Titan Prometheus, was the brother, oddly enough, of your friend, the late, unlamented Captain Aag. Not that they ever got on. Couldn't stand each other, in fact" (150).

6. Immortality Now: Luka and the Fire of Life

This odd kinship is Rushdie's further manipulation of the myth: Rushdie is playing with fire and delighting in the many ways this element can be manipulated. Thus, it is the fire bug that spies on Luka and his friends and alerts the gods at the Heart of Magic of their presence. The gods then sound the fire alarm, which alerts the inhabitants of the Heart of the intruders. Fiery characters such as Captain Aag represent fire as a destructive element, an epitome of uncontrollable rage. Soraya's red hair, however, signals another kind of fire: quick to anger on the one hand yet kind and loving on the other, she represents the Otter way of being in the world. Her fiery nature is seen as a positive trait. The red dragon, formerly imprisoned by Captain Aag and set free by Luka, is also a fiery element, but one that helps Luka on his quest. Thus fire comes to represent both an attitude to life (being "fiery") and an element that carries the mythological connotations of a primary life force, one that burns as long as a person lives. Soraya's Ott Pott with its Ott Potatoes is another pun on the qualities of fire: the "hot potatoes" seem to be an emblem of her fiery nature and the nature of her "over the top" people, who are hot natured and quick to anger.

Luka's quest to steal the fire of life and thus awaken his sleeping father hinges on what his father had told him about the nature of his disagreement with the Aalim about the concept of time. Thus, as I have shown, the Aalim's control of time rivals the storyteller's abilities to manipulate time, to disrupt its linear and irreversible nature and offer instead a more fluid version of time as a river. Rashid tells Luka a bedtime story that Luka remembers just as he is about to face the powers of the Aalim:

> Our dreams are the real truths—our fancies, the knowledge of our hearts. We know that Time is a River, not a clock, and that it can flow the wrong way, so that the world becomes more backward instead of less, and that it can jump sideways, so that everything changes in an instant. We know that the River of Time can loop and twist and carry us back to yesterday or forwards to the day after tomorrow [157].

This concept of time is at odds with the Aalim's view:

> Their view of Time is strict and inflexible: yesterday, then today, then tomorrow, tick, tock, tick. They are like robots marching along to the beat of the disappearing seconds. What Was, Jo-Hua, lives in the Past; What Is, Jo-Hai, simply is right now; and What Will Come, Jo-Aiga, belongs to a place we cannot go. Their Time is a prison, they are the jailers, and the seconds and the minutes are its keys [157].

Rashid concludes by telling Luka that he is the Aalim's enemy, and he positions his version of time as the truth and their view as lies: "I've spent my life telling people that this is the truth about Time, and that the Aalim's clocks tell lies. So naturally the Aalim are my mortal enemies, which is just fine, because as a matter of fact I am their deadly foe" (158). The rivalry between gods and men is another of Rushdie's gestures towards the Promethean myth. Prometheus's act of stealing the fire for mankind represents the rift between gods and men. In the Greek collective imagination, represented by mythological tales, the state of harmony between gods and men is shattered forever by Prometheus's act of betrayal. From now on, a new relationship between gods and men emerges, one based not on unity but on separation of spheres. Men and gods are no longer part of the same (sometimes harmonious) universe. Rather, man becomes an antagonist to the gods. His independent status is a threat to the gods' dominion. The Promethean myth signals this moment of rupture. From now on, man will try to appease the gods. He will give them symbolic offerings that further enhance the separation between the spheres of the sacred and the profane. The gods' role will no longer be as dominant in men's lives, but their symbolic presence will remain as a structuring force of men's experiences in the world. Rushdie's retelling of this myth in novelistic form, employing the new narrative mode of the computer game, demonstrates the ongoing life of the myth in contemporary representation. The power of the myths over us, says Rushdie, is never-ending. Within this space of a "fictional truth," they live on in new and surprising ways. Rushdie's novel is meant to be read by children and adults alike, thus showing how this mythological legacy is now, as in the past, to be handed down from generation to generation by a telling and retelling of the tales.

Thus fictionality becomes a different kind of truth, much like the dreams that disrupt the ordered notion of time. The words *mortal* and *deadly* signal the idea of mortality as the foe. The imagined/fantastic/science-fictional view of time is the counter-narrative to this ordered narrative of time. The re-imagining of time as fluid, rather than linear and irreversible, is both a narrative tool and an aesthetic truth. Rashid poses his own storytelling powers as another form of godlike control of the world, one at odds with the notion of order and linear structure. If *Luka* is, as I suggested at the outset, Rushdie's endeavor to re-enchant a disenchanted world, then Luka's quest in the Heart of Magic enacts this attempt to rethink time and mortality; time is not a straight arrow but a river, and the notion of death and life is recast in game form to suggest that the imaginative rule over time may be more powerful than the man-made notions of clocks and calendars. It is this victory of one concept of time over another, the victory of Rashid's magical story world over that of the Aalim and the other gods in the Heart of Magic, that is at the center of Luka's final challenge. To win it, he must harness his father's alternate mythology and use it to prove to the gods that their existence depends on storytelling and myth-making.

Towards a "More Sensible Relationship with Time"

The final encounter in the novel takes place with the gods of the ancient worlds who apprehend the Fire Thief, Luka, in the "left handed" dimension of the World of Magic. An angry group of gods and goddesses, led by Ra the Supreme, who speaks "Hieroglyph," (171)[2] which Soraya's emissary, the red squirrel Ratatat, has to translate for Luka's benefit, charge Luka with stealing the fire of life and aiming to take it across the "forbidden frontier" into the "Real World" (179). This act is a violation of order or, as the gods call it, Maat (178).[3] Luka's response to this accusation begins with "[a] fire of his own making" that "had risen in his breast, and blazed through his eyes" (180). As I have shown, Rushdie plays with fire as he takes this motif and recasts it in many different forms: from the actual to the metaphoric and back again. The fire in Luka's breast helps him challenge the gods and keep the "real" fire of life. Luka's fiery speech, which he "hollers" (180) at the assembled gods, reflects the passion of his beliefs and is an echo of Soraya's Otter nature, his mother's Soraya's equally fiery nature, and his father Rashid, the Shah of Blah's impassioned rhetoric. The speech enacts Luka's fiery nature: "'It's my turn to speak now,' Luka hollered at the assembled Supernatural Beings, 'and believe you me, I have a lot to say about all this poppycock, and you had better listen closely, and listen well, because your future depends upon it as much as mine does'" (*Luka*, 180). Luka reveals the interconnectedness of the two worlds: Rashid's World of Magic and the real world inhabited by Luka and his family. Luka's intimate knowledge of his father's fictional world allows him to make this connection explicit, in ways that are inaccessible to the fictive beings that inhabit Rashid's world:

> You see, I know something about this World of Magic ... *it isn't your World!* It doesn't even belong to the Aalim, whoever they are, wherever they are lurking right now. *This is my father's World.* I'm sure there are other Magic Worlds dreamed up by other people, Wonderlands and Narnias and Middle-earths and whatnot — but this one, gods and goddesses, ogres and bats, monsters and slimy things, is the World of Rashid Khalifa, the well-known Ocean of Notions, the fabulous Shah of Blah [*Luka*, 180].

Rushdie here gestures back to *Haroun and the Sea of Stories* and recasts the figure of the storyteller as the "Ocean of Notions." This evocation of the earlier novel at this crucial point in the narrative demonstrates the link between the two texts: Both dramatize the power of storytelling as a life-giving force. In both novels, the existence of the alternate world is conterminous with the real world. Luka's passionate speech returns to the concerns of the earlier novel as he comments on his father's role as a maker of worlds:

> He put it together that way, he gave it shape and laws, and he brought all of you here to populate it, because he has learned about you, thought about you, and even dreamed about you all his life. And I know about it because I've been hearing about it every day of my life, as bedtime stories and breakfast sagas and dinner-table yarns, and as tall tales told to audiences all over the city of Kahani and the country of Alifbay. So in a way, this is now my World, too [*Luka*, 180–181].

The son's quest to save the father hinges on this incorporation of his father's world. As Luka tells the assembled gods and goddesses, he must save his father and thus save their own existence: "If I don't get the Fire of Life to him before it's too late, he isn't the only one who will come to an end. Everything here will vanish too ... because let's be frank, how many people other than Rashid Khalifa are really bothering to keep your story going nowadays?" (*Luka*, 181). Rashid's role, as Luka presents it here, is to "keep the stories going"; he has to keep the magic alive in an age that no longer believes.

In Tzvetan Todorov's work on the fantastic, he makes an interesting observation on the role of magic. Relating to the opposition between religion and magic as one closely linked to the themes of self and Other he had discussed as the main themes of the fantastic genre, Todorov, following Mauss, claims that, unlike mystical or religious rites, "magic cannot do without language" (Todorov, 153). It is this language of magic that Rushdie accesses in *Luka and the Fire of Life*. It is also the language of literature in

6. Immortality Now: Luka and the Fire of Life

a broader sense. As Todorov notes, the fantastic genre "permits the description of a fantastic universe, one that has no reality outside language" (92). In that sense, fantasy is a particularly evocative example of what makes the literary text "literary." Rushdie's meditations on the nature of literature in both *Haroun* and *Luka* employ the fantastic or science fictional mode to present the province of the literary text as a magic world made of words, always already under threat of extinction in one form or another. The magic world exists only if its author is able to continue imagining it and only if there are readers who continue to read it, thus keeping it alive.

Luka's speech identifies his father's storytelling as a force that makes and destroys worlds. He tells the gods that their very existence depends on his father's creation: the magic world that they inhabit would not exist without Rashid's invention and retelling of the tales. The gods' power no longer comes from people believing in them but from the will to suspend disbelief for a time and surrender to the stories' alternate truth — the truth of the imagination. Thus Rushdie recasts the power of mythological tales as a life-giving force. The gods would not exist without someone to tell their story. But Rashid's life depends on the ability to tell. In *Haroun*, the loss of storytelling powers almost leads to Rashid's undoing. In *Luka*, the father's ebbing life can only be restored by an appeal to the power of tales to make and unmake worlds. The only way Luka can get away with his seemingly wrong act of stealing the fire of life is by showing the gods and goddesses in his father's fictional universe that their very lives depend on stories. The qualified happy ending of Luka's quest must then hinge on the acceptance of the force and importance of old and new mythologies. If Rushdie's endeavor in *Luka* is to re-enchant a world that has lost its magic, then Luka's speech can be seen as an impassioned call to the readers; only by keeping the stories alive can we truly live. The relationship between the magic world of fiction and the real world is of reciprocity: the readers of the tale have an active duty in keeping it alive by the act of reading.

Luka's call for the importance of tales as a life-affirming force echoes Rushdie's fictional endeavor. In interpreting the Promethean myth as a story about creative abilities and man's unique powers to create life, Rushdie is providing us with yet another version of this myth for our postmodern times. In this novel, Rushdie's last novel to date (at the time of writing), we find that the author's investment in the power of storytelling takes on a new and yet old twist. Rushdie may borrow the trope of the computer game as a narrative device, as I have shown, but, much like the P2C2E in

Haroun, Rushdie parodies his own distrust of scientific and technological explanations. In his alternate universes, science and scientific explanations that explain the way things work remain, as in the forever childish eye of the author, magical.

In my reading of Rushdie's oeuvre, from his earliest science fictional novel to his latest fantastic adventure, I chart the magical worlds he creates in his fiction. Although the mature Rushdie is pondering his own demise, as least as an imagined possibility to be averted in *Luka and the Fire of Life*, his creative fire has not ebbed.

In my conclusion, I look at Rushdie's memoir as a text that enacts the generic hybridity that characterizes his science fictional novels. *Joseph Anton*, a memoir written in the third person, begins as a horror story. Evoking Hitchcock's *The Birds*, the third person narrator recalls the day when his life was turned upside down: "Afterwards, when the world was exploding around him and the lethal blackbirds were massing on the climbing frame in the school playground, he felt annoyed with himself for forgetting the name of the BBC reporter, a woman, who had told him his old life was over and a new, darker existence was about to begin" (3). This striking beginning demonstrates Rushdie's playful manipulation of multiple genres: The beginning evokes another well-known and filmic text, while manipulating both the verbal and the visual signifier "blackbird" to hint at the Muslim fanatics, as well as a more general evil (or darkness). The second part of the sentence takes up the issue of memory (and "forgettery," to use Rushdie's phrase) and locates the story of this new life in a more realistic frame, without losing the metaphorical significance of both the Hitchock allusion and what the narrator (and reader) attribute to this notion of "darkness."

Rushdie's memoir moves between genres: from domestic drama to detective thriller, from horror to the comic antics of the author in hiding. I shall examine the ways in which generic "bleeding," one genre melding into another, becomes a way of re-inventing the memoir form as a hybrid construction. Looking at what the British SF writer China Mievelle has termed "The New Weird," a new generic hybrid, I suggest we view Rushdie's latest work as participating in the spirit, if not the thematic and stylistic tropes, of this highly political brand of fiction. For Rushdie's unique memoir is a literary hybrid. In that sense, it evokes the postcolonial experience of hybridity as a state of constant "becoming." As Jessica Langer insightfully notes in *Postcolonialism and Science Fiction*:

6. Immortality Now: Luka and the Fire of Life

[the] matter of the "hybrid"—the person, the planet, the society—is a common trope in science fiction, so much so that it has become almost a cliché. The hybrid is terrifying because it is uncannily both us and not-us, and is wildly hopeful for the same reason: in hybridity lies the potential for humanity to be either subsumed or enhanced, or perhaps both [107].

This dynamic also characterizes the postcolonial condition where "the spectre of the stranger, the Other, who is both self and not-self, who is human but dismissed as 'animal' is a common central issue in science fiction and postcolonial theory" (107). I suggest then that we look to Rushdie's oeuvre as participating in this project of hybridity, not only as a person writing about a society and the multiple worlds we inhabit, but also in its generic resistance. Rushdie's work is, as I have suggested, science fictional in the broadest sense of the term, but its generic hybridity, or its refusal to fit into a neat generic category, is what makes it so much his own.

Conclusion: The Genre That Isn't: Rereading Rushdie

> *This in the end was who he was, a teller of tales, a creator of shapes, a maker of things that were not.* — Joseph Anton
>
> *There are things that one can do with the fantastic as an aesthetic in fiction, and indeed in other media, that you can't do with realist fiction.* — China Mieville, "Weird Fiction"
>
> *I know always that I'm an outsider. This I have known ever since I stretched out my fingers to the abomination within that great gilded frame; stretched out my fingers and touched* a cold and unyielding surface of polished glass. — H.P. Lovecraft, "The Outsider"

Rushdie's memoir, entitled *Joseph Anton* after the alias he employed at the time of the *fatwa*, was released in September 2012. As I have suggested, the book's title, Rushdie's alias, indicates to what extent the notion of a borrowed identity is central in a reading of Rushdie's trajectory as a writer. My claim for Rushdie's investment in the fantastic aspects of nationhood and selfhood finds a chilling expression in his own life as he was forced to live under an assumed identity in the years following the *fatwa*. I have chosen not to address the book that caused this edict on Rushdie's life directly, but its spirit hovers over my reading of Rushdie's figure as a teller of tales, a word and world conjurer who constructs fictional worlds in which he finds solace from the personal and collective traumas of nationhood. As noted in the introduction, Rushdie presents his earlier experiences in England in science fictional terms. He borrows the figure of the science fictional "little green men or Slime from Outer Space" (26) to describe that overwhelming sense of alienation which he experiences later on as "Joseph Anton."

My aim in this book, as stated in the introduction, has been to trace Rushdie's work as a writer of postcolonial SF. I have shown how Rushdie's work, from his first unpublished novel *The Antagonist* to *Luka and the Fire of Life*, engages in the spaces of imagined possibilities offered by science fiction in the broadest sense. In her meditation on the possible futures of postcolonial science fiction, Jessica Langer comments on India as "an emerging centre of science fiction production, despite its being mostly ignored by mainstream SF channels until very recently" (156). However, notes Langer, "a few SF writers in the Indian diaspora are also finding success. Along with the forays into SF of Amitav Ghosh and the great Salman Rushdie, younger and emerging talents such as Vandana Singh are beginning to gain prominence in the science fiction community" (156).

As I have shown, what Langer terms Rushdie's "foray" into SF has in fact been a driving force in his oeuvre since its inception. I therefore suggest we look to the future of SF, evident in the writings of young British SF writers such as China Mievelle, as a model for the kind of generic hybridity that Rushdie's texts enact and perform. China Mievelle, a British writer of fantasy/SF and a Marxist activist, calls for the reemergence of a genre he names "The New Weird." Mievelle conjures up a literary movement that began in the late 19th century and whose founding father is H.P. Lovecraft and his "Weird" brand of horror tales. Mievelle published a manifesto statement entitled "Long Live the New Weird" in 2003 in the magazine *The Third Alternative*. In this manifesto, a term linking Mievelle's literary endeavors to his Marxist ideology, Mievelle comments on the fluidity of genre categories. According to Mievelle, genres, which are "fuzzy sets at the best of times, are now fuzzier than ever" (35). Mievelle relocates a sub-genre, or what he terms "a rather breathless and generically slippery macabre fiction" ("Weird Fiction," 510), in the works of H.P. Lovecraft and others associated with the pulp magazine *Weird Tales*, as a generative moment in the history of fantasy/SF. In Mievelle's reading, Weird Fiction "may serve as the bad conscience of the Gernsenback/Cambell sf paradigm, and as rebuke to much theorizing that takes that paradigm's implicit self-conception as its starting point" (510). This move questions the history of SF/fantasy's originary moment, located, as John Rieder points out in his description of the founding moment of the genre, in "the emergence of a set of conventions and explanations that presented itself as a market niche, on the one hand (as the publishing entrepreneur Hugo Gernsback, the man most responsible for promulgating the term 'science fiction,' recognized), and as a creative possibility, on the other" (15).

This challenge to the accepted genesis of SF/fantasy as a genre and as

Conclusion

a creative possibility highlights the problematics at the heart of this categorizing endeavor. For Mievelle's own fictional works, as Grace Dillon points out, participate in the project of reinvigorating generic expectations by writing a brand of sf/fantasy that is politically aware and conscious of its role as a formative text for postcolonial sensibilities. Dillon reads Mievelle's work as representing what she terms a "totemic" significance:

> Sf often hyperbolizes contemporary social interests (after J.G. Ballard's fashion) and recaptures social concerns (in Jean Baudrillard's sense of hyperreality). The question surfaces, then, whether contemporary sf that depicts totemic relationships among humans and animals extends popularized misreadings, or whether sf thought experiments reveal the conundrums created by social science, figuratively asserting that totemism as conceived by these ethnographers is an illusion [1].

Dillon locates Mievelle's brand of SF as participating in the project of "recovery of totemic significance" and "[renewing] an indigenous conception of personhood" (1). In other words, Dillon reads contemporary SF narratives, such as Mievelle's, in terms of their revision of ethnographic misconceptions of the Other, while seeing SF's "thought experiments" as a corrective to these misconceptions.

In this sense, we can read the works I have discussed in this book as participating in the science fictional "thought experiment": In *Luka and the Fire of Life*, for one, we see Rushdie shifting the focus from the predominantly Western Promethean myth in favor of the indigenous or Native American version of the tale, placing the figure of the Coyotte/Trickster at the center alongside other non–Western myths. Rushdie's own playful manipulation of the Prometheus myth as a computer game further stresses the ways in which his thought experiment works to subvert the known hierarchy of mythical tales as an allegory for the human condition. In Rushdie's retelling of this key myth, and in his revisionary retelling of key events in Indian and Western history, he participates in this project of remaking.

Mievelle's renaming gesture harks back to an earlier pronouncement by the cyber-punk author, Bruce Sterling. In 1989, a crucial year in world history and for Rushdie, the ominous year of the *fatwa*, Sterling published an essay on a new kind of fiction he saw emerging in SF and fantasy. He called this new formless form "slipstream." Sterling asserted that this new category in fiction resembles science fiction, but is not quite SF: "This genre is not 'category' SF; it is not even 'genre' SF. Instead, it is a contemporary kind of writing which has set its face against consensus reality. It is a fantastic, surreal, sometimes speculative on occasion, but not rigorously so" (Sterling, 2). Sterling further delineates what this genre is about: "It seems to me that at the heart of slipstream is an attitude of peculiar aggression against 'reality.' These are fantasies of a kind, but not fantasies which are 'futuristic' or 'beyond the fields we know.' These books tend to sarcastically tear at the structure of 'everyday life'" (3). This "aggression against reality," or at least a suspicious attitude towards what constitutes reality, characterizes Rushdie's novels. As Sterling claims:

> Some such books, the most "mainstream" ones, are non-realistic literary fictions which avoid or ignore SF genre conventions. But hard-core slipstream has unique darker elements. Quite commonly these works don't make a lot of common sense, and what's more they often somehow imply that nothing we know makes "a lot of sense" and perhaps even that nothing ever could [3].

This kind of writing, then, "simply makes you feel very strange; the way living in the late twentieth century makes you feel, if you are a person of certain sensibilities" (3). This "strange" feeling at the heart of what Sterling calls "slipstream" is also at the heart of the novels I discuss in this book. Perhaps it is nowhere more apparent than in *Joseph Anton*. For this is a book about this "strange" feeling of the "late twentieth century man" beset by dark forces. In this sense, Rushdie's memoir may be what Sterling terms a "slipstream" text: Its generic hybridity represents its thematic strangeness; Rushdie retells his life story as a fantastic text, focusing on the most strange event in his life and on suddenly becoming an object of murderous hate. This, of course, is Rushdie's perception. The strangeness he describes is seen differently by his critics, both in the Muslim world and in the West. But as an author, writing about his life, Rushdie chooses generic slipperiness over more conventional forms. This choice is significant and places *Joseph Anton* in line with Rushdie's overtly fictional texts.

What Sterling first called "slipstream" in 1989 becomes in 2006, for James Patrick Kelly and John Kessel, the editors of *Feeling Very Strange: The Slipstream Anthology*, a way of readdressing the question of genre and generic ghettos. As they rightly point out in the introduction: "Science fiction has not been well served by its seventy-year long war of definition" (x–xi). However, "[slipstream] raises fundamental epistemological and ontological questions that other kinds of fiction are ill prepared to address" (xi). It is not a genre but "a psychological and literary effect that cuts across genre" (xi). The editors do present some attributes of "slipstream," among which are "[violating] the tenets of realism," being "playfully postmodern" and "[paying] homage to various popular genres and their conventions" without being "science fiction stories, traditional fantasies, dreams, historical fantasies, or alternate histories" (xii).

One could say, then, that Rushdie's work, which I have addressed in this book, fits some of these attributes. As I have shown, however, Rushdie does engage in alternate histories, and in some cases, like *The Ground Beneath Her Feet*, this alternate history is at the heart of the novel. But even then Rushdie's alternative history novel, as I pointed out in my discussion of the novel in Chapter 2, is unlike other works in this mode. Its playful twist on the histories of East and West dramatizes the strange feeling that Kelly and Kessel evoke as the defining characteristic of "slipstream." The novel dramatizes the feeling we experience when the world as we know it slips off its hinges and becomes "strange." But the other novels discussed here also fit into this category as they all offer a strange version of everyday realities and historical events. Rushdie's novels engage in an imaginative reinvention of historical facts. Rushdie's project, however, like the more traditional works of SF, does create alternate worlds, whether the computer game world of *Luka and the Fire of Life* or the imagined postcolonial conflicts in *Fury*.

Kelley and Kessel cite Jorge Luis Borges as a major influence on their project. Borges' essay "Kafka and His Precursors" becomes a template for the kind of generic hybridity advocated by Sterling and later by Kelley and Kessel. Borges' statement that "every writer creates his own precursors" (xiv) leads Kelley and Kessel to note that the founding writers in the SF genre (Mary Shelley, H.G. Wells and Jules Verne) were not identified as science fiction writers at the time, but "in retrospect they can be identified as such once the genre has been 'invented'" (xiv). In the same way, in the works of such diverse writers as Borges, Coover, Calvino and Bartheleme, we can "discern the shape of slipstream" (xiv).

As Kelley and Kessel point out, "Borges, as devoted to the word as any writer in the last century, did not make high-vs.-low genre distinctions. He drew on Poe and Wells and Chesterton — writers ignored or discounted by the modernist canon — without embarrassment, or even awareness that he ought to be embarrassed" (xiv). The same claim can be made about Rushdie. This lack of embarrassment is one of his defining characteristics as he draws on high and low culture alike. If for Rushdie the Greek myth meets the computer game as a matter of course, pop music icons reenact mythological love stories, cyberspace meets postcolonial revolutions, and the historical tales of national birth and national trauma meld with tales of telepathy and living bombs detonated by lovemaking, then we have a prime example of generic crossing. This delight in boundary crossing is, as I have shown, a thematic and aesthetic concern in Rushdie's oeuvre.

If, however, we look to projects such as Kelley and Kessel's slipstream anthology, we note that the editors have "confined [themselves] to writers active today, primarily in the period since Sterling's essay" and "have taken only stories published in the United States" (xiv). This geographic and linguistic limitation (the anthology only features works written in English) also indicates how this project remains somewhat limited. The editors note this limitation but seem not to focus on its social and political ramifications. I would suggest, then, that if we are to view Rushdie's genre crossing, we can think of it as both participating in what may be termed slipstream, at least to some extent, but we can also view it, as in this book, in terms of its postcolonial thematics as they meet the science fictional form.

I would therefore like to return to one of the key metaphors outlined in my introduction, that of the broken mirror. The notion of "living on a broken mirror," the image employed by Rai, the narrator in *The Ground Beneath Her Feet,* best demonstrates this feeling of strangeness at the heart of Rushdie's brand of postcolonial science fiction. The broken mirror image, as shown in the introduction, also meets Appiah's figure of the ultimate cosmopolitan, Sir Burton, and what I suggested calling Rushdie's "imagined cosmopolitan" sites. The more sinister aspect of the cosmopolitan ideal, however, outlined by both Appiah and Rushdie, finds expression also in the literary reimagining of the personal and the communal as sites of fracture: The mirror is broken and perhaps reflects the many versions of the shape-shifting entity that is the migrant, the cosmopolitan and the writer.

It is interesting to note, then, how this mirror image figures in a tale of identity and its discontents, written by H.P Lovecraft in 1921, aptly named "The Outsider," from which is taken part of the epigraph for this chapter. In Lovecraft's tale, the narrator sees an image that represents all he believes to be horrifying and monstrous in the world. When he reaches out to touch this being, he discovers that the entity he so loathes and fears

Conclusion

is himself. The ending of the tale locates the narrator in front of a "great gilded frame," the mirror of the self, as it meets and realizes its existence as always already Other. This narrative move destabilizes the readers' expectations. In *Science and Destabilization in the Modern American Gothic*, David A. Oakes chooses this tale as an example of the ways Gothic fiction destabilizes its readers by "[inspiring] its readers to ask questions about themselves, their society, and the cosmos surrounding them. It serves as a cultural artifact, reflecting the concerns and fears not only of the time in which it was written but also of the time in which it is read" (1).

These tales, then, "have held up a mirror that captured the dark side" (1) of American society. If we look to Lovecraft, as Mievelle suggests, as the founding father of "Weird Fiction," we can see how this tale touches on the weirdness, or to use Sterling's term, strangeness in the very notion of selfhood. The realization that Lovecraft's narrator faces is that the "monster" is his image in the mirror. He therefore chooses to remove himself from civilized society. The narrator describes what his new existence is like:

> Now I ride with the mocking and friendly ghouls on the night-wind, and play by day amongst the catacombs of Nephren-Ka in the sealed and unknown valley of Hadoth by the Nile. I know that light is not for me, save that of the moon over the rock tombs of Neb, nor any gaiety save the unnamed beasts of Nitokris beneath the Great Pyramid: yet in my new wildness and freedom I almost welcome the bitterness of alienage.

The "monster" finds its freedom and a wild new life amidst a non–Western setting: the Pyramids serve as a site of ultimate otherness, which the narrator embraces in his alien state. What Lovecraft's narrator calls "alienage" is presented then in terms of a removed geography (Egypt) that is also a mental state (the "unknown valley" is the symbolic representation of the psyche's unknowable and dark side). This estrangement is dependent upon an Orientalist view of the East as always a ready Other. In Rushdie's work, "alienage" is a central trope. But his presentation of the outsider, or the antagonist, both reflects and resists colonial, Orientalist, or racialized perceptions. Rushdie's Shechrezade becomes Saleem Sinai; Haroun Al Rashid is now Rashid, the stand-in for the author, and Sinai is both a name and an attribute of the two Saleems of *The Antagonist* and *Midnight's Children*.

In *Joseph Anton* Rushdie describes what he feels like as a "new self" in the wake of the *fatwa*:

> He was a new self now. He was the person in the eye of the storm, no longer the *Salman* his friends knew but the *Rushdie* who was the author of *Satanic Verses*, a title subtly distorted by the omission of the initial *The*. *The Satanic Verses* was a novel. *Satanic Verses* were verses that were satanic and he was their satanic author, "Satan Rushdy," the horned creature on the placards carried by the demonstrators down the streets of a faraway city. How easy it was to erase a man's past and to construct a new version of him, an overwhelming version, against which it seemed impossible to fight [5].

This version of Salman Rushdie as "Satan Rushdy," the monstrous version of the author as a satanic figure, at first seemingly "impossible to fight against," is finally "fought against" over and over again in Rushdie's own constructed versions of his own life and the history of his country.

The creative making of other worlds is performed in Rushdie's rewriting of his nation's historical past and conflicted present. Even in novels that do not deal explicitly with the vexed relations between India and England or the India-Pakistan conflict, such as *Haroun* and *Luka*, the two "children's books" dedicated to Rushdie's sons, the historical conflict and Rushdie's personal tale are at the heart of the novels. It is Rushdie's genius as a writer that he manages to create such diverse fictional worlds, which always end up telling us something about the world we live in now. As I have pointed out, the science fictional imaginings of a postcolonial dilemma are at the heart of the novels I have chosen to discuss. But Rushdie's oeuvre as a whole engages in these sites of imagined possibilities. As I have shown, generic hybridity becomes for Rushdie a way of enacting the personal and collective state of the migrant figure. Rushdie's fictional alter egos are all storytellers and world makers, in one way or another. All reflect Rushdie's description of himself in the final pages of his memoir as a "teller of tales, a creator of shapes, a maker of things that were not" (629–630).

What remains to be seen is how Rushdie's future work will continue to engage with the science fictional mode in its literary and filmic forms. I believe Rushdie's oeuvre will continue to explore the links between science fiction and the postcolonial condition in new and surprising ways. Rushdie's science fictional texts examined here remain highly relevant, engaging as they do with the social and political realities of the time. His works perform what SF does at its best, offering us a broken mirror of the world(s) we inhabit and envisioning an elsewhere that is also the here and now.

Chapter Notes

Preface

1. Rushdie made a cameo appearance in the hit film *Bridget Jones's Diary* in 2001 and a famous *Seinfeld* episode centers on Kramer's (mistaken) sighting of Rushdie in the subway, to name just two examples. Rushdie's marriage to Padma Lakshmi, model and celebrity chef, added to his fame. The recent filmic adaptation of *Midnight's Children* shows that Rushdie is still at the center of public attention.

2. Zoe Heller calls Rushdie to task for what she calls his "exaggerated claim to naiveté" regarding the "offensive" nature of his book. She further claims that Rushdie is making a case for "fiction's immunity from political and religious anger." Heller's most resounding accusation against Rushdie has to do with what she sees as his changing view of Islam and his lack of tolerance regarding Islam: "Now he regards any efforts to separate reactionary forms of Islam from Islam itself as dishonest and wrong." ("The Salman Rushdie Case." *The New York Review of Books.* December 20, 2012).

3. These two conflicting views of the author appear in *Haroun and the Sea of Stories*, Rushdie's fictional response to the *fatwa*. Rushdie is getting back at his critics here, but also reflecting their view of him as a writer of intricate fictions which lack a political or moral commitment.

Chapter 1

1. Rushdie commented on this work in a 1983 interview with Rani Dharker, in which he explains the reasons why he "disliked" his first novel. Rushdie comments on the "fantastic" nature of the text and its disassociation from "actuality": "[F]antasy is not interesting when you separate it from actuality, it's only interesting as a mode of dealing with actuality" (*Salman Rushdie Interviews*, 52). In *Fury*, Rushdie engages with this space of actuality and explores the consequences of the intervention of the fictional in the actual.

2. As Rushdie's fame (or notoriety) came largely in wake of the *Satanic Verses* affair, it would seem audacious to make this claim. What I am suggesting, however, is that Rushdie's writing is *political* in a way that resists what Aurora calls "tractor art." In his extended commentary on the *Satanic Verses* affair, "The Cultural Politics of Rushdie Criticism," Timothy Brennan claims that in that novel Rushdie had written a "500-page epic that realigned English literature, making it more rife with possibilities, more uproarious ... less European—but above all more 'Political' in the grand sense of that word, where history becomes a burr in the flesh of the imagination, taking us back to the fictive musings over sweeping movements of social change" (112).

3. See Elana Gomel's work on the science fictional and fantastic modes as constructing versions of the world. Gomel describes the fantastic, a literary mode that includes science fiction, as a mode offering "different approaches to unreality" (Gomel, 17). The fantastic thus "produces literary dream lands" (23) and "constructs versions of the world" (24). The fantastic mode's main artistic device is its projection of a fictional world, a self sufficient realm: "It is the construction of such a world, into which the reader escapes in search of 'recovery,' 'escape' and 'consolation' that is the primary goal of the fantastic text" (32). The fantastic and science fictional texts may function therefore as possibly healing sites, as is the case in the Rushdie novels I discuss.

Gomel distinguishes between the postmodernist and the fantastic texts. Employing Brian McHale's notion of the ontological dominant of postmodernist fiction, Gomel claims that the fantastic differs from the postmodern text in both rhetoric and ideology. Whereas the fantastic is usually a conservative mode that mimics realistic discourse, postmodern fiction blatantly draws attention to itself as text: "The ontological preoccupation of post modernism is on the illustration of modern fragmentation of reality; the ontological 'dominant' of the fantastic is both an early symptom of, and an unconscious attempt to heal, this fragmentation" (38–39). Although the Rushdie novels I discuss at times share this postmodernist project by foregrounding their own textuality, the attempt to heal fragmented reality is also very apparent in Rushdie's novels. The novels I discuss at length all partake in this project of the fantastic and science fictional modes. Rushdie's literary "dream lands" function then as possibly redemptive sites for the readers or at least as temporary spaces for recovery and consolation.

4. See, for example, Dubravka Juraga's scathing critique of *Midnight's Children* in which Rushdie's novel is described as "a fundamentally Western one that has been elaborately tricked out with ornamentation derived from Indian culture" (184).

5. See also Ghosh's analysis of Aurora's role in *When Borne Across*. Ghosh contends that Aurora is a representative of Mother India in the novel and also India's "best historian" (87). The "mother-son symbiosis" in the novel "depicts the central social imaginary of Indian nationalism" (88). On the other hand, in a paternalistic India, it is the hidden (god) father in the form of Abraham Zogoiby who destroys the social imaginary embodied by Aurora.

6. See Paul Cantor's discussion of *The Moor's Last Sigh* in his "Tales of the Alhambra." Cantor claims that "[in] works such as *The Moor's Last Sigh*, Rushdie has created a fictional world that mirrors the problematics of postcoloniality, a strange kaleidoscopic universe in which figures out of Indian mythology ... rub elbows with characters out of American popular culture, a hybrid landscape in which a Spaniard and an Indian can communicate only because they have seen the same Hollywood Westerns" (14).

7. Appiah's own mixed ethnic background seems to play a significant role in his optimistic belief in the power of border crossing "conversations." But although it would seem this position links him to Rushdie's endorsement of border crossing hybridity, I believe the Rushdean stance is less moralistic than Appiah's and more complex. I believe Rushdie's vexed position as author/migrant does not allow him the comfort of espousing such an optimistic position. He remains forever in doubt—not only about truth value and moral absolutes—but also, and more importantly, about the power of the literary (and cinematic) work to effect change in the world.

8. This anti-religious position is not a far cry from Rushdie's own beliefs. Rushdie repeatedly reiterates his belief in the power of doubt over the certainty offered by religion. In *Joseph Anton* this becomes even more evident. Rushdie's father, Anis, is "a true scholar of Islam, who was also entirely lacking religious belief" (23).

9. See Rushdie's *The Wizard of Oz*, in which he continually draws parallels between

the migrant condition and the film's imagining of the ultimate elsewhere that is "Oz." Thus, for example, he compares the Wizard's tactics as a "migrant" with Dorothy's behavior as she arrives at Emerald City: "But Dorothy learns that meekness isn't enough, and the Wizard finds that ... his command of hot air isn't all it should be. It is hard for a migrant like myself not to see in these shifting destinies a parable of the migrant condition" (54).

10. In *The Wizard of Oz*, Rushdie relates to his own memory lapses: "My bad memory—what my mother would call a 'forgettery'—is probably just as well. I remember what matters" (9).

Chapter 2

1. The tension between the genre's "popular" nature and its status as "Literature" features in numerous contemporary debates. See, for one, Barr, where she calls for a "war" against literary critics who see the genre as inferior. Her "one all-important objective" is "to argue that science fiction should be taken seriously as Literature with a capital 'L'" (430). This tension is reflected in *Fury* as Solanka's cyber saga "Let the Fittest Survive" is commodified and becomes a popular culture phenomenon, much like his first fictional creation, Little Brain. However, the text's philosophical and moral implications are at the core of Solanka's artistic endeavor. Rushdie calls for an engagement with science fiction as a vehicle for expressing moral dilemmas. Moreover, he sees this mode as the best vehicle for such an engagement in the fictional realm.

2. Sarah Brouillette argues that the novel echoes Rushdie's own authorial anxiety about his possible participation in the power structures he seeks to critique in his work. The commodification of Solanka's creation—Little Brain, who breaks away from her author to become a media celebrity—as well as the fate of his cyberspace saga hint at Rushdie's fear of losing control of his artistic integrity and sharing in the orgy of American consumerism that he describes in the novel's opening. Brouillette claims, "[W]ith Rushdie's career in mind, the novel's more significant solipsism is its paranoia about the way mass media make cultural products available for highly politicized forms of approbation or interpretation that betrays the controlling intentions of their authors" (140).

3. Subsequent references to *Fury* are to this edition and are cited by page number in the text.

4. Rabkin and Scholes note that the "designation 'Golden Age' is typical of the American science fiction scene. It is overstated, self-approving, and quite uncritical" (51). Yet they concede that "there is a certain amount of truth buried in that overstated designation after all" (51). It is interesting to note here that Rushdie's narrator refers quite uncritically to this term but chooses to include non-American writers as well, most notably Stanislaw Lem. For example, Solanka relishes the "high brow sci-fi of *Solaris*" (*Fury*, 170).

5. Judi Nitsch reads Solanka as a "Globetrotter" who "never questions the possibly exploitative production" (4) as he admires the commodities on offer: "Though Solanka crosses continents we never glimpse a sweatshop or slum. Indeed Rushdie resolves his narrative with Solanka's return to the metropole to claim his role as middle-class father" (Nitsch, 9). This reading fails to take into account the ironic note in Solanka's view of himself as "egalitarian by nature and a born-and-bred metropolitan of the countryside-is-for-cows persuasion" (6). The multiple ironies in this statement alone problematize Nitsch's condemnation of Rushdie as participating "in the new global economy" as a "curative for Solanka's anxieties of age, gender and identity" (5). Rushdie's novel, as I try to show, is a far more sophisticated exploration of these anxieties.

6. Margaret Wertheim offers an interesting analysis of the early stages of the cyber revolution. She locates the move from the early stage when "cyberutopians were proffering a vision of a new age in which the Internet would enable everyone toe become equal participants in the knowledge society" (Wertheim, 216) to the orthodoxy of the new Internet, where "the market has replaced the temple as the epicenter of our social landscape" and concludes it was "naïve to imagine that cyberspace would provide a more 'pure' foundation for our dreams" (Wertheim, 225). A similar move can be traced in *Fury* where Solanka's earlier enthusiasm gives way to a realization of the commercial nature of his dream of the Web and the disillusionment following the first utopian impulse that led him to author his cyber-saga.

7. Andrew Teverson comments on the links between the internet as a literary form and Rushdie's fictions: "Rushdie believes that the Internet functions in ways that are not dissimilar from his own fictions: it permits the constructions of anti-linear narrative sequences of *Midnight's Children*, and it allows for a degree of narrative interactivity that is also apparent in the complex textualities of *Haroun*. The Internet, in that respect, operates as one more in a long line of metaphors, from the oral narrative tradition in *Haroun* to popular music in *The Ground*, that are designed to be paradigmatic of Rushdie's own writing: heterotopian spaces in which multitudes of influences blend creatively and clash dynamically" (Teverson, 191).

8. Judi Nitsch reads this episode in the novel as another instance of Solanka's problematic relationship with women: "Rushdie's only portrayal of nationalist revolution is tainted by its intersections with his protagonist's love interest" (Nitsch, 7). The revolution is "tainted," I would add, by its own agenda, as Rushdie shows us. Nitsch reads the revolution in the text, however, as "a disturbing example of this mimic man's overt interpretation of world events as gendered threats to his heterosexual fantasy: revolution becomes a vehicle for Solanka to exorcise his insecurities over retaining his younger lover. Accentuating the 'man' in 'mimic man,' Rushdie is placing 'heterosexual lover' as the identity that overrides Solanka's ambivalent colonial self and any subversive ambiguity that lurks therein" (Nitsch, 7).

9. Zahir-un-din Muhammad Babur (1483–1530) was the founder of the Mughal dynasty of India and the author of the *Babur-nama* (Memoirs of Babur). As S.M. Edwards tells us in *Babur: Diarist and Despot*, this fascinating figure "appears before us in the diverse roles of ruler, warrior, sportsman, craftsman, author and a devoted student of Nature" (Edwards, 1). Edwards reads Babur's character in positive, nigh romantic terms, and comments that despite the ruler's "barbarian ancestry" (2), "he was endowed with certain finer qualities" (2). It is this mixture of "diarist," or man of letters, and "despot" that seems to be at the core of fascination with this figure. Rushdie invests his fictional Babur with the cruelty and ruthlessness of his namesake but with none of his "broad minded" attitudes. Rushdie's Babur is a narrow minded despot who insists on his own twisted version of the world and forces Neela to vow that the sun never sets on his new empire (*Fury*, 245). Rushdie's fascination with this figure resurfaces in a later novel, *The Enchantress of Florence* (2008), in which Akbar the Great, Babur's grandson (who shared his grandfather's love of music, poetry and gardens) appears as a main character.

10. In a similar vein, Mila's father Milo Milosevic, a Serb poet, returns to former Yugoslavia and dies there almost as arriving at the scene of conflict. Although Milo hates his namesake, he nonetheless retains his loyalties to the Serbian cause and ends up dying for it.

11. See for one Donna Haraway's call (in "A Manifesto for Cyborgs") for the "pleasure in the confusion of boundaries" and her claim that "the boundary between science fiction and social reality is an optical illusion" (Haraway, 50). Haraway does not ignore

the real "struggle over life and death" (50) but rather constructs a utopian framework that offers transcendence of both gender and genesis.

12. The Prime Directive is a common trope in science fiction, referring to any code of conduct that artificially limits the choices available to the protagonist. It made its most famous appearances in *Star Trek* and in Isaac Asimov's *Three Laws of Robotics*. Rushdie employs it to describe Kronos' edicts to his created beings.

13. Rushdie may be alluding here to J. D. Salinger's *The Catcher in the Rye*, in which the word "phony" becomes the marker of Holden Caulfield's teenage angst and his feelings of alienation, reflected here in the aging Solanka's petulant, at times almost adolescent, reflections.

Chapter 3

1. Rushdie comments on this aspect of his novel and alludes to the fact that he chose to open the plot in 1989 with Vina's death in a Mexican earthquake. In an interview with Peter Kadzis, he recounts his doubts about leaving this autobiographical reference in the text: "I vacillated a great deal about whether to leave that date in or not. There was a bit of me that thought it was digging the reader in the ribs too hard to leave it in. In the end I did, simply because I thought, well, one of the reasons I'm writing a novel about cataclysms in people's lives, about earthquakes, about the fact that the world is provisional and the life you think is yours can be removed from you at any moment ... is because of what happened in my life, and I may as well acknowledge that fact" (224).

2. Linguanti's model is akin in many ways to Wolfgang Iser's discussion of possible worlds. As I have shown in my introductory chapter, I find Iser's model a very useful way of approaching Rushdie's novels. In my reading of *The Ground Beneath Her Feet*, however, I focus on a more strictly "science fictional" model as it allows me to examine the unique narrative techniques employed in the novel.

3. It is interesting to note that two other alternative history novels, both overtly science fictional ones, Philip K. Dick's *The Man in the High Castle* (which depicts an imaginary world where the Germans and the Japanese have won World War II) and Philip Roth's *The Plot Against America* (which imagines a different scenario of Nazi domination and does not have any science fictional elements), are ideologically invested in ways that Rushdie's novel is not. Both texts *do* engage, unlike Rushdie's, with imagining a world where one central event (World War II) has veered off its "proper" historical track, and they try to gauge how the world as we know it is shaken by this dramatic "twist" in history.

4. And this, as Saint-Gelais shows, is what Rushdie's novel has in common with *The Man in the High Castle*, in which "the otherness of the fictional world is gradually revealed, not through a detailed and explicit expose but rather through the dispersion of details throughout the text" (29).

5. For a detailed discussion of the different Greek and Latin mythological allusions in the novel, see Rossi, 23–41, and Monti, 43–52.

6. For a discussion of Rai's dual role as narrator/photographer and its implications, see Concilio, 117–27.

7. Rushdie here refers to a real cartoon by Gary Larson that shows Rushdie and Elvis in a hotel room. His version of the cartoon in the novel thus alludes to Rushdie's own celebrity status.

8. For a discussion of the novel in terms of the classical Greek narrative of the hero's journey into the underworld in search of his lost love, see Rachel Falconer's "Bounc-

ing Down to the Underworld: Classical Katabasis in *The Ground Beneath Her Feet*." Falconer suggests that Ormus, Vina and Rai all make this journey to the underground but only one finally returns: "If *The Ground Beneath Her Feet* is about descending to hell and returning, it is as well to remember that this journey starts and all but ends upside down, with two of the protagonists in lowest hell, and only one of them returning to the surface. So, if from one perspective, the novel traces a journey from periphery to center of the world and back, from another perspective, this journey moves from deepest hell upward, and then back down" (Falconer, 6). Falconer concludes that the novel's "ultimate optimism" is to be found in the new family that Rai finds at the end of the novel: "In the last chapter, Ormus and Vina are dead, but Mira is now Hope to Rai (replacing Rai as 'Hope' to Vina), Rai is now Music to Mira, and Mira's child Tara looks uncannily like Vina, although she is tone deaf and unmusical. It is not only art that proves to be unstoppable; individuals also survive by repeating themselves, as do whole culture and cities" (Falconer, 20–21).

9. It is interesting to note the parallels between Ormus and Rushdie as famous migrants who are both revered and attacked for their art. In a revealing comment Rushdie makes in an interview with Peter Kadzis, he talks of Ormus as a modern day Orpheus figure: "I think of the end of the Orpheus myth, in which the head of Orpheus, having been torn from his body, is thrown into the river and goes on singing. That's the meaning of that story. You can destroy the singer, but you can't stop the song. And I think that for fairly obvious reasons, that's an important thought for me to have and to hold on to" (224). In the same interview, Rushdie also relates to Rai's figure as a photographer/narrator and hints at the close links between author and narrator figures. When asked why he chose to have a photographer as narrator and why Rai is tone deaf, Rushdie briefly replies, "Well, he can't sing because I can't sing. That's very simple" (226). Rushdie thus aligns himself with Rai and Ormus as his fictional alter egos.

10. For a discussion of Bombay's role in the novel, see Concilio, 129–149. Concilio claims that "Bombay is the certainly the most imposing character in *TGBHF*" (130) and Bombay becomes both the "text" and "texture" for narration in the novel.

11. Bassi traces the trajectory of the Orpheus figure — from its appearance in Greek mythology to the Renaissance and modern day rewritings of the Orpheus myth — and compares Ormus's role as a modern day Orpheus to Freddie Mercury, another famous migrant singer.

12. Andrew Teverson comments on the role popular music plays in the novel. He claims, "[Like] the novel form itself, pop music is imagined as a dialogical and heteroglossic aesthetic medium that is by definition antagonistic to singular conceptions of self and society. *The Ground Beneath Her Feet*, in this sense, is not just a novel about pop music; pop music is also about the novel" (Teverson, 186).

13. For a discussion of the biblical allusions in the text, see Marchesi, 56–68.

14. Tara is named after a mythological goddess. This choice of name allows Rushdie to add an ironic touch to her very "earthly" comments regarding Ormus and Vina as god and goddess figures. Further, Tara sounds like "Terra" or earth, and she becomes the "firm ground" beneath Rai's feet at the end of the novel.

Chapter 4

1. See, for example, Josna E. Rege's defense of Rushdie as a writer committed to the national idea of India. Rege claims that despite the novel's "conceptual freshness and vitality, *Midnight's Children* remains very much emotionally committed to the narrative

of nation. In the end, it can only reconfigure ideological categories, not step out of them altogether" (274).

2. See Teresa Heffernan's reading of the novel, where she argues that the novel "is ... suspicious of the very model — with its apocalyptic underpinnings — of the modern nation," and therefore "explores an alternative, though equally apocalyptic, concept of the nation, the Islamic umma" (2). Heffernan claims that "securing these models is the figure of the (un)veiled woman, who tacitly calls into question the very apocalyptic language of 'unveiling' on which they both rest" (2).

3. As Andrew Teverson demonstrates in his reading of the novel, Rushdie "promotes an anti-Enlightenment historiography that is determined to deconstruct Enlightenment concepts of cultural coherence and historical progress" (134). This view of historical narrative resists the mythology of endings as they participate in acts of colonial violence: "Mythologies of endings, in this context, have tended to justify acts of colonialism and accompanying acts of violence" (134). One may say then that the ending of *Midnight's Children* resists this act of colonization by refusing to offer an ending that would accord with its narrator's *own* mythologizing acts of narration.

4. Ram Mohan Roy (1722–1833), an Indian reformer and educator, was best known for his effort to abolish *sati*. He sought to integrate Western culture with features of Indian tradition. Rushdie chooses his figure to symbolize the ability to reconcile the two cultures. Roy lived in England for the last years of his life and was buried there. He acted as the ambassador of the Mughal emperor, Akbar II, who conferred on him the title of raja. Rushdie's fascination with the figure of the first Mughal emperor, Akbar, appears in *Shalimar the Clown*. This possibility of peaceful coexistence between England and India is shattered by political realities but still remains a utopian option in Rushdie's oeuvre.

5. In "Intimations of Lifelessness," Stephen Handzo comments on Sirk's manipulation of the woman's picture genre: "Sirk employs the convention in order to emphasize the limitations of those conventions and to show the need for a larger more ideological world-view. No wonder Sirk said of *Imitation of Life:* 'I would have made it for the title alone'" (http:www.brightlightsfilm.com/18/18_lana.html).

Chapter 5

1. In Andrew Teverson's favorable reading of Rushdie's text, he mentions such claims made by Srinivas Aravamudan, who accuses Rushdie of writing a "banal didactic fiction that demonstrates ... everything that is wrong with liberal assumptions about literature" (Teverson, 452, quoting Aravamudan).

2. This is only one of a number of Kafka allusions in the text. The novel's magical sea of stories, for one, is populated by Plentimaw Fishes, described as "hunger artists," after Kafka's well known tale. In the land of Chup, or the land of silence, we encounter a "Shadow Warrior" who cannot speak but gestures instead. His only utterance is "Gogogol" and "Kafkakafka," in what may be Rushdie's homage to the two literary giants.

3. We may assume Rushdie is alluding here to the former Pakistani leader, although "Snooty Buttoo" is a figure for corrupt politicians everywhere.

4. Rushdie is alluding here both to the Walrus in *Through the Looking Glass*, who "talks of many things" and is a kind of "scientist" or "egghead" figure, and to the John Lennon song, inspired by Carroll's text, "I am the Walrus."

5. Yuvraj Singh is also the name of a very famous cricket star, the son of a famous Bollywood star of the same name. Yuvraj junior achieved one of his most impressive successes on the cricket field in 2005, the year Rushdie's novel came out.

6. As Andrew Teverson points out in "Rushdie's Last Lost Homeland," "[If] there is one redeeming element in *Shalimar*, it resides in the next generation, as was the case in *Midnight's Children*." Teverson describes Kashmira as a "hybrid being who lives in America and loves her American father, but who is also in the process of discovering who her father really is, what he has done and what her mother was. Global politics may be such that old Kashmir no longer exists, Kashmira's story tells us, but globalization has also generated new combinations, new ethnicities, that exist in complex relationships with the power systems that have produced them, and in which the possibilities of new forms of political equilibrium resides—neither fully sympathetic to the U.S., nor in the arms of absolutist militants" (Teverson, 3–4). My reading of Kashmira's role is similar, but I focus more on the poetics of Rushdie's endings and the roles played by his hybrid sons and daughters in establishing this poetics.

Chapter 6

1. Rushdie comments on his choice to write children's books in an interview for *The Times*. Commenting on Martin Amis's scathing dismissal of writing a children's book, Rushdie comments: "I said to Martin that the line that rings truest to me is something E.B. White said, around the time he wrote *Charlotte's Web*. He said, 'You don't write down to children: you write up to them.'"

2. Rushdie reproduces the "Hieroglyphs" in the novel, thus creating a different "language" to be "translated" alongside his many playful insertions of Hindi words and phrases, as in the Aalim's names.

3. Maat is both the ancient Egyptian concept of justice and the name of an Egyptian goddess who represents this view of "order" and "justice."

Works Cited

Aarseth, J. Epsen. *Cybertext*. Baltimore: Johns Hopkins University Press, 1997. Print.
Ahmed, Sara. *Strange Encounters*. London: Routledge, 2000. Print.
Aji, Aron R. "'All Names Mean Something': Salman Rushdie's Haroun and the Legacy of Islam." *Contemporary Literature* 36.1 (Spring 1995): 103.
Appiah, Anthony. *Cosmopolitanism: Ethics in a World of Strangers*. New York: Norton, 2006. Print.
Asimov, Isaac. *I, Robot*. New York: Bantam, 2008. Print.
Atwood, Margaret. *In Other Worlds: SF and the Human Imagination*. London: Virago, 2011. Print.
Aupers, Stef. "'Better than the Real World': On the Reality and Meaning of Online Computer Games." *Fabula* 48.3/4 (2007): 250–69. Print.
Barr, Marleen S. "Textism: An Emancipation Proclamation." *PMLA* 119.3 (2004): 429–41. Print.
Bassi, Shaul. "Orpheus's Other Voyage: Myth, Music and Globalization." In *The Great Work of Making Real: Salman Rushdie's* The Ground Beneath Her Feet, ed. Elsa Linguanti and Viktoria Tchernichova, 99–114. Pisa: ETS, 2003. Print.
Baudrillard, Jean. *The Transparency of Evil*. Trans. James Benedict. London: Verso, 1993. Print.
Baum, Frank L. *The Wonderful Wizard of Oz*. London: Penguin, 1995. Print.
Bauman, Zygmunt. *Mortality, Immortality and Other Life Strategies*. Cambridge: Polity, 1992. Print.
Blake, William. "To Old Nobodday." In *Poems of William Blake*, ed. William Butler Yeats. London: New York: Routledge, 2002. Print.
Bould, Mark. *Science Fiction*. London: Routledge, 2012. Print.
Brennan, Timothy. "The Cultural Politics of Rushdie Criticism: All or Nothing." In *Critical Essays on Salman Rushdie*, ed. Keith M. Booker, 107–28. New York: G.K. Hall, 1999. Print.
_____. "*Midnight's Children*, History and Complexity: Reading Rushdie after the Cold War." In *Critical Essays on Salman Rushdie*, ed. Keith M. Booker, 283–314. New York: G.K. Hall, 1999. Print.
_____. *Salman Rushdie and the Third World: Myths of the Nation*. London: Macmillan, 1989. Print.
Bronfen, Elizabeth. "Risky Resemblances: On Repetition, Mourning and Representation." In *Death and Representation (Parallax: Re-visions of Culture and Society)*, ed. Sarah Webster Goodwin and Elizabeth Bronfen, 103–129. Baltimore: Johns Hopkins University Press, 1993. Print.
Brouillette S. "Authorship as Crisis in Salman Rushdie's *Fury*." In *Journal of Commonwealth Literature* 40.1 (2005): 137–56. Print.

Works Cited

Buchan-Terrell, Allison. "Salman Rushdie: When Censorship Is Mislabelled Respect." *The Inside Agenda Blog*, 3 January 2011.
Bukatman, Scott. *Terminal Identity: The Virtual Subject in Post-Modern Science Fiction*. Durham: Duke University Press, 1993. Print.
Cantor, Paul. "Tales of the Alhambra: Rushdie's Use of Spanish History in *The Moor's Last Sigh*." *Studies in the Novel* 29 (1997): 323–42. Print.
Chakravarty, Sumita, S. "Fragmenting the Nation: Images of Terrorism in Indian Popular Cinema." In *Cinema and Nation*, ed. Mette Hjort and Scott MacKenzie, 222–35. London: Routledge, 2000. Print.
Chauhan, Pradyumna, ed. *Salman Rushdie Interviews: A Sourcebook of His Ideas*. Westport, CT: Greenwood, 2001. Print.
Clark, Alex. *Luka and the Fire of Life* (Review). *The Guardian*, 16 October 2010.
Coleridge, Samuel, Taylor. "Kubla Khan." In *The Norton Anthology of English Literature*, ed. M.H. Abrahams, 1505–06. New York: W.W. Norton, 1996. Print.
_____. "The Rime of the Ancient Mariner." In *The Norton Anthology of English Literature*, ed. M.H. Abrahams, 1487–504. New York: WW. Norton, 1996. Print.
Concilio, Carmen. "The City as Text(ure): Bombay in Salman Rushdie's *The Ground Beneath Her Feet*." In *The Great Work of Making Real: Salman Rushdie's* The Ground Beneath Her Feet, ed. Elsa Linguanti and Viktoria Tchernichova, 129–49. Pisa: ETS, 2003. Print.
_____. "'Worthy of the World': The Narrator/Photographer in Salman Rushdie's *The Ground Beneath Her Feet*." In *The Great Work of Making Real: Salman Rushdie's* The Ground Beneath Her Feet, ed. Elsa Linguanti and Viktoria Tchernichova, 117–27. Pisa: ETS, 2003. Print.
Cundy, Catherine. *Salman Rushdie: Contemporary World Authors*. Manchester: Manchester University Press, 1996. Print.
Dick, Philip K. *The Man in the High Castle*. London: Penguin, 2000. Print.
Dillon, Grace. "Totemic Human-Animal Relationships in Recent SF." *Extrapolation*, 22 March 2008.
Edwards, S.M. *Babur Diarist and Despot*. New Delhi: Universal Voice, 2010. Print.
Evans, Katherine, A. "Luka Pilgrim Saves the World." *The Critical Flame: A Journal of Literature and Culture*. 31 July 2012.
Falconer, Rachel. "Bouncing Down to the Underworld: Classical Katabasis in *The Ground Beneath Her Feet*." *Twentieth Century Literature* 47 (2001): 467–509. Web: ProQuest, 7 Aug. 2008.
Fiedler, Leslie A. *Cross the Border— Close the Gap*. New York: Stein and Day, 1973. Print.
Gerber, Richard. *Utopian Fantasy: A Study of English Utopian Fiction Since the End of the Nineteenth Century*. London: McGraw-Hill, 1973. Print.
Ghosh, Bishnupriya. *When Borne Across: Literary Cosmopolitics in the Contemporary Indian Novel*. New Brunswick: Rutgers University Press, 2004. Print.
Gomel, Elana. *Woman as Monster: Images of Women in Nineteenth Century Fantastic*. Dissertation, Tel Aviv University, 1988. Print.
Gonzalez M . "Artistic 'Fury' in the Information Age: Nostalgia for the Real." *Information, Communication and Society* 11.6 (2008): 765–80. Print.
Graham, L. Elaine. *Representations of the Post/Human*. New Brunswick: Rutgers University Press, 2002. Print.
Haraway, J. Donna. "A Manifesto for Cyborgs: Science, Technology and Socialist Feminism in the 1980." In *Feminism/Postmodernism*, ed. Linda J Nicholson, 190–233. New York; London: Routledge, 1990. Print.
Hawely, C. John. "Mapping Utopia: Spatial and Temporal Modes of Meaning." In *The

Works Cited

Utopian Fantastic: Selected Essays from the Twentieth International Conference on the Fantastic in the Arts, ed. Martha Bartter, 17–22. Connecticut: Praeger, 2004. Print.

Heffernan, Theresa. "Apocalyptic Narratives: The Nation in Salman Rushdie's *Midnight's Children*." *Twentieth Century Literature* 46.4 (2000): 470–92.

Heim, Michael. "The Erotic Ontology of Cyberspace." In *Cyberspace: First Steps*, ed. Michael Benedikt, 59–80. Cambridge, MA: MIT Press, 1991. Print.

Heller, Zoe. "The Salman Rushdie Case." *The New York Review of Books*, 26 December, 2012.

Hoegland, Erica, and Reema Sarwal, eds. *Science Fiction, Imperialism and the Third World*. Jefferson, NC: McFarland, 2010. Print.

Hutcheon, Linda. *A Poetics of Postmodernism: History, Theory Fiction*. London: Routledge, 1988. Print.

Iser, Wolfgang. *The Fictive and the Imaginary*. Baltimore: Johns Hopkins University Press, 1993. Print.

James, Edward, and Farah Mendlesohn, eds. *The Cambridge Companion to Science Fiction*. Cambridge: Cambridge University Press, 2003. Print.

Jameson, Fredric. *Archaeologies of the Future: The Desire Called Utopia and Other Science Fictions*. London: Verso. 2005. Print.

———. "Utopianism and Anti-Utopianism." In *The Jameson Reader*, ed. Michael Hardt and Kathi Weeks, 382–92. Oxford: Blackwell, 2000. Print.

Juraga, Dubravka. "'The Mirror of Us All': *Midnight's Children* and the Twentieth Century Bildungsroman." In *Critical Essays on Salman Rushdie*, ed. Keith M. Booker, 169–87. New York: G.K. Hall, 1999. Print.

Kelley, James Patrick, and John Kessel, ed. *Feeling Very Strange: The Slipstream Anthology*. San Francisco: Taychon, 2006. Print.

Kuchta, Todd. "Allegorizing the Emergency: Rushdie's *Midnight's Children* and Benjamin's Theory of Allegory." In *Critical Essays on Salman Rushdie*, ed. Keith M. Booker, 205–24. New York: G.K. Hall, 1999. Print.

Langer, Jessica. *Postcolonialism and Science Fiction*. New York: Palgrave, 2011. Print.

Legatt, Judith. "Other Worlds, Other Selves: Science Fiction in Salman Rushdie's *The Ground Beneath Her Feet*." *Ariel* 33.1 (2002): 105–25. Print.

Levi-Strauss, Claude. *Structural Anthropology*. Trans. Claire Jacobson and Brooke Schoepf. New York: Basic, 1953. Print.

Linguanti, Elsa. "Different Whatness." In *The Great Work of Making Real: Salman Rushdie's* The Ground Beneath Her Feet, ed. Elsa Linguanti and Viktoria Tchernichova, 151–63. Pisa: ETS, 2003. Print.

Lovecraft, H.P. "The Outsider" (1921). Web, HP Lovecraft http://www.hplovecraft.com/writings/texts/fiction/o.aspx. Accessed 29 May 2013.

Marchesi, Maria Serena. "'*No sermons on the mount*'": Salman Rushdie's Use of the Bible in *The Ground Beneath Her Feet*." In *The Great Work of Making Real: Salman Rushdie's* The Ground Beneath Her Feet, ed. Elsa Linguanti and Viktoria Tchernichova, 55–68. Pisa: ETS, 2003. Print.

McHale, Brian. *Postmodernist Fiction*. New York: Methuen, 1987. Print.

Mievelle, China. "Weird Fiction." In *The Routledge Companion to Science Fiction*, ed. Mark Bould et al., 510–15. New York: Routledge, 2009. Print.

———. "Long Live the New Weird." *The Third Alternative* 35 (2003): 3.

Monti, Allesandro. "A Hoarding of Goats and Rumours of Mermaids: Puzzling Out Myth in *The Ground Beneath Her Feet*." In *The Great Work of Making Real: Salman Rushdie's* The Ground Beneath Her Feet, ed. Elsa Linguanti and Viktoria Tchernichova, 43–53. Pisa: ETS, 2003. Print.

Works Cited

Morrissey, J. Thomas. "Not So Blind Hope: An Introduction." In *The Utopian Fantastic: Selected Essays from the Twentieth International Conference on the Fantastic in the Arts*, ed. Marthat Barrter, 1–9. Westport, CT: Praeger, 2004. Print.

Moulthrop, Stuart. "Misadventure: Future Fiction and the New Networks." *Style* 33.2 (Summer 1999): 184–203.

Nelson, Davia. "Salman Rushdie and the Sea of Stories." *American Theatre* 20.3 (March 2003): 26–40. Print.

Nitsch, J. In *Writing the Postcolonial*. 2002 MMLA http://www.case.edu/affil/sce/Texts_2002/Nitschptr.html Web. Accessed 16 December 2013.

Nora, Pierre. "Between Memory and History." In *Realms of Memory: Rethinking the French Past*, vol. 1, trans. Arthur Goldhammer, ed. Lawrence D. Kritzman, 1–20. New York: Columbia University Press, 1996. Print.

Oakes, David A. *Science and Destabilization in the Modern American Gothic: Lovecraft, Matheson, and King*. Westport: Greenwood, 2000. Print.

Orphanos, Spyros D. "Mythos and Logos." *Psychoanalytic Dialogues* 16.4 (July/August 2006): 481–99. Print.

Pitkin, Annabella. "Salman Rushdie Loses His Cheerfulness: Geopolitics, Terrorism and Adultery." *Journal of International Affairs* 61 (2007): 257–62. Print.

Plato. *Timaeus*. Trans. Benjamin Jewett. The Hermetic Library. http://classics.mit.edu/Plato/timaeus.html

Raja, Masood Ashraf, Ellis Jason, and Nandi Swaralipi, eds. *The Postnational Fantasy*. Jefferson, NC: McFarland, 2011. Print.

Rank, Otto. "The Promethean Complex." *A Psychology of Difference: The American Lectures of Otto Rank*, ed. R. Kramer, 201–10. Princeton, NJ: Princeton University Press, 1996. Print.

Reder, Michael. "Rewriting History and Identity: The Reinvention of Myth, Epic and Allegory in Salman Rushdie's *Midnight's Children*." In *Critical Essays on Salman Rushdie*, ed. Keith M. Booker, 225–49. New York: G. K Hall, 1999. Print.

Reje, Josna E. "Victim into Protagonist? *Midnight's Children* and the Post-Rushdie National Narratives of the Eighties." In *Critical Essays on Salman Rushdie*, ed. Keith M. Booker, 250–81. New York: G. K Hall, 1999. Print.

Ricoeur, Paul. *A Ricoeur Reader: Reflection and Imagination*, ed. Mario J. Valdes. New York and London: Harvester, Wheatsheaf, 1991. Print.

_____. *Lectures on Ideology and Utopia*, ed. George H. Taylor. New York: Columbia University Press, 1986. Print.

Rieder, John. *Colonialism and the Emergence of* Science *Fiction*. Connecticut: Wesleyan University Press, 2008. Print.

Roberts, A. *Science Fiction*. Routledge: London, 2006. Print.

Roberts, Daniel. "Rushdie and the Romantics: Intertextual Politics in *Haroun and the Sea of Stories*." *Ariel*, 1 Oct. 2007. The Free Library. http://www.thefreelibrary.com/Rushdie+and+the+Romantics%3a+intertextual+politics+in+Haroun+and+the...-a0182047192> Web. Accessed 16 December 2013.

Rollason, Christopher. "'Rushdie's Un-Indian Music': *The Ground Beneath Her Feet*." http://yatrarollason.info/files/RushdieGFupdated.pdf Web. Accessed 16 December 2013.

_____. "An Unsurprising World of Magic? Review of Salman Rushdie, *Luka and the Fire of Life*." *Bilingual Culture Blog*, 22 Feb. 2011.

Rose, Jacqueline. *States of Fantasy*. New York: Oxford University Press, 1998. Print.

Ross, J.W. *Conversations with Salman Rushdie*. Jackson: University Press of Mississippi, 1982. Print.

Works Cited

Rossi, Elena. "'Against an Amnesiac Culture': Greek and Latin Mythology in *The Ground Beneath Her Feet*." In *The Great Work of Making Real: Salman Rushdie's The Ground Beneath Her Feet*, ed. Elsa Linguanti and Viktoria Tchernichova, 23–41. Pisa: ETS, 2003. Print.

Roth, Philip. *The Plot Against America*. London: Vintage, 2005. Print.

Rushdie, Salman. *The Antagonist*. Salman Rushdie Papers Archive, Box 43. Atlanta, Emory University, 1975. Print.

———. "Contemporary Authors." Interview by W. Jean Ross. In *Conversations with Salman Rushdie*, ed. Michael R. Reder, 1–7. Jackson, MS: University Press of Mississippi, 2000. Print.

———. "A Dream of Glorious Return." In *Imaginary Homelands: Essays and Criticism 1981–1991*, 180–209. London: Granta, 1991. Print.

———. *The Enchantress of Florence*. London: Jonathan Cape, 2008. Print.

———. "'Errata': Or, Unreliable Narration in *Midnight's Children*." In *Imaginary Homelands: Essays and Criticism 1981–1991*, 22–25. London: Granta, 1991. Print.

———. *Fury*. London: Vintage, 2002. Print.

———. *Grimus*. New York: Modern Library, 2003. Print.

———. *The Ground Beneath Her Feet*. London: Vintage, 2000. Print.

———. *Haroun and the Sea of Stories*. London: Penguin, 1990. Print.

———. *Imaginary Homelands*. London: Granta, 1991. Print.

———. "Influence." In *Imaginary Homelands: Essays and Criticism 1981–1991*, 62–70. London: Granta, 1991. Print.

———. *The Jaguar Smile: A Nicaraguan Journey*. New York: Random House, 2008. Print.

———. *Joseph Anton*. London: Jonathan Cape, 2012. Print.

———. "The Location of Brazil." In *Imaginary Homelands: Essays and Criticism 1981–1991*, 118–25. London: Granta, 1991. Print.

———. *Luka and the Fire of Life*. London: Random House, 2010. Print.

———. *Midnight's Children*. London: Jonathan Cape; New York: Penguin, 1991. Print.

———. *The Moor's Last Sigh*. New York: Vintage, 1997. Print.

———. "Notes on Writing and the Nation." In *Imaginary Homelands: Essays and Criticism 1981–1991*, 58–69. London: Granta, 1991. Print.

———. "Salman Speaks." Interview by Peter Kadzis. In *Conversations with Salman Rushdie*, ed. Michael R. Reder, 216–27. Jackson: University Press of Mississippi, 2000. Print.

———. *The Satanic Verses*. London: Viking/Penguin, 1988. Print.

———. *Shalimar the Clown*. New York: Random House, 2005. Print.

———. *Step Across This Line: Collected Nonfiction 1992–2002*. New York: Modern Library, 2003. Print.

———. *The Wizard of Oz*. London: BFI, 1992. Print.

Saint-Gelais, Richard. "Impossible Times: Some Temporal Labyrinths in Science Fiction." Trans. Carolyn Perkes. In *Worlds Enough and Time*, ed. Garry Wesfahl, George Slusser and David Leiby, 25–36. Connecticut: Greenwood, 2002. Print.

Salinger, J.D. *The Catcher in the Rye*. New York: Little, Brown. 2001. Print.

Sanga, Jaina. *Salman Rushdie's Postcolonial Metaphors*. London: Greenwood, 2001. Print.

Scholes, R., and E.S. Rabkin. *Science Fiction: History, Science, Vision*. Oxford: Oxford University Press. 1977. Print.

Sen, Suchismita. "Memory, Language and Society in Salman Rushdie's *Haroun and the Sea of Stories*." *Contemporary Literature* 36.4 (Winter 1995): 654. Print.

Sterling, Bruce. "Slipstream." *SF Eye 5*, July 1998.

Su, John J. "Epic of Failure: Disappointment as Utopian Fantasy in *Midnight's Children*." *Twentieth Century Literature* 47 (2001): 545–568. Print.

Suvin, Darko. *Metamorphoses of Science Fiction: On the Poetics and History of a Literary Genre*. New Haven, CT: Yale University Press, 1979. Print.
Teverson, Andrew. "Fairy Tale Politics: Free Speech and Multiculturalism in *Haroun and the Sea of Stories*." *Twentieth Century Literature* 47.4 (Winter 2010): 444–66. Print.
_____. "Rushdie's Last Lost Homeland: Kashmir in *Shalimar the Clown*." *The Literary Magazine* 1.1 (2005).
_____. *Salman Rushdie: Contemporary World Writers*, ed. John Thieme. Manchester: Manchester University Press, 2007. Print.
Todorov, Tzvetan. *The Fantastic: A Structural Approach to a Literary Genre*. Trans. Richard Howard. New York: Cornel University Press, 1975. Print.
Wertheim, Margaret. "Internet Dreaming: A Utopia for All Seasons." In *Prefiguring Cyberculture*, ed. Darren Tofts, AnneMarie Jonson and Allessio Cavallero, 216–27. Cambdrige: MIT Press, 2002. Print.
Wharton, Thomas. "A Return to the Land of Haroun." Review. *Saturday's Globe and Mail*. 19 November 2010.
Wilde, Oscar. *The Artist as Critic: Critical Writings of Oscar Wilde*. Ed. Richard Ellmann. Chicago: University of Chicago Press, 1969. Print.
Wolpert, Stanley. *India and Pakistan: Continued Conflict or Cooperation?* Berkeley: University of California Press, 2010. Print.
Žižek, Slavoj. "Is It Possible to Traverse the Fantasy in Cyberspace?" In *The Žižek Reader*, ed. Elizabeth Wright and Edmund Wright. Oxford: Blackwell Publishers, 1999. Print.

Index

Ahmed, Sara 6, 7
Alice (in Wonderland, Through the Looking Glass) 42, 129, 151
alienation 2, 4–8, 17, 62, 83, 88, 178, 184, 191n13
alterity 2–4
apocalypse 99, 101
Appiah, Quame Anthony 11, 16–20, 24, 25, 183, 188n7
Arabian Nights 122–123, 125, 162; see also *A Thousand and One Nights*
art 2, 11–14, 16, 18, 20, 21, 30, 31, 70, 77, 80, 88, 90, 96, 122, 125, 130, 136, 139, 188n3, 193n2
atom bomb 90

Baudrillard, Jean 91, 150, 180
Bauman Zigmunt 59, 61, 62, 69, 72, 73
The Birds 176; see also Hitchcock, Alfred
Blake, William 149–151
Bombay 12, 15, 67, 85, 86, 105, 106, 108, 109, 117, 119, 192n10
Bowie, David 51
Brazil 24, 50; see also Gilliam, Terry
Brennan, Timothy 12, 187c1n2
Burton, Sir Richard Francis 18–21, 183

Chup 121, 124, 126–129, 132, 136, 137, 139, 162, 193c5n2
cinema 24, 47, 50, 79, 81, 84–86, 89, 91, 92, 115–119, 123, 141, 188n7
Cleopatra 88
clone 45, 51, 64–66
computer game 11, 28, 149–156, 165, 169, 172, 175, 180, 182
cosmopolitan 2, 11–21, 24, 183
Coyote 170

cyberspace 8, 10, 30–39, 41, 43, 44, 46–48, 183, 189n2, 190n6
cyborg 30, 38, 40, 41, 190n11

Delhi 15, 86
desert 78, 87, 88, 93–96, 99
Dickens, Charles 154
diva 52, 57, 58, 62
double (doppelganger) 45, 63–65, 115, 150, 168
dream 16, 23, 24, 27, 31, 40, 46, 47, 73, 76, 89, 100, 102, 109, 113, 122, 129, 131, 135, 138, 141, 142, 144, 147, 149, 150, 151, 169, 171, 172, 174, 182, 188n3, 190n6

Egypt 84, 88, 117, 184, 194n3
Elvis 51–53, 62, 191n7
empire 6, 10, 26, 31, 40, 46, 47, 76, 78, 80–82, 84, 88, 92–95, 159, 190n9
The Enchantress of Florence 190n9
Englishness 158
Eurydice 51, 57, 60, 61

the fantastic 4, 27–29, 32, 33, 51, 75, 79, 100–103, 114, 119, 123, 124, 126, 128, 130, 137, 143, 169, 172, 174–176, 178, 181, 187c1n1, 188n3
femme fatale 65

Gandhi, Indira 87
Gandhi, Mahatma 85–87, 89, 100
Gatsby 46
Gilliam, Terry 24, 50; see also *Brazil*
globalization 7, 17, 67, 194n6
God 34, 37, 40, 43, 52, 72, 73, 105, 118, 150

Index

gods and goddesses 42, 52, 57, 58–60, 69–71, 71–72, 146, 151, 164, 165, 173–175, 192n4, 194n3
golden age 4, 33, 46, 189n4
Gulliver's Travels 38, 39, 42, 47; see also Swift, Jonathan
Gup 121, 124, 126–128, 132–134, 136, 139, 140, 158

Hitchcock, Alfred 64, 176; see also *The Birds*
home (homeland) 3, 4, 12, 14–16, 24, 31, 33, 34, 38, 39, 45, 46, 47, 50, 61, 63, 69, 70, 72, 83, 108, 119, 129, 131, 138, 140, 145, 147, 154, 194n6

icon 26, 48, 51, 52, 58, 59, 62, 68, 69, 71, 183
Imitation of Life 115–116, 118, 193c4n5; see also Sirk, Douglass
immortality 11, 28, 57, 59, 62, 71, 72, 73, 148, 149, 151, 153, 155, 158, 169
imperial 2, 4, 6, 8, 17, 47, 74, 76, 78, 92, 93, 158, 159
Indianness 4, 15, 88, 170
Iser, Wolfgang 8, 21–24, 115, 191n2

Jameson, Fredrick 10, 11, 44

Kashmir 27, 28, 48, 85, 86, 89, 108, 109, 121, 124, 127, 130, 131, 134, 135, 139, 140–147, 194n6
Kathakali theatre 136, 137
Kipling, Rudyard 84

Langer, Jessica 5, 6, 176, 179
Lilliput-Blefuscu 30, 33, 36, 38–41, 43, 46
London 31, 39, 47, 82, 95
loop 33, 59, 62, 69, 71, 149, 171
Lovecraft, H.P. 178, 179, 183, 184

Madonna (icon) 58
Madonna (singer) 51, 58
Magical Realism 1, 3
martyr 58
McHale, Brian 52, 74, 188n3
melodrama 80, 86, 96, 105, 107, 115–117
memory 9, 26, 39, 62, 65, 70, 72, 74, 101, 105, 110, 147, 176, 189n10

migrant (immigrant) 2–4, 9, 12, 14, 19, 24, 25, 27, 29–30, 33, 67, 79, 82, 84, 94, 95, 137, 162, 183, 185, 188n7, 189n9, 192n9
Monroe, Marilyn 51, 52, 58
The Moor's Last Sigh 11, 12, 14, 15, 19, 27, 107, 147, 188n6
Mother India 9, 12, 15, 16, 27, 79, 96, 107, 188n5
Mudra 136, 137

New York 30, 31, 34, 45, 46, 82
nostalgia 47, 56

Orpheus 51, 53, 60, 61, 67, 68, 192n9
Other 174, 177, 180, 184, 191n4
"Ozymandias" 48

Pakistan 26, 83, 84, 87–89, 91–93, 101, 108, 110, 130, 136, 185, 193c5n3
postcolonial SF 2, 5, 179, 183
postcoloniality 1–3, 5–7, 9, 11, 25, 30–33, 36, 38, 47, 53, 54, 176–180, 182, 183, 185, 188n6; see also postcolonial SF
Prometheus 71, 152, 164, 167, 168, 170, 172, 180
prophet 71, 78, 94, 96–99, 102, 108, 109–111, 117, 167
puppet 25, 30, 40, 41, 44, 45

Ramesses 84
Reider, John 5, 7, 8, 21, 179
religion 19, 71, 160, 164, 174, 188n8
revolution 4, 10, 25, 30, 34, 36, 38, 40, 41, 44, 100, 102, 183, 190n6
rivers of blood 15, 130
rock n' roll 26, 50, 51, 52, 58, 62, 67, 70, 154, 164
Rose, Jacqueline 75, 76, 100, 119
Rugby (school) 4, 95

The Satanic Verses 1, 82, 123, 159, 185, 187c1n1
Scheherazade 97, 103
Shakespeare, William 161
shape-shifter 2, 9, 137, 170
Sirk, Douglass 115–116, 118, 193c4n5; see also *Imitation of Life*
state 12, 14, 24, 29, 34, 59, 66, 75–77,

202

78, 83, 90, 95, 100, 103, 104, 107, 109, 112, 113, 117, 119, 120, 131, 136, 144, 172, 176, 184, 185
strangeness 2, 5, 6, 7, 8, 16, 18, 32, 38, 42, 106, 134, 140, 144, 159, 162, 177, 181, 182, 183, 184, 188n6
subversiveness 9, 44, 120, 190n8
survival 44, 116, 137
Suvin, Darko 8, 9, 32
Swift, Jonathan 38–40, 42; *see also Gulliver's Travels*

A Thousand and One Nights 103

uchronia 54–56
Utopia 10, 11, 25, 30, 44, 45, 47, 52, 56, 67, 68, 74, 145, 190n6, 193c4n4

veil 96, 101–103, 129, 193c4n2

war 4, 38, 80, 83, 84, 87–91, 93, 94, 105, 106, 121, 124, 126, 130, 134, 136, 139, 141, 144, 146, 147, 158, 181, 191n3
The Wizard of Oz 3, 50, 72, 92, 123, 128, 129, 153, 166, 188n9, 189n10
worlds: actual 39, 49, 165, 173; alternate(imagined) 2, 7, 14, 19, 24, 25, 28, 32, 33, 39, 49, 52, 57, 70, 74, 114, 134, 150, 155, 177, 182, 185; parallel 53, 54; possible 54, 165, 166, 191n1

Žižek, Slavoj 35, 36, 65

www.ingramcontent.com/pod-product-compliance
Ingram Content Group UK Ltd.
Pitfield, Milton Keynes, MK11 3LW, UK
UKHW042006140426
5217IPUK00015B/1016

9 780786 474967